LUTHER'S LIVELY THEOLOGY

A Study Based on Luther's Small Catechism

*With Over 400 Quotations
from Other Works by Martin Luther*

DEL JACOBSON

Lutheran University Press
Minneapolis, Minnesota

LUTHER'S LIVELY THEOLOGY
A Study Based on Luther's Small Catechism
by Del Jacobson

Copyright 2019 Lutheran University Press, an imprint of 1517 Media. All rights reserved. No part of this publication may be reproduced, stored in a retrieval system, or transmitted in any form or by any means, electronic, mechanical, photocopying, recording, or otherwise, without written permission of the publisher: 1517 Media Permissions, PO Box 1209, Minneapolis, MN 55440-1209, or copyright@1517.media.

Cover illustration by Thursday Jacobson.

ISBN 978-1-942304-32-6
eISBN 978-1-942304-66-1

For Katherine

"*A good wife does not come by chance and without God's guidance; she is a gift.*"

MARTIN LUTHER
WA 43:377 [LW 4:335]

TABLE OF CONTENTS

Foreword 7

Preface 9

Introduction 11

Part One—The Ten Commandments 15
Background of the Ten Commandments 15
The First Word 20
"You shall not make for yourself a graven image. . . ." 26
"You shall not take the name of the LORD your God in vain." 29
"Remember the Sabbath day to keep it holy." 33
"Honor your father and your mother. . . ." 33
"You shall not kill." 37
"You shall not commit adultery." 41
"You shall not steal." 43
"You shall not bear false witness. . . ." 44
"You shall not covet . . . ." 47
"I, the LORD your God am a Jealous God" 47
The Commandments and Jesus 50
The Commandments and Christians 54

Part Two—The Apostles' Creed 57
Background of the Apostles' Creed 57
"I believe in . . . ." 61
"I believe in God the Father . . . Son . . . Spirit. . . ." 68
"I believe in God the Father almighty" 77
"I believe in Jesus Christ, God's only Son, our Lord." 91
"He was conceived by the Holy Spirit, born of the Virgin Mary." 93
"He suffered under Pontius Pilate, was crucified, died. . . ." 100
"He . . . died, and was buried." 107
"He descended into hell." 107
"On the third day he rose again." 108

"He ascended into heaven. . . ." 113
"He . . . is seated at the right hand of the Father." 115
"He will come again to judge the living and the dead." 116
"I believe in the Holy Spirit. . . ." 118
"I believe in . . . the holy, catholic church. . . ." 129
"I believe in . . . the forgiveness of sins. . . ." 140
"I believe in . . . the resurrection of the body. . . ." 141
"I believe in . . . the life everlasting." 142

Part Three—The Lord's Prayer 143
Background of the Lord's Prayer 143
"Our Father. . . ." 153
"Hallowed be your name." 158
"Your kingdom come." 164
"Your will be done. . . ." 170
"Give us today our daily bread." 174
"Forgive us our sins. . . ." 177
". . . as we forgive those who sin against us." 180
"Lead us not into temptation" / "Save us from the time of trial" 183
". . . and deliver us from evil." 184
"For the kingdom, the power, and the glory are yours. . . ." 184
"Amen" 185

The Sacraments 187

Part Four—The Sacrament of Holy Baptism 193
Origins of the Sacrament of Holy Baptism 193
What Is Holy Baptism? 197
The Continuing Reality of Holy Baptism 203
Infant Baptism 210

The Office of the Keys 217

Confession 219

Part Five—The Sacrament of Holy Communion 221
Origins of the Sacrament of Holy Communion 221
What Is Holy Communion? 222
Differences in Understanding the Lord's Supper 238
Celebrating the Lord's Supper 244

Endnotes 248

Works of Martin Luther Cited 261

Acknowledgments 264

FOREWORD

Here is a gathering of fresh insights into Luther's Small Catechism, growing out of the author's lifetime of experience as a pastor and teacher in parishes, public schools, and a theological seminary. He has mined materials from the reformer himself as well as from a constellation of modern authors ranging from Raymond Brown and Martin Buber through Roy Harrisville, Ernst Käsemann, C. S. Lewis, Hans Küng, and others.

The author's goal is to shine light from these resources onto the Catechism in order to illuminate its relevance for our own time. I have used this material with profit in connection with a Lenten series on the Catechism. If I were to teach a class of confirmation-age students or preach to a congregation reviewing the basics of the faith with the help of the Catechism, I would want to have *Luther's Lively Theology* within reach.

JAMES LIMBURG
Professor Emeritus of Old Testament
Luther Seminary

Cover of the 1536 edition of Luther's Small Catechism

PREFACE

The Purpose of this Book

Martin Luther's Small Catechism is the template and springboard for the comments in this book, the purpose of which is to add to what Luther teaches in the Small Catechism and to fill in its blanks as it were:

1. By expanding on the catechism, theme by theme, with over 400 quotations from other works by Luther along with 50 quotations by other authors or speakers.
2. By identifying the background of the five major parts of the catechism and by addressing issues that are not addressed in the catechism, such as the teaching and preaching ministry of Jesus.

Luther's Lively Theology

British theologian Gordon Ruff once wrote: "Luther is the least typical of all Lutherans, the least typical of Protestants [and] invariably more disconcerting and alive than . . . his traditional and modern interpreters."[1]

Many of Luther's comments quoted here are not typical of twenty-first century Lutherans and are quite surprising, somewhat disconcerting, and always lively. Here, as examples, are the opening lines of a few of Luther's spirited, thought-provoking comments quoted later in this volume:

> True Christian religion begins, not at the highest as other religions do, but at the lowest. . . .
>
> Faith without love is not enough; it is not faith at all, but. . . .
>
> Christ wants no one to boast of being a Christian, saying, 'I am baptized. . . .
>
> The Word, the Word, I say, merits more regard than the whole sacrament with all that it is and can do. . . .
>
> To make progress [as Christians] is nothing else than always to begin. . . .

These pages also address such extraordinary expressions of Luther's evangelical faith as "law and gospel," "the priesthood of all believers," "the rule of faith vis-à-vis the rule of love," "*simul justus et peccator*," and "the theology of the cross versus the theology of glory."

Luther's theology of the cross, and its dispute with what he calls "the theology of glory," runs all through Luther's theology, most often without being identified as such. And it runs throughout his comments quoted here. One might say, as he once wrote, "The cross alone is our theology."[2] It is a theology that addresses the question: "What enables us to become right with God?" Is it obeying God's law? Is it faithful religious practice? Is it standing up for justice? Is it doing to others what we would have others do to us? Is it simply trying our best?

In contrast to the assumption that such positive actions bring us into a right relationship to God (an aspect of the theology of glory), Luther would say that none of these fine things can put us right with God. No matter how hard we try, we don't measure up. In Luther's own words: "It is certain that a human being must utterly despair of his or her own ability before being prepared to receive the grace of Christ."[3]

There is simply nothing we can do to eradicate our self-centered, sin-sick nature. Only God can do so, and has and does—through the crucified, resurrected Jesus—as we are led by God's Spirit to give up on ourselves and to turn to rely on Christ Jesus alone. This is the essence of the theology of the cross.

The biblical texts quoted in this book are based on Revised Standard Version and New Revised Standard Version translations of the original languages, but use inclusive language.

The endnotes identify the sources of all quotations. The endnotes that identify the sources of Luther's quotations often refer to the sources of other comments made by Luther on the same subject. This is especially important when Luther's comments are unusual or controversial.

INTRODUCTION

Martin Luther

Martin Luther was born in Germany over 500 years ago (November 10, 1483). In those days the Christian church in Europe had strayed from its biblical roots. The pope and his top officials were more interested in money and personal power than in people's relationship with God. Human practices had become more important than the Bible. A system of church sacraments had replaced the gospel of Jesus as the center of church life.

As a young man, Martin Luther became a monk and a priest. Later his vicar general ordered him to become a student and teacher of the Bible. As he studied the Bible, Luther began to realize how far the leaders of the church had drifted away from the gospel.

Church officials led the people to believe that they were right with God when they received the sacraments of the church and lived lives of good deeds. Luther did not deny the importance of the sacraments or the value of good deeds. But he realized, as the New Testament teaches, that people can never make up for their sins and failures by the things they do. We are put right with God only through faith in God's saving action in Jesus. In Luther's words:

> The kingdom of Christ is nothing else than the kingdom of faith in the Word of God—namely, that salvation comes to us not by our own strength, not by our own merits or righteousness, but out of the gracious mercy of God, who, as Paul says in Romans (5:10), loved us even when we were still God's enemies, who sent the Holy Spirit into our heart to be the effective cause of our calling on the name of the Lord, in whom alone we must be saved.[4]

Lutherans

Luther did not want people to be called by his name—Lutherans. He wanted them to be called Christians, that is, "those who belong to Christ." Luther writes:

> I ask that people make no reference to my name; let them call themselves Christians, not Lutherans. What is Luther? After all, the teaching is not mine. Neither was I crucified for

anyone. St. Paul, in 1 Corinthians 3, would not allow Christians to call themselves Pauline or Petrine, but Christian.[5]

Why, then, do some people call themselves Lutherans? They do so to identify themselves as people who believe as Luther did—that Jesus Christ alone is God's way of saving human beings from sin and evil. As Luther wrote on another occasion:

> Christ alone died for you. He alone is your Master, and you should confess yourself a Christian. But if you are convinced that Luther's teaching is in accord with the gospel, then you should not discard Luther completely, lest with him you discard his teaching also. For Luther's teaching is not really his, but Christ's teaching.
>
> Paul also writes thus to Timothy in 2 Timothy 1: "Do not be ashamed then of testifying to our Lord, *or to me*, a prisoner for his sake."
>
> As Christ says in Matthew 10 concerning those who proclaim him: "Whoever receives you receives me and whoever rejects you rejects me." Why this? Because holding thus with his messengers, those who bring his word, is the same as holding with Christ himself and with his word.[6]

The Catechism

The word catechism comes from a Greek verb that means "to teach" or "to make one's self understood." In Luther's words: "Catechism means the instruction in which those who want to be Christians are taught and guided in what they should believe, know, do, and leave undone, according to the Christian faith."[7]

Luther wrote his Small Catechism in 1529 CE[8] to give people a simple handbook for learning and for teaching the basic doctrines of Christian faith. It is called the Small Catechism to distinguish it from the Large Catechism that Luther wrote primarily for pastors.

The Bible is the source and foundation of the Small Catechism. In Luther's words, "The Catechism is a brief survey and summary of all the Holy Scriptures."[9] The Small Catechism is made up of five main parts:

> Part One: The Ten Commandments
> Part Two: The Apostles' Creed
> Part Three: The Lord's Prayer
> Part Four: The Sacrament of Holy Baptism
> Part Five: The Sacrament of Holy Communion

Luther included biblical texts and instructions on the sacraments because of their great importance for Christian faith and life. Part Five, on Holy Communion, also includes sections on the Office of the Keys and Confession.

Each part of *The Small Catechism* includes two types of material: one, the *text* of the Commandments, Creed, Lord's Prayer, etc.; and two, Luther's simple *explanation* of each portion of the text. Luther's personal suggestion for learning the catechism is, first, to learn the *text* of each part, and, second, to learn the *explanation* of each part. For Luther the *text* is most important.[10] When he used the word "catechism" he always meant, first and foremost, the *text*.

We often think of the Small Catechism as a handbook for young people. That it is. But Luther had people of all ages in mind when he wrote it.

Luther's German language editions introduced each of the five main parts of the Small Catechism with words that, in translation, read:

> In the plain form in which
> the head of the household shall teach his family.

The Latin title, in translation, reads:

> Small Catechism for the Use of Children in School:
> How, in very Plain Form,
> Schoolmasters Should Teach their Students.

The Small Catechism, then, is designed for parents and family, for teachers and students. Many believe the Small Catechism is one of the finest Christian writings of all time.

People come to appreciate the catechism more and more as they grow older. Perhaps this is because its simple truths take hold of our hearts and imaginations more and more with the passing years. As Luther himself puts it:

> Though I am a doctor and preacher of the church, yet, I do as a child who is being taught the catechism [the *text* of the commandments, creed, etc.]. Every morning, and whenever else I have time, I read and recite word for word the Lord's Prayer, the Ten Commandments, the Creed, the Psalms, etc. I must still read and study the catechism daily, yet I cannot master it as I wish, but must remain a child and pupil of the catechism and I do it gladly.
>
> It is highly profitable and fruitful daily to read the catechism and make it the subject of meditation and conversation. In such reading, conversation, and meditation the Holy Spirit is present and bestows ever new and greater light

and fervor, so that day by day we relish and appreciate the catechism more greatly. This is according to Christ's promise in Matthew 18:20, 'Where two or three are gathered in my name, there am I in the midst of them.'"[11]

PART ONE

THE TEN COMMANDMENTS

Background of the Ten Commandments

What we know as the Ten Commandments are based on two texts in the Old Testament, Exodus 20:1-17 and Deuteronomy 5:5-21. But what we call commandments are introduced in these texts as the "words" of God (Exodus 20:1; Deuteronomy 5:5). Elsewhere they are called the Ten Words, that is, ten pronouncements—ten audible, hear-able words from the mouth of God (Exodus 34:28; Deuteronomy 4:13, 10:4).

As Exodus 20:1 puts it, "God *spoke* all these *words, saying.* . . ." Each of the three Hebrew words translated here as *"spoke" "words," "saying"* has to do with audible language. Here, then, is an essential aspect of what we call the Ten Commandments:

- God speaking. God addressing those whom both Exodus and Deuteronomy identify as a people set apart for God's purposes.
- God saying, *"I* am the LORD your God." God saying, *"You..."* (and here the pronoun *you* is singular), *"You* shall have no other gods. . . . *You* shall not kill. . . . *You* shall not covet."

The God who speaks is the LORD, the God of Abraham, Isaac, and Jacob. The persons to whom God speaks are the descendants of Abraham, persons whom the LORD has delivered out of bondage in Egypt and with whom the LORD is now making a covenant.

God addresses the people as individuals so that each of them may respond personally to the Ten Words. But, of course, with these words God calls each of them to live in community with all the others, so they can be forged into a people capable of representing God in the world.

Luther, too, identifies God as "one who speaks." He says:

> All the patriarchs believed in God, not as in a creator, but in a God who spoke with them. They did not have a speechless God . . . but One who spoke. . . . We, too, have a communicating God who speaks to us daily through ministers of the Word and the sacraments.[12]

God's Covenant Promise

In making a covenant with the people of Israel God's first words are a gracious promise. As we read in Exodus 20:1, God declares:

1. *"I am the LORD your God. . . ."* These words assure the people of the relationship the LORD (the God of Abraham, Isaac, and Jacob) is establishing with them, choosing them out of all earthly people to be God's special people.
2. *". . . who brought you out of the land of Egypt, out of the house of bondage."* These words remind the people of God's merciful action in their behalf, delivering them out of slavery in Egypt.

God's gracious promise is given before God's commands. The gospel, the good news of *God's redeeming action* for Israel, precede God's law. This means God's grace (*merciful action*) is the foundation of God's covenant with Israel. And God's grace is the reason for the people of Israel—and for us—to trust in God and to obey God's commandments. Furthermore, God's commandments are themselves expressions of God's grace, commandments given to guide and benefit God's people. As Luther writes:

> Nothing is lacking to those who live by the Word and believe that we shall be under God's care in all things and through all things. It is just as Peter says (1 Peter 5:7): "Cast every care upon God, because God cares for you;" and Psalm 34:10: "Those who seek God shall lack no good thing." To understand these and similar wonderful and faithful promises of God is truly to understand the promise of the First Commandment, in which God says: *"I am the LORD your God." "Yours, yours,"* God says, *"who will show and display myself to you as God and will not forsake you, if only you believe this."* All such promises depend on and flow from the First Commandment.[13]

God's Call to Abram

The LORD God first chose, called, and made a covenant with Israel's ancestor Abraham (at first named Abram), c. 2000 BCE:

> The LORD said to Abram: Go from your land, your kindred and your father's house to the land that I will show you. I will make of you a great nation. I will bless you and make your name great so that you will be a blessing. Those who bless you I will bless and whoever curses you I will curse; and in you all the families of the earth will be blessed (Genesis 12:1-3).

Notice first that the LORD called Abram to separate himself from his systems of support (land, clan, and family) and to rely on the LORD. Notice second that the LORD made a four-fold promise to Abram:

1. To give him a "land."
2. To make of him "a great nation."
3. To "bless" him and make his name great.
4. In Abram and his descendants to bless "all the families of the earth."

As Luther says:

> God summoned Abraham out of his homeland and promised him that by his descendants all nations should be blessed. This promise Abraham believed and obeyed and thereby was justified and became a friend of God. In the same book (Genesis) this promise to Abraham is cited significantly and repeatedly, enlarged and clarified, until Isaac is promised to him, who was to be the seed from which Christ and every blessing should come.[14]

The Exodus from Egypt and the Covenant at Mt. Sinai

During a famine in Canaan, Abraham's descendants moved to Egypt. After a time they were enslaved by the Egyptians. When they had become great in number and in agony cried for help, God mercifully delivered them out of slavery (c. 1280 BCE). From that time on that event (the Exodus) has been of central importance for the Hebrew people. By that great saving event God established a special relationship with Abraham's descendants that was to be the foundation of their faith, life, and purpose.

After rescuing the descendants of Abraham out of slavery in Egypt, the LORD God established a covenant with them at Mount Sinai:

> The LORD said to Moses, "You shall say this to the house of Jacob and to the people of Israel: You have seen what I did to the Egyptians, and how I carried you on eagle's wings and brought you to myself. Now therefore, if you will obey my voice and keep my covenant, you shall be my own possession among all peoples, for all the earth is mine; and you shall be to me a kingdom of priests and a holy nation" (Exodus 19:3-6).

With these words God reminded the people that it was by God's gracious action that they had been delivered out of slavery.

"You have seen what I did to the Egyptians"—God's power

"And how I carried you on eagle's wings"—God's salvation

"And brought you to myself"—God's presence

God established the terms of the covenant: "If you will obey my voice and keep my covenant. . . . You shall be my own possession among all people." God's goal for the chosen people was clear: "You shall be to me a kingdom of priests" [ministers to all people] and a holy nation" [*set apart* for God's purposes].

The response of the people was faith in what God had said. They said, "All that the LORD has spoken we will do" (Exodus 19:8).

It was on this basis that God gave them the Ten Words as a vital part of the covenant. God gave these "words" to a people already chosen and saved out of slavery. God gave "the words":

- To guide the covenant people in their life and purpose together.
- To restrain evil and to promote justice among themselves.
- To protect and promote the welfare of each person in the community.

As Luther says, "The purpose of all earthly laws is peace, harmony, and quiet or . . . love." Certainly the purpose of the Ten Words is peace, harmony, and love.[15]

Why God Chose Israel

The LORD's choice of Israel was not based on some special quality of the people. The authors of Deuteronomy quote Moses to say:

> It was not because you were more in number than any other people that the LORD's love has been set upon you to choose you, for you were the fewest of all peoples. It is because the LORD loves you, and is keeping the oath sworn to your forebears, that the LORD has brought you out with a mighty hand and redeemed you from the house of bondage (Deuteronomy 7:7-8).

> Do not say in your heart, "It is because of our righteousness that the LORD has brought us in to possess this land," . . . for you are a stubborn people. . . . Rather, the LORD's heart has been set in love upon your forebears and the LORD chose their descendants after them, you above all peoples (Deuteronomy 9:4, 6; 10:15).

In Luther's words:

> Here Moses himself testifies that the Jews were not brought into the land of Canaan because of their righteousness or penitence, but by virtue of the promise God had sworn to the patriarchs.[16]

Of course, the Scriptures declare that God loves all humanity. But why then were the people of Israel chosen to be God's "own possession among all peoples"? God chose them to be representatives of that love; God appointed them to be priests to all nations of the blessings of God. Cf. Genesis 12:1-3; Exodus 19:3-6; Isaiah 49:5-6. In the same way, Christians have been set aside for God's gracious purposes. In the words of Jesus according to John 15:16: "You have not chosen me, but I have chosen you and appointed you to go and bear fruit."

As Luther says:

> This is the great distinction Christians have through Christ. In the first place, Christ has called and chosen them through his Word to be his beloved branches and to have everything he gained for them, victory and dominion against sin, death, and the power of the devil. In the second place, we are also to be his servants and to lend a hand in spreading his kingdom, to do much good. This he calls "bearing much fruit, fruit that abides" forever before God.[17]

The Ten Words as Torah

> The LORD said to Moses, "Come up to me on the mountain. Wait there; and I will give you the tablets of stone, with the law (*Torah*) and the commandment (*Mitzvah*) that I have written for their instruction" (Exodus 24:12).

The Hebrew word *Torah* occurs well over 200 times in the Old Testament. It comes from the root-word "throw," meaning "to point" or "to give direction." The Torah points the way. It is God's guidance or teaching for those whom God delivered out of slavery in Egypt.

Torah arises out of God's gracious action for Israel. It is anchored in the good news of what God has done:

- Saving the Hebrew people out of slavery in Egypt.
- Choosing them as a peculiar possession among all earthly people.
- Establishing a covenant with them.
- Commissioning them to be a kingdom of priests to all nations.
- Leading them through the desert.
- Giving them the land of Canaan.
- Caring for them and blessing them day after day.

The Ten Words are central to God's Torah, but the Torah includes guidance and direction that go beyond these sayings of the LORD.

Throughout Israel's history God gave the people Torah in the varied form of declarations, testimonies, stipulations, guidelines, advice, commands, injunctions, warnings, promises, and examples, but always in order to guide, to point the way, to instruct the people.

It is *God's* Torah for *God's* people. It is not meant to be separated from God and to stand on its own as a universal standard or model for living. Taken out of the context of God's *"I-you"* relationship with the chosen people, the Torah, including the Ten Words, tends to become something rigid and confining. Luther describes the on-going value of the Torah for Christians, saying:

> The law must not be cast aside because of the promise of grace, but must be taught so that discipline and the teaching of good works may be retained and we may learn to know and humble ourselves when we have sinned. This is the true and necessary use of the law.[18]

The First Word: I am the LORD your God. . . . You shall have no other gods before me (Exodus 20:2-3).

This, the initial *word* of the Ten Words is the first in order and the first in importance. In Luther's thinking this "word" is, at one and the same time, an affirmation and a command that calls us to trust in the LORD in every situation, good or bad. As Luther writes:

> As the First Commandment teaches, the worship of God consists in this: that you know, honor, and love God with your whole heart; put all your confidence and trust in God; never doubt God's goodness, neither in life nor in death, neither in sin nor in doing good.[19]

> We are not only reminded, admonished, and persuaded by this commandment to hope in and to love God, but it is commanded to us on penalty of the greatest punishment and obligation.[20]

As an affirmation and a command, this word has a double intent. As an affirmation, its intention is to create faith in those of us who hear God's word, "I am the LORD your God." As a command, its intention is to undermine the unbelief of those of us who will not hear and respond to God's affirmation. To apply a well-know construction of Luther's, the proper work of the first word is to affirm God's merciful goodness to those who hear God's promise. The alien work of this word is to bring judgment upon those who do not accept the promise.

In any case, God's promising word and God's threatening demand have the same goal—to turn us to trust in the LORD as the one true source of goodness, life, and salvation. In Luther's words: "No richer consolation or voice is more plainly heard or ever will be heard, yet none harder or severer, than the voice of the First Commandment: 'I am the Lord your God.'"[21]

Of First Importance

Even if we do not realize it, God is of first importance in our lives *because* God has created us and because it is only by God's goodness and power that we continue to live. But God wants to be more than an impersonal force in our lives. God wants to be closely connected to us as *our* God, *our* Savior, *our* Lord.

There are "other gods," of course. The people of Israel never denied the existence of other gods. What they denied was that these gods are living and true. To this day people worship and follow other gods.

As Luther says:

> Whatever it is that makes a person do something, that motive is that person's god. . . .[22] Whatever you cling to and trust is your god.[23]

It could be money or a habit or some created thing or person. But only the true, living God can be trusted to give direction, meaning, and fullness of life to us. For this reason God says to us, as to the people of Israel, "I am the LORD your God. . . . You shall have no other gods before me."

Luther's Explanation

Luther explains what the first commandment means for us by saying: "We are to *fear*, love, and trust God above anything else."[24]

What are we to make of the word *fear*? Is Luther saying we should be afraid of God? In one sense of the word, yes. The German word *fürchten*, that Luther uses in explaining the first commandment, means "fear" in the sense of "deep seated awe or respect." Elsewhere Luther writes, "This is what it means to fear God: to have God in view, to know that God looks at all our works, and to acknowledge God as the Author of all things."[25]

But what about passages such as Matthew 10:28 or Hebrews 10:31: "Do not fear those who kill the body, but fear the One who can destroy both body and soul in hell" (Matthew 10:28). "It is a fearful thing to fall into the hands of the living God" (Hebrews 10:31).

These passages remind us that God is just and upright, that our sins have consequences, and that God's judgment is real and serious. They remind us not to take our sins lightly or to dismiss God's judgment as if it doesn't matter how we act. After all, the first commandment is *law*; which means that when we fail to "fear, love, and trust God," the first commandment exposes our failure, and shows us that we need to confess our failure and turn to God for mercy and forgiveness.

But we should never forget the declaration that stands back of and goes with the first commandment. God assured the people of Israel: "I am the LORD your God who brought you up out of the land of Egypt, out of the house of bondage." This is why they could respond to God's commands not simply with fear, but with reverent confidence. And because God in Christ has delivered us from bondage to sin and death, we too can respond to God's commands with deep seated awe, love, and trust in God above all things.

Again, Luther explains what the first commandment means by saying: "We are to fear, *love*, and trust in God above anything else." But how can we possibly love God, whom we have never seen? Scripture gives us the answer: "In this the love of God was made known to us, that God sent the only Son into the world that we might live through him" (1 John 4:9) "We love because God first loved us" (1 John 4:19).

In Luther's words:

> Christ has already begun and has laid the first stone. He suffered for me. He has his gospel preached and has me baptized before I have asked for it or have known about him, as Paul says in Ephesians 1:4. And in 1 John 4:19 we read: "He first loved us."[26]

Indeed, when we hear the good news of God's love in action for us, there is stirred up within us a responding love for God. In a similar way, God's action of delivering the people of Israel out of slavery in Egypt stirred up a response of love for God.

This means that love is not an emotion or an attitude that *we* devise or decide to exercise. Love is, rather, the grateful devotion to God that arises within us in response to God's prior love for us. In fact, love is the result of God's Spirit at work in us, as we hear the Good News of God's caring action for us proclaimed in the gospel. As Luther writes:

> This King rules and works through the preaching of the gospel. The nature and the power of this Word and preaching is able to draw people to come willingly to God. . . . Every other power must force us.
>
> Through the Holy Spirit God works in our hearts so that we can take hold of this comfort and so begin to obey God. . . .
>
> And so, comforted and raised up by this faith, a person receives new ideas about God, a new mind and disposition,

> *begins* to love God . . . and receives a desire and a love for God's Commandments. . . . Although this obedience is still weak, although it is impure and imperfect, and although much disobedience still stirs within, such a person has the comfort of God's grace and forgiveness in Christ.[27]

Finally Luther explains what the first commandment means by saying: "We are to fear, love, and *trust* in God above anything else." Elsewhere Luther writes:

> The first commandment admonishes, "You shall have no other gods" This means, "Since I only am God, you shall place all your confidence, trust, and faith in me only and in no one else." For you do not have a god just by using the word "god" outwardly with your lips, or worshiping that god with your knees or bodily gestures; but only if you trust that god with your heart and look to that god for all good, grace, and favor, whether in works or suffering, in life or death, in joy or sorrow.
>
> As the Lord Jesus said, "Whoever wants to worship God must worship in spirit and in truth." This faith, this trust, this confidence from the heart's core is the true fulfilling of the First Commandment. Without such faith, no work at all can satisfy this commandment.[28]

As with love for God, our trust in God is brought about by the work of God's Spirit within us as we hear the good news of God's redeeming action in Christ proclaimed to us in the gospel. As Paul writes: "Faith comes from what is heard, and what is heard comes by the preaching of Christ" (Romans 10:17). Through the gospel, God's Spirit appeals to us—convincing us of our sins, revealing our need for God's mercy, and calling us to trust in God's saving action for us. In this way *trust* in God is created within us in response to the awesome wonder of what God has done for us.

The First Word and Idols

As the authors of the Bible declare, there is all the difference in the world between the LORD and the gods of the nations round about Israel. In the words of Jeremiah, the LORD alone lives, speaks, acts, and creates (10:10-13). The gods of the nations are nothing but idols patterned after human imagination and/or fashioned by human hands. Such gods are no more alive and awesome than "scarecrows in a cucumber field" (10:5).

But, of course, there is more to idolatry than falling down before a human-made image. As Luther writes:

> Idolatry does not consist merely of erecting an image and praying to it. It is primarily in the heart, which pursues other things and seeks help and consolation from creatures, saints, or devils.
>
> There is, moreover, another false worship that is the greatest idolatry that has been practiced up to now. . . . It concerns that approach to life which seeks help, comfort, and salvation in one's own works.[29]

In Luther's judgment, then, to turn from the living God to any created thing, no matter how lovely or beneficial, is idolatry. But worst of all is the idolatry or false worship of trusting only or primarily in myself.

In contrast to such idolatry or false worship, Luther joins the psalmists, prophets, and apostles in identifying *praise that springs up out of faith* as the true worship of the LORD.[30] For believers, such praise is the perfect antidote for idolatry. As Rolf Jacobson writes: "Because praise evokes a world in which the Lord alone reigns, biblical praise is always both praise of the true Lord and praise against false lords—human and non-human—who seek to set themselves up in God's place."[31]

Responding to God "Above All Else"

Why "fear, love, and trust God *above anything else*" as Luther puts it? Is it because God has a need to be worshiped? No. Is it because God is jealous of the very things God has created? No. We are the ones with a need. It is easy enough to get side-tracked from what is important in life. Things, especially good things, can occupy so much of our time and energy that we miss out on what is most essential in life—a healthy relationship with God, with ourselves, with other human beings, and with the creation of which we are a part.

Furthermore, we have a need to "fear, love, and trust God *above anything else*" in order to keep from worshiping ourselves or to keep from attempting to re-create God in our image.

Most important, we have a need to "fear, love, and trust God *above anything else*" because God is the source of everything—the source of life, the source of meaning in life, the source of love, hope, and the very reason for our being. Luther writes:

> . . . the nature and scope of this commandment requires that a person's whole heart and confidence be placed in God alone, and in no one else. . . . God wishes to turn us away from everything else and to personally draw us close, since God is the one, eternal good.

This, I think, is why we Germans from ancient times have called God by a name more elegant and worthy than any found in other languages, a name derived from the word 'good' because God is an eternal fountain which overflows with sheer goodness and pours forth all that is good in name and in fact.[32]

To realize our purpose in life, we need God *above anything else*. As Colossians 2:9-10 puts it: "In Christ the whole fulness of God dwells bodily, and you have come to fullness of life in him."

The First Word and the Others

Luther considers the first commandment to be the foundation of all the others. He does so because, as we have seen, he considers God's promise, "I am the LORD your God," to be part, parcel, and essence of the command, "You shall have no other gods before me." Luther writes:

This commandment is the very first of all commandments and the highest and the best, *from which* all the others proceed, *in which* they exist, and *by which* they are judged and assessed.[33]

The first commandment is the measure and yardstick of all others, to which they are to yield and give obedience. . . . It contains the whole sum and fulfillment of all the commandments that follow.[34]

The third commandment, like the second, should be nothing other than a doing and keeping of the first commandment, that is, of faith, trust, confidence, hope, and love toward God so that in all the commandments the first may be the captain, and faith the chief work and life of all other works."[35]

Where the heart is right with God and this commandment is kept, fulfillment of all the others will follow of its own accord.[36]

If I were to keep the commandments of the Second Table perfectly and would want to trust in that and boast of it before God, then I would be sinning against the first commandment, which teaches that I have received everything and can give nothing.[37]

Jews and Reformed Christians (Presbyterian, Christian Reformed, and others) number the Ten Words differently than Lutherans, Roman Catholics and Orthodox Christians. In this book we will follow the precedent of the authors of the Old Testament by identifying the commandments by their content rather than by a number.

The Ten Commandments | 25

"You shall not make for yourself a graven image . . ."
(Exodus 20:4).

> You shall not make for yourself a graven image, or the likeness of anything that is in heaven above, or that is on the earth beneath, or that is in the water under the earth. You shall not bow down to them or serve them" (Exodus 20:4-5).

In the ancient Middle East the purpose of cultic images was to *represent* the "gods" being worshiped. Only rarely was an image considered to be identical with the "god" being worshiped. Why, then, is making images of the LORD prohibited?

It is prohibited, first, because it is impossible to make a sensible image of the high and holy God of Israel. The LORD God of Israel is unique—completely *distinct* from any creature of heaven or earth and absolutely different from any "god" imagined by human beings. The "gods" of ancient Canaan, Egypt, and Babylon were represented by images of animals and other earthly forms. Further, these "gods" were identified with the sun, moon, and stars. Not so with the LORD, the creator of animals, earth, sun, moon, and stars. The LORD is transcendent: completely *other* than any created thing; and yet, at the same time, the LORD is present and at work among us within creation.

Making images of the LORD is prohibited, second, because it would be *misleading* to make a *particular* image of God. No single image or likeness can adequately represent God. According to the Bible, down through the ages the LORD has appeared to various people in many forms (angels, clouds, fire, smoke, people) and in a variety of modes (dreams, visions, trances). But precisely because the LORD may use almost anything as a means of self-revelation, no *single* image is adequate to represent the LORD.

To this day, the LORD God may act and/or appear any place, any time, in any way. And it is certainly true that the LORD is actively at work in and through persons and events of human society. The LORD is the God of here and now, who addresses us particularly through the gospel of Jesus Christ our Savior. Luther puts it well:

> It is surely a great thing for God to appear to a human being and for God's promises to be fit to a particular individual. For this reason many consider the saintly fathers far more blessed in this respect than we are, since they had such definite and individual comforts and appearances from God through the ministry of the angels.
>
> I answer: You have no reason to complain that you have been visited less than Abraham or Isaac. You, too, have

appearances, and in a way they are stronger, clearer, and more numerous than those they had, provided that you open your eyes and heart and take hold of them. You have Baptism. You have the Sacrament of the Eucharist, where bread and wine are the species, figures, and forms in which and under which God in person speaks and works into your ears, eyes, and heart. Besides, you have the ministry of the Word and teachers through whom God speaks with you. You have the ministry of the Keys, through which God absolves and comforts you. "Fear not," God says, "I am with you."[38]

Making images of the LORD was prohibited, third, because the LORD is *the God of the name and the Word*. Unlike other nations of the ancient Middle East, the people of Israel were directed (as are we), not to a cultic image representing the LORD, but to the LORD's self-revealed name and clearly declared Word—a name defined and empowered by the LORD's very words and deeds.

In Luther's understanding, the LORD's *declaration*, "I am the LORD your God" means "I reveal myself through the Word. . . ."[39] As Luther declares elsewhere, God appears to us, not in naked majesty, but "clothed and revealed in the Word."[40] Luther goes on to say: "This God, clothed in such a kind appearance and, so to speak, in such a pleasant mask, that is to say, *dressed in promises*—this God we can grasp and see with joy and trust."[41]

We might prefer the tangible security of more direct contact with God, but no. We would be overwhelmed by God's majesty. We might like to have God at our beck and call through an established religious system, but no. The LORD cannot and will not be restricted to religious things or sacred places. Neither can the LORD be reduced to an image or an idea that we can control for our purposes.

"I will be who I will be," says the LORD—free to speak and to act when, where, and however God chooses to do so.[42] Yes, the God of the Word *promises* to be near to all those who trust in God and who pray in time of need. Nevertheless God *calls* us to walk by faith, not by sight. Unfortunately we have a tendency to equate God with *our* thoughts and desires. We create, as it were, idols or images in our minds, thinking we know what God should do or desire. But over the course of time, the reality of *things as they are* tends to shatter our cherished concepts of God. In the mean time, God's hidden action among us is designed to keep us in suspense. Why? So that we remain dependent on faith (not sight) in the God whose name is sacred and sure and whose promise to be present and at work for our good never fails.

God Prohibits What God Has Done

> God said, "Let us make humans in our image, after our likeness. . . ." So God created humans in the image of God, male and female God created them (Genesis 1:26-27).

Human beings, then, were created to be images of God in the world. The words translated "likeness" in Genesis 1:26 and "image" in Exodus 20:4 are based on the same Hebrew root word.

But haven't we said no image can adequately represent the true and living God? Yes. And that is certainly true of human beings. We constantly misrepresent and distort who and what God is. As Luther understands the Scriptures, the image of God in us has been "obscured and corrupted," if not "lost" because of our sinfulness.[43] And yet, in contrast to human-made images (idols), even though distorted and corrupted, God-created images (human beings) are alive and active. In the words of Psalm 135:15-17: "The idols of the nations are silver and gold, the work of human hands. They have mouths, but they speak not, they have eyes, but they see not, they have ears, but they hear not, nor is there any breath in their mouths." Idols tell us little or nothing about the nature of their creators. Human beings, at least, reflect the fact that God lives, speaks, sees, hears, and acts.

"The Image of the Invisible God"

> "Christ Jesus is the image of the invisible God, the firstborn of all creation" (Colossians 1:15).

> "He reflects the glory of God and bears the very stamp of God's nature" (Hebrews 1:3).

Christ Jesus is *the* image of the invisible God. Not only does "the whole fullness of God dwell in him bodily," as the letter of Colossians goes on to say (2:9), he is *the most fully human* being who has ever lived. He is what every human being is meant to be—"the express image" of God as an older English version of Hebrews 1:3 puts it.

In the words of Dietrich Bonhoeffer:

> Jesus lacks nothing that is human. There is nothing offered by this world or by human beings which Jesus Christ did not take. Of Jesus alone is it really true that nothing human remained alien to him. Of this man we say, "This is God for us."[44]

In his humanness Jesus reflects exactly who and what God is. In his words, actions, and relationships with others, God is revealed. In his self-giving death for our sins and in his resurrection from the dead, the living, forgiving God is active and at work for us. This is the conviction and confession of those who have been led to believe in him.

But not only did Jesus give himself to rescue us from the power of sin and death, he also came to transform us, to reshape our lives so that we might be more fully human in our living, our speaking, our actions, and our relationships with one another, with God, and with all creation. As Paul wrote to the Corinthians: Those who trust in Christ "are being changed into the *likeness* of Christ by the working of the Holy Spirit" (2 Corinthians 3:18). Cf. Romans 8:29; 2 Corinthians 4:16; Ephesians 4:24; Colossians 3:10

In Bonhoeffer's words: "Christ is the new creation. He is the restored creation of our spiritual and bodily existence. . . ."[45] We discover our humanity in him."[46]

And because believers are "being changed into the likeness of Christ," who is *the* image of God, we are being equipped to be what human beings are meant to be—God's *active representatives* on earth, exercising the justice, care, and love for the earth and for others that is true of God.

Had Luther considered the image command to be the second word from God he might have explained it as follows: "We are to fear and love God so we do not misrepresent God or idolize ourselves or others, but worship and trust the Lord as the one and only true and faithful God."

"You shall not take the name of the LORD your God in vain" (Exodus 20:7).

In the Bible, words are more than simply labels for something and names are more than simply terms for identifying certain persons. Hebrew is a precise, concrete language with words that describe actual things only.[47] Hebrew has no words for concepts such as *matter, material, substance,* and *solid* because these are not actual things. Things we might categorize as *material,* for example, Hebrew identifies for what they are: "wood," "iron," "water," "silver," "gold," etc.

In a similar way, names in Hebrew are used to express what a person actually is or is meant to be. For example:

> David, meaning "beloved," is said to have been deeply loved by both God and the Hebrew people.
>
> Hannah, meaning "gracious," was exactly that kind of person.
>
> Barnabas, meaning "son of encouragement," practiced a ministry of encouragement as an early follower of Jesus.

Furthermore, in Hebrew thinking, a name is a person's *renown*; not simply renown in the sense of "reputation," but renown in the sense of "power to influence."[48] This is why it was common practice among the ancient Hebrew people to give their children names to which, in their minds, good forces were attached. Of course, a person may be quite different from the meaning of the name by which she or he is called. And people can change, which is why the Bible, at times, speaks of people receiving new names. Your name is what you make of it of course. We've all heard that a few times. But whatever our names may be, the most important thing is what we are and are becoming day by day.

The Name of Israel's God

The Bible uses several terms to describe God, but only one name. The primary biblical text concerning God's name is Exodus 3:12-15 (along with Exodus 33:12-34:9). This text describes God's call to Moses to lead the Hebrew people out of slavery in Egypt into the land of Canaan. In response to God's call, Moses asked: "If I come to the people of Israel and say to them, 'The God of your fathers has sent me to you,' and they ask me, 'What is God's name?' what shall I say to them?" God replied:

> I Will Be Who I Will Be. Say this to the people of Israel, "I Will Be has sent me to you." Say to them, "The LORD (YHWH), the God of your fathers, the God of Abraham, the God of Isaac, and the God of Jacob, has sent me to you." This is my name forever, and this is how I am to be known from generation to generation.

YHWH, then, is God's self-revealed name, a name that declares *"God will be what God will be"*—free, sovereign, autonomous. This name occurs over 6,700 times in the Old Testament. It is an awesome, mysterious name that is unpronounceable and untranslatable. Some Old Testament English versions translate YHWH as "Yahweh." Other versions mistranslate it as "Jehovah." Most versions follow Jewish tradition in making no attempt to translate the name, and so, use the title "LORD."

As a *proper* name, YHWH distinguishes the God of Israel from any other god. As a *personal* name, YHWH declares the unique character of the one true God. As an *anonymous* name, YHWH asserts the sovereignty of God to act freely, independent of any outside influence. Ancient Middle East people believed that to know a god's name enabled a person to influence and even to control that god. According to Exodus 3, the God of Israel personally qualified the meaning of the name YHWH with two important declarations. God said, *"I Will Be Who I Will Be"* (3:14) and repeatedly declared, "I *Will Be* with you" (3:12; 4:12, 15). In these two phrases, two letters from God's mysterious name H-Y-H occur over and over again in the dynamic, active verb HYH. This play-on-words declares both *the sovereign freedom* and *the active presence* of the living God.

At the same time, God said, "I am the God of your fathers, the God of Abraham, the God of Isaac, and the God of Jacob" (Exodus 3:6, 15, 16). This designation declared the faithfulness of God in upholding the covenant promises made first with Abraham, then with Isaac, then with Jacob. In fact, the declaration, "I am the God of your fathers," may have assured Moses that what God had been to each of the patriarchs, in turn—"the *Shield of Abraham*" "*the Fear of Isaac,*" and "the *Rock* of Israel (Jacob)"—God would now be to their descendants, "the *Shield*, the *Fear*, and the *Rock*" of the whole people of Israel.[49]

This, then, is YHWH, the distinctive, powerfully active sovereign of all creation; forever faithful to covenant promises and purpose. In the words of Deuteronomy 32:3-4: "I will proclaim the name of the LORD . . . whose work is perfect and whose ways are justice; a God of faithfulness and without iniquity, just and right!"

There can be no question, then, of controlling the God of Israel. The very name YHWH declares God's freedom from human control, and at the same time, declares God's active presence in human life and events. Yet, it is possible to misuse God's name in a *false* or *worthless* way. This is why the name command (Exodus 20:7) declares: "You shall not take the name of the LORD your God in vain; for the LORD will not hold anyone guiltless who takes God's name in vain."

The Word "Vain"

The word "vain" refers to any action that is empty, false, without value.

> Flattery (praising someone falsely or in an excessive manner) is "vain," that is to say, deceitful, without value or truth.
>
> Going through the motions of religious practice without faith in God is "vain," that is, worthless, empty of meaning.
>
> To take a language course and manage to pass the course, but to fail to truly learn the language is "vain," that is, worthless, a waste of time.

Examples of "taking God's name in vain":

- To tell someone a lie, and to say, "I swear to God it's true," is to take God's name in vain.
- To pray to God for forgiveness while you refuse to forgive another person is to take God's name in vain.
- To tell a person who holds a grudge against someone else, "It's okay. God accepts you no matter what," is to take God's name in vain.

- To profane God's name with filthy words takes God's name in vain.

As Luther comments in his Large Catechism: "It is a misuse of God's name if we call upon the Lord God in any way whatsoever to support falsehood or wrong of any kind."[50]

Luther's Explanation

Luther explains in this way: "We are to fear and love God so that we do not use God's name superstitiously, or use it to curse, swear, lie, or deceive, but call on God in prayer, praise, and thanksgiving."[51]

Notice three things:

1. Luther explains this commandment and all the others, beginning with the words, "We are to fear and love God so that . . ."[50] In this way Luther ties all the commandments to the first and most important command. For surely, if we "fear, love, and trust in God above anything else," we will want to obey all of God's commands.

2. As with each of the other commandments, Luther's explanation here has a positive element ("call on God in prayer, praise, and thanksgiving") as well as a negative element (*do not* use God's name superstitiously").

    As Luther says elsewhere: "It is to be understood in this command that you should use the name of God well, to the honor and praise of God. This is done when you call upon God's name in time of need, as God has commanded: 'Call upon me in the day of trouble; I will deliver you, and you shall glorify me'." Here, then, Luther uses the name command as a call to prayer as well as an exhortation "to use it in the service of truth and all that is good . . . for the advantage of our neighbor."[52]

3. We might ask, why did Luther leave out of this and his other explanations the all-important word "trust," that he used in explaining the first commandment?" It's difficult to say. Perhaps because "fear (awe) and love for God" is an expression of the trust awakened in us in response to God's prior love for us.

    For Luther, at any rate, to fear God and to trust God belong together. As he comments: "To fear God and to trust God is alone true religion. Where these two are in correct balance, there the whole life is righteous and holy."[53]

"Remember the Sabbath day, to keep it holy" (Exodus 20:8).
"Honor your father and your mother" (Exodus 20:12).

As Martin Buber points out, these two commands differ from one another in content, yet stand together within the framework of the commandments.[54]

First of all, as the following outline of Exodus 20:3-17 indicates, each one of these two commands is *positive* in contrast to the negative commands that precede and follow them. In the Hebrew text of Exodus 20, the first word of each negative command is *Lo*, translated here as "never." In contrast, the positive commands begin with the *action* verbs "remember" and "honor."

> **NEVER** shall you have other gods before me.
> **NEVER** shall you make yourself a graven image. . . .
> **NEVER** shall you bow down to them.
> **NEVER** shall you serve them.
> **NEVER** shall you take the name of the LORD in vain.
> *Remember* the Sabbath day to keep it holy. . . .
> *Honor* your father and your mother. . . .
> **NEVER** shall you kill.
> **NEVER** shall you commit adultery.
> **NEVER** shall you steal.
> **NEVER** shall you bear false witness. . . .
> **NEVER** shall you covet. . . .'"

Second, it seems clear that the Sabbath commandment is related to the commands that precede it, which concern a person's relationship to God, while the parental commandment is related to the commands that follow it, which concern a person's relationship to other human beings.

The third way in which the positive commandments relate to one another concerns *the days* of a person's life. The repeated remembering of the Sabbath promotes a renewal of life (week by week) that contributes to a person's stability. This "rhythm of the weeks," as Martin Buber calls it, is as important for a healthy life as proper eating, exercise, work, recreation, and sleeping. The faithful honoring of one's parents promotes a vitality in family life that provides stability from one generation to another. This "rhythm of the generations," in Buber's words, fosters a love between family members that gives meaning to life and strengthens the worth of each person.[55]

Daily renewal is the key to every kind of human growth, whether it be physical, mental, social, or spiritual. We might wish that we could learn a language in ten easy lessons. We might wish that we could be skilled in music or sport without practice. We might wish that we could become effective Christians once and for all, simply by giving our life to Christ. But this is not how things work. Every one of us needs the renewal of body, mind, and soul that comes "slowly and in community." This is why God calls us to "Remember the Sabbath day to keep it holy." This is why God calls us to "Honor your father and your mother."

The fourth way in which the positive commandments relate to each other is that each one has a reason added to it for obeying it. The reason given for keeping the Sabbath commandment (cf. Exodus 20:11) is that, after creating heaven and earth, "God rested on the seventh day." The Hebrew word *sabat* means "to stop" or "to rest"—in this case to stop or rest from labor. The Hebrew people were commanded to stop or rest from their daily work so that they, their servants, and their cattle might be refreshed and renewed before the work of the coming week.

The authors of Deuteronomy give another reason for God's command to rest. They say, "Remember, you were slaves in Egypt and the LORD brought you out . . . therefore the LORD orders you to keep the Sabbath day" (Deuteronomy 5:15). It is as if they are saying, as slaves you had no rest, but because the LORD delivered you from slavery you are free to rest and to honor the LORD accordingly on the Sabbath day. The reason given for honoring one's father and mother is "that your days may be long in the land that the LORD God gives you." These reasons are practical ones. Everyone needs rest. And everyone needs the positive value of family love and harmony, however long or short their lives may be.

What It Means to "Remember"

The Hebrew word *zakar*, which we translate into English as "remember," emphasizes the present as it relates to the past. It is a word that calls for an active response here and now to an enduring command or person or reality.

According to Exodus 20:8-11, the LORD commands the people of Israel to "remember" the Sabbath day by keeping it holy. That is, they are to set aside the seventh day each week so that they, their children, their servants, and their cattle, along with the strangers among them, might "rest," and so, be renewed in body and spirit as well as be renewed in their relationship to the LORD who created them (Exodus 20:10-11) and redeemed them (Deuteronomy 5:15).

As Martin Buber has argued, the Sabbath, in its origin, was "a day not ordered for cultic reasons, but freed of all authority of command except that of the one Lord."[56] That is, the original purpose of the Sabbath was not to set aside a special day to worship God (a daily practice for God's people).

Its purpose was *to set aside* (make holy) a day when *only God's authority* would apply; a day when all human authority—master over slave, mistress over servant, manager over worker; owner over beast of burden—would be set aside. Why? For a two-fold reason: first, as a reminder that "every realm of life" (not simply religion) was to be subject "to the absolute authority" of the LORD as savior, master, and leader of the chosen people; second, so that slaves, hired hands, and animals, might "rest" from their labors and "catch their breath" or "be refreshed" as the Hebrew word of Exodus 23:12 puts it. But note that this humane purpose was given, not simply for the sake of the slaves, workers, and animals, but so that the whole people of God, the powerful and the weak, might be drawn together under the LORD's leadership, to become what God intended them to be—a people made fit to bring God's blessing to all the earth.

As Christians, we also have a special day of rest. We celebrate Sunday, the first day of the week, the day that God raised Jesus from the dead, a day in which we, in turn, are renewed in body and spirit through Jesus our Lord and in which we are called to look out for those among us who need "to catch their breath" and to "be refreshed."

What It Means to "Honor"

The Hebrew root-word *kabod*, which we translate into English as "honor" simply means "weight" or "heaviness." As a noun the word is often translated as "glory," and refers to *what a person really is*—his or her "substance" or "weight." As a verb the word is often translated as "honor" or "glorify," and it means "to respect a person for what he or she truly is," "to give due weight to a person's true value or authority." To honor one's father and mother, then, means to give due weight to what they are, and to the love, energy, and responsibility they give or have given, in caring for their children to the best of their abilities.

According to Exodus 20, this commandment is directly related to God's covenant promise to Abraham of life in the promised land. That is, such an honoring of one's parents fosters a family harmony which insures stability from generation to generation. As Luther writes: "Here you see how important God considers this commandment. Not only is it an object of pleasure and delight to God, but also an instrument intended for our greatest welfare, to lead us to a quiet, pleasant, and blessed life."[57]

It has never been easy to be a parent. It takes time, energy, money, love, skill, patience, and a lot more. What a blessing to parents when their children understand the responsibility their parents have! What a blessing to parents when their children support them with love and respect, and forgive them when they err!

Honoring Our Parents for a Lifetime

So often we think "honor your father and mother" refers to a young person's duty to trust and obey her parents. While that is true enough, there is strong reason to suggest that this command was *originally designed* for adult children to care and provide for their aging parents. Such devotion to aging parents was the "social security system" of thousands of years ago, and remains so in much of the world to this day. Certainly that is the understanding of the commandment as Jesus taught it (cf. Mark 7:9-13). 1 Timothy 5:4, 8 indicates that same understanding. We read:

> The children or grandchildren of a widow should first learn their sacred duty to their own household, to make some repayment to their parents; for this is pleasing in God's sight. . . . Whoever does not provide for relatives, and especially for family members, has denied the faith and is worse than an unbeliever.

Luther, too, applies the commandment to grown-up children as well as to young people. He writes: "When you hold your parents in honor, this teaches you not to let them suffer want, to lack food, and perish with hunger, but to give them the best you have in the house, the most precious treasure that God has given to you in order that you may honor them."[58]

But we might ask, how do we explain Jesus' admonition to honor our parents (Mark 7:9-13) when, on another occasion, he boldly declared that, *for his sake*, we must be willing to turn against our parents, spouse, children, brothers, and sisters (Matthew 10:34-37; Luke 14:26)? As Luther points out, these two statements of Jesus are not contradictory.[59] The challenge to forsake all relationships for Jesus' sake concerns faith. Only if family and friends hinder or oppose our relationship to Jesus are they to be set aside. In Luther's words: "It is on account of faith in Christ that everything should be forsaken."[60] But Luther also teaches us: "After faith in God nothing greater than obedience to parents."[61]

Luther's Explanations

Luther's Small Catechism explanations of the Sabbath and parental commands remind us that *trusting* in God is the key to keeping all the commandments. In explaining the Sabbath command, Luther writes: "We are to fear and love God so that we do not neglect God's Word and the preaching of it, but regard it as holy and gladly hear and learn it."[62]

In his Large Catechism Luther identifies the Sabbath as "a day to rest and be refreshed" as well as a day to hear God's Word,[63] and then writes:

We Christians should make every day a holy day . . . that is, occupy ourselves daily with God's Word and carry it in our hearts and on our lips."[64]

In his Small Catechism Luther explains the parental command, saying:

We are to fear and love God so that we do not despise or anger our parents and others in authority, but respect, obey, love, and serve them.[65]

Elsewhere Luther speaks of the parental command as "the golden chain" that parents wear as God's representatives, who are accountable to God in raising their children.[66] As Luther writes in his Large Catechism, "God has given and entrusted children to us with the command that we train and govern them according to God's will; otherwise God would have no need of father and mother."[67]

"You shall not kill" (Exodus 20:13).

This word is God's command to the people of Israel. It is a word designed to restrain evil among that people for the good of all. But surely it is a word for God's New Covenant people in Christ as well. "You shall not kill"—this seems clear and straight. Does this word, then, apply to us at all times and in every situation? Yes and no.

Yes. The Hebrew word used here (*ratsach*) is quite different from other Hebrew words translated as "kill." It is a word that refers to killing motivated by retaliation, by getting even, by revenge. This, for God's people, is wrong at all times no matter what. In the words of Paul: "Repay no one evil for evil. . . . Never avenge yourselves, but leave it to the wrath of God; for it is written, 'Vengeance is mine, I will repay,' says the Lord" (Romans 12:17-20).

No. In an absolute sense, "You shall not kill" does not seem to apply to us under certain circumstances. In defense of their country, soldiers are duty-bound to shoot to kill invaders. In the line of duty, police officers may be forced to kill criminals in self-defense. In fact, anyone under attack may be forced to kill in self-defense. Killing in such cases is done, not out of revenge, but out of necessity, and so, it would seem, is not a violation of the command against killing.

But wait. It's true that the Hebrew word *ratsach* is a technical term that refers to killing motivated by hatred or revenge, and yet, as Patrick Miller points out, that very word is used elsewhere in the Old Testament to refer to killing that is not premeditated or motivated by revenge.[68] And so, it would seem, we are not in a position to make a clear cut distinction between killing by premeditation or otherwise. In the end we must say, "To kill another person is tragic whatever the circumstance." To destroy another person can never be right, even when it is done in self-defense or in the line of duty. Everyone is precious in God's sight. Every person is priceless and cannot be replaced.

What about other kinds of killing, which are committed neither in retaliation nor in the line of duty? What about suicide, abortion, and euthanasia?

Suicide. Again we say, destroying life is always a tragedy and never right. Why would a person throw life away by committing suicide? Is it because life has become too much to handle or meaningless? Is it because the person is mentally ill? God is the judge of such actions, of course. We are not. But there is help to be had, short of such action. However depressed, lonely, or overwhelmed we may be, good friends, pastors, doctors, and others can help to restore us to health and a better life.

Abortion. Abortion is common today and in every case a tragedy. From the moment of conception in a woman's womb, a human being is being created. Who has the right to destroy this living being? Surely abortion as a method of birth control is wrong. At times an abortion may be a tragic necessity in order to save the life of a woman who is pregnant or when it is determined that the expected child is brain dead. But what if a woman is raped and made pregnant? What if a young girl becomes pregnant long before she has grown up herself? These are difficult questions which require tragic moral choices which will be hard to live with.

Euthanasia. What, then, of euthanasia? Consider a person with incurable cancer, facing great suffering and medical bills which will ruin his or her family. Should such a person be allowed to choose to die instead of to live? Or, should a person who is brain-dead be kept alive or be allowed to die naturally by starvation? These are difficult questions with no easy answers. But again, destroying life is always a tragedy. As the psalmist declares: "No ransom can be given for a person's life" (Psalm 49:7).

Capital punishment. What about capital punishment? Should a person who is found guilty of murder be put to death? Such was the law of Israel (Leviticus 24:17; Numbers 35:30--31). And such is the law of some states in our country. Many U.S. citizens today are opposed to capital punishment even for those who commit murder. Some argue that such extreme punishment does not fit the spirit of life and mercy we see in Jesus.

Actually the New Testament has no teaching regarding criminal law. What Jesus teaches and stands for concerns our everyday relationships to God, to ourselves, and to one another. His life and teachings should not be seen as a way of living that is intended to overrule or eliminate civil or criminal law in society. As Martin Luther once said:

> If any one attempted to rule the world by the gospel and to abolish all temporal law and sword, claiming that all people are baptized and therefore Christian . . . what would such a person be doing? He or she would be loosing the chains of the savage wild beasts and letting them tear and mangle every one.[69]

As Christians we are governed by the gospel and the Spirit of God. But whether we are Christians or not, in human society we are governed by the law and the sword which restrain evil among sinful human beings. What, then, might be a reason to oppose capital punishment? Perhaps to give the criminal time to reform. To give him or her the opportunity to be reached by the Good News of Christ, and through the work of God's Spirit, to be reborn. In any case, a person who deliberately kills someone else deserves to be put in prison, in most cases, for life.

Killing in war. What about the killing that takes place in war? War is never good. As someone has said, "There are no winners in war, only losers, no matter who comes out on top." And yet, isn't war necessary at times in order to repel invaders or to free those who have been taken captive against their will?

Some people, including some Christians, believe war is never justified under any circumstances. Such persons are known as "pacifists," from the Latin word *pacificus*, meaning peaceable. Christian pacifists believe that the best response to those who make war is passive resistance— opposing the enemy without violence. Sometimes such Christians quote Jesus, who said: "Do not resist one who is evil. But if anyone strikes you on the right cheek, turn the other also . . . and if anyone forces you to go one mile, go also the second mile" (Matthew 5:39, 41).

Others who hate war as much as pacifists do think passive resistance against invaders is not enough. They believe the words of Jesus quoted above are addressed to individual followers of Christ. The Lord urges us to respond to *personal* abuse in a non-violent way. They believe Christ's words do *not* apply to our duties as citizens of a country. In defense of others, when peaceful efforts to make things right have failed, they believe it is proper to oppose an aggressor by force. Luther, for one, is quite convinced about the need to support the government in the defense of peace and well-being. He writes: "It is certain and clear enough that it is God's will that the temporal sword and law be used for the punishment of the wicked and the protection of the upright."[70]

Luther's Explanation

Luther's explanation to the commandment, "You shall not kill," begins with the words, "We are to fear and love God so that. . . ." As with every commandment, our motive for obeying this command is trust in the LORD, whose actions and commands are intended to guide us and to enrich our lives. The phrase, "so that we do not hurt our neighbor in any way," expresses the *negative* half of Luther's explanation.[71] It is easy enough to "hurt" another person by our actions or our words. Children sometimes chant, "Sticks and stone may hurt my bones, but words will never hurt me." But it's not true. Words can hurt us deeply. A person's feelings are as important to well-being as bodily health.

Not only can sticks, stones, and words hurt us. Silence can hurt us as well. To be ignored is an awful thing. To be left out hurts. One of the finest things we can do as Christians is to include others in our activities. For example, what could be more thoughtful than for Christian young people to purposely look for a lonely classmate to sit with in the cafeteria or to visit with while waiting for a bus? What could be more thoughtful than for Christian adults to visit a lonely person or to invite for coffee some neighbor whom almost everyone dislikes and avoids? This is why Paul, following the urging of Psalm 37:27, writes: "See that none of you repays evil for evil, but always seek to do good." And this is why Luther, also commenting on Psalm 37:27, writes: "The expression 'do good' refers not only to returning good for good, but to offering good."[72]

". . . but help in all our neighbor's physical needs,"[73] is the *positive* side of Luther's explanation. As Luther puts it in the Large Catechism:

> This commandment is violated not only when a person actually does evil, but also when a person fails to do good to a neighbor or, though having the opportunity, fails to prevent, protect, and save the neighbor from suffering bodily harm or injury.
>
> It is God's real intention that we should allow no one to suffer hram, but show to everyone kindness and love . . . expcially to our enemies.[74]

Luther refers to Jesus' words:

> Love your enemies and pray for those who mistreat you. . . . For if you love those who love you, of what benefit is that? Isn't that true of the worst rascal? And if you are gracious only to your brothers and sisters, in what way are you doing any more than any one else? Don't even unbelievers do the same? (Matthew 5:44, 46-47).

Then Luther comments:

> Here again we have God's Word by which we are encouraged and urged to true, noble, exalted deeds, such as gentleness, patience, and in short, love and kindness toward our enemies. God always wants to remind us to think back to the First Commandment, to remember that the LORD is *our* God who (in the case of this commandment) wishes to help and protect us and subdue any desire we may have for revenge.[75]

"You shall not commit adultery" (Exodus 20:14).

The commandment on adultery forbids God's people to have sexual intercourse with anyone other than their own spouses. Why? Isn't sexual intercourse a good thing? Isn't sexual intercourse one of the blessings of life? Not only is sexual intercourse a good thing, it is one of the wonderful pleasures of life. That's how God intents it to be. That is, God intends that we enjoy the wonder of such sexual giving and receiving with *one* other human being, our spouse.

But why? If sexual intercourse is so wonderful, if it is the greatest expression of human love any one can have with another human being, why not enjoy this experience with other human beings as well as with one's spouse? Simply because it doesn't work. Adultery is quite common in our society, of course. We hear about it, read about it, and see it on TV and movie screens over and over again. But it is not what it might seem to be. True enough, the act of sexual intercourse can be a stimulating pleasure in and of itself. But to experience the *fullness* of joy and love that God intends for us as sexual beings, something more is required. That something more is the commitment and companionship that is experienced in a life-long relationship of trust, love, and faithfulness.

Luther speaks of the staying power of such love and loyalty:

> When a husband and wife really love one another, have pleasure in each other, and thoroughly believe in their love, who needs to teach them how they are to behave one to another, what they are to do or not to do, say or not to say, or what they are to think? Confidence alone teaches them all this, and even more than is necessary.[76]

It is God's intention that every married couple experience such love. This is why Jesus quotes Genesis 2:24, saying, "Therefore a man leaves his father and mother and is joined to his wife, and the two become one flesh." This means that a married couple's loyalty is primarily to each other. Other relationships (friends, parents, brothers, sisters, and children) are important, but secondary. This means the two of them are united in a life-long adventure with all its joys, challenges, and difficulties. To succeed, their adventure together requires trust, openness, honesty, and respect as well as patience, understanding, and forgiveness. In a word, their relationship requires personal commitment to each other.

Adultery is a violation of marriage. It is an act that threatens to destroy the trust and respect so necessary to any relationship. And it can inflict great harm on children and others it betrays. Equally important, adultery with someone else's spouse is a violation and threat to that other person's marriage. For after all, as Patrick Miller emphasizes: "All of the commandments in the second table are aimed at protecting the well-being of members of the community by placing upon each one a responsibility for the other/neighbor."[77]

Psychiatrist Paul Tournier not only calls adultery "childish," but "an infantile regression."[78] Indeed, adultery may very well be psychological in nature. It may be a means of mutual solace for the two persons involved. It may be a search for something more in life. It may be the outcome of some other deep seated issue or hangup. In any case, adultery is a flight from reality; an escape from the challenges of everyday living.

The relationship between two persons involved in adultery may seem to be quite wonderful, but it is an illusion. If and when an adulterous pair divorce their mates and marry each other, they soon discover that things are not quite so wonderful. As is often the case, they discover that their solace in each other fades and the something more they seek is unfulfilled. Moreover, if those involved in adultery are Christians, their relationship with God is disrupted by the guilt they experience because of their betrayal. No wonder Luther's explains this commandment by writing: "We are to fear and love God so that in matters of sex our words and conduct are pure and honorable, and husband and wife love and respect each other."[79]

God's Purposes for Marriage

According to the opening chapters of Genesis, God created human beings to live in community with others. And quite clearly the *primary* community the authors of Genesis have in mind is the partnership of marriage. True enough, there are those who, as Jesus says, are especially gifted to be single (Matthew 19:11). And there are those who, for a variety of reasons, establish no relationship with another. But in the overall perspective of the Bible, the very order of creation indicates the primary importance of the marriage partnership. Furthermore, for several biblical writers, the marital relationship is the model or analogy of God's special relationship with the chosen people.[80]

With their marital vows, a couple bind themselves together as lovers, companions, and partners. There may be some ongoing magic in this relationship, but for the most part it is work. Often it is great fun and sometimes it is just plain sweat and tears. *This is the way it is meant to be.* Not only does marriage provide companionship and partnership; of practical necessity it requires that each spouse adapt and adjust to the other.

Marriage has other God-given purposes as well—bringing children into the world, providing a stable home for children and parents alike, giving stability to community life, and providing companionship to the couple. But surely one of God's purposes for marriage is the *development*, *shaping*, and *renewal* of each spouse within the give-and-take, challenges, joys, and difficulties of life together.

You shall not steal" (Exodus 20:15).

As with every commandment, the *first* purpose of God's commandment against stealing is to keep order, to restrain evil, and to promote harmony among God's people. Clearly stealing upsets good order. It is evil. And it disrupts harmony in the community. Even if a thief is not caught, the fact that robbery has taken place disrupts relationships, causing suspicion and distrust within the community.

Just as important, stealing disrupts the life of the person who steals. The very act of stealing robs the thief of the well-being he or she is meant to experience as a creature of God. It reveals that we are sinful and need redemption (which is the *second* purpose of God's commandments). It is because we are sinful that we are tempted to steal, cheat, and deceive to get what we want. It is because we are sinful that we are tempted to take such shorts cuts in order to avoid the hard work of study or labor, or in order to compensate for a lack of ability in our studies or work. We see other people cheat, steal, and deceive, and in our sinfulness we think, "Why shouldn't I?"

Why? Because we are meant to be better than that. Because of who we are—children of God, redeemed by Christ. Because of the damage to our own self-image and well-being. If we fail, we can be forgiven, of course, as we confess and make good on what we have stolen. But how much better to life a life of honesty. And we can, with God's help.

Stealing takes many forms: Cheating on an exam is stealing. Copying someone else's homework is stealing. Reproducing music or printed material without permission is stealing. Charging more for something than it is worth is stealing. Lying on your income tax return is stealing. Drawing a salary, but not putting in an honest day's work is stealing.

Every such form of stealing disrupts the human community and robs the one who steals of self-respect and personal confidence. This is why God commands us, "You shall not steal." And this is why Luther explains this commandment by writing, "We are to fear and love God so that we do not take our neighbor's money or property, or get them dishonestly, but help to improve and protect our neighbor's property and means of making a living."[81]

Honest living begins with "fear and love for God." To trust in God, rather than in our selfish attempts to make it easy on ourselves by stealing, cheating, and lying, will give us strength to resist temptations. Furthermore, to trust in God brings us the hidden power and guidance of the Holy Spirit in our lives, and enables us to live in ways that help our neighbors and bolster our communities.

Luther puts it this way in the Large Catechism:

> Surely the Lord is sufficient for your needs and will let you lack or want for nothing. And so with a happy conscience you can enjoy a hundred times more than you could scrape together by dishonesty and wrong doing.[82]

"You shall not bear false witness. . . ." (Exodus 20:16)

This is one of the very worst sins. As Luther says: "This commandment seems insignificant, and yet it is so great that whoever would rightly keep it must risk life and limb, property and reputation, friends and all that he or she has."[83]

There are at least three ways in which we can bear false witness against our neighbor by deliberately lying about our neighbor—by passing on something we hear about our neighbor without knowing if it is true, and by keeping silent when someone says something against our neighbor that we know is false.

Why would anyone lie about someone else? Out of jealousy perhaps; out of meanness; to get even; to bring that person down (and make the liar look better). Whatever the motive, to deliberately lie and ruin a person's reputation is not only inexcusable, it is a betrayal. We might call it treason on a personal level. To pass on an ugly rumor about someone, whether we know it is true or not, is almost as bad as a deliberate lie about that person. True or not, the person's reputation is damaged just the same. To keep silent when someone says something about our neighbor that we know is false, is not only wrong, but downright cowardly.

Again, as with every commandment, the first purpose of God's commandment against false witness is to keep order, to restrain evil, and to promote harmony within the community of God's people. A second purpose of the commandment is to reveal our sinfulness.

The Tale of the Tongue

Someone has said, three things do not return—an arrow shot into the air, an opportunity missed, and a word quickly spoken. Many of us are too quick to speak. Sometimes we speak before we think. Sometimes we misunderstand another person's words or actions and react in anger, saying things for which we are sorry later. Sometimes we hear a rumor and tell it to someone else without knowing if it is true or not.

The ability to speak is a wonderful thing. The ability to hold our tongues and to listen is just as wonderful. The authors of the Bible (and of the inter-testamental books) have a great deal to say about this:

> Set a guard over my mouth, O LORD, keep watch over the door of my lips! (Psalm 141:3).

> There is one whose rash words are like sword thrusts, But the tongue of the wise brings healing (Proverbs 12:18).

> Those who watch their mouth and hold their tongue stay out of trouble (Proverbs 21:23).

> Let another praise you, and not your own mouth; a stranger, and not your own lips (Proverbs 27:2).

> Do you see someone who is hasty in speaking? There is more hope for a fool than for such a person (Proverbs 29:20).

> Many have fallen by the edge of the sword, but not so many as have fallen because of the tongue (Sirach 28:18).

> Never repeat a conversation and you will lose nothing at all. Do not report it with a friend or a foe; and unless it would be a sin, do not disclose it, for someone may have heard you and watched you, and in time will hate you. Have you heard something? Let it die with you. Be brave! It will not make you burst (Sirach 19:7-10).

Gossip

Perhaps nothing is as common in our society as gossip, which someone has called "careless talk" or "thoughtless chatter." Gossip tends to be destructive because it is usually made up of nasty comments or delicious rumors about others (behind their backs). Some of the world's wisest people are those who refuse to spread rumors or to downgrade other persons. A good example is a respected politician who, when someone suggested that he put down his opponent, refused. He said: "My mother taught me years ago that if you can't say something good about a person, say nothing at all."[84]

Few things in human society can be more harmful to our relationships with others than idle gossip. As Ephesians 4:29 puts it: "Let no evil talk come out of your mouths, but only what is uplifting, as fits the occasion, that it may impart grace to those who hear."

Luther's admonition says much the same. He says:

> It does not lie within your power to prevent evil talk from arising and to prevent hearing the world; but it behooves you to be vigilant and not to give way to it but to ward it off wherever it raises its head.[85]

Luther's Explanation

Luther explains God's commandment against false witness by saying, "We are to fear and love God so that we do not betray, slander, or lie about our neighbor, but defend, speak well of, and explain our neighbor's actions in the kindest ways."[86]

Again, Luther's opening words remind us that faith in God is the best preparation for living by the commandments as a whole. For surely, if we trust in God, we will not want to betray, slander, lie, or gossip about our neighbor. And surely, if we trust in God, we will be led to defend and speak well of others when they are under attack, and to forgive them when they have done wrong. The phrase "explain their actions in the kindest ways" is tremendously important. In the words of an older translation, "put the best construction on all that they do."

Too many of us make judgments before we understand or have all the facts before us. In Luther's striking words:

> Knowledge of sin does not entail the right to judge it. I may see that my neighbor sins, but to make my neighbor the talk of the town is not my business. If I interfere and pass sentence on him or her, I fall into a greater sin than his or hers. When you become aware of a sin, simply make your ears a tomb and bury it.[87]

It would be wonderful if we could learn to "put the best construction on what others do," including when others jump to conclusions before they have the facts. Not only would such a habit benefit others; it would give us a positive self-image at the same time. Again, in Luther's words: "It is a particularly fine, noble virtue always to put the best construction on all that we may hear about our neighbor."[88]

"You shall not covet . . ." (Exodus 20:17).

"You shall not covet" is the one forbidden *attitude* among the Ten Words. The command is not to covet what belongs to someone else —that person's spouse, property, or personal belongings. This doesn't mean it's wrong to want something *such as* a neighbor has. It means it's wrong to want *the very thing* a neighbor has. Because we live in a sinful world, we seldom enjoy all the benefits or privileges that certain others do. We may think, "It isn't fair. I deserve better." Such an attitude sometimes leads to the *actions* forbidden in other commandments of the Second Table of the Law.

In any case, to covet what belongs to another person disrupts the harmony of friendship, neighborhood, family, community, and/or one's inner self. Ambition, good planning, and working hard to obtain things *such as* our neighbor's can be good, as long as such things don't rob us of wholesome relationships with others. To covet what rightfully belongs to someone else always leads to unhappiness and *dis-ease*.

In explaining this commandment, Luther writes:

> We are to fear and love God so that we do not desire to get our neighbor's possessions by scheming or by pretending to have a right to them, but always help our neighbor to keep those possessions.[89]

Elsewhere he beautifully concludes:

> Now let us weave all the commandments into a garland, the last into the first. In them all you will find these two things: you should fear God and trust God. If you fear God, you will not mistrust God, you will not blaspheme, you will not be disobedient to your parents, you will not kill or do anyone physical harm, but rather help him or her; and so with all the rest of the commandments.[90]

"I the LORD your God am a jealous God . . ." (Exodus 20:5).

Luther completes his Small Catechism explanations of the Ten Commandments with the words of Exodus 20:5-6:

> I the LORD your God am a jealous God. I visit the iniquity of the parents upon the children to the third and the fourth generation of those who hate me, but I show steadfast love to thousands of those who love me and keep my commandments.

These words underscore the gravity of God's triple command: "*Never* shall you make yourself a graven image; *never* shall you bow down to them; *never* shall you serve them" (Exodus 20:4-5).

Luther goes further. He understands these words as part of the first commandment, but declares: "Although primarily attached to the First Commandment . . . this appendix ought to be regarded as attached to each individual commandment, penetrating and pervading them all."[91]

Luther asks, "What does this mean for us?" He answers:

> God threatens to punish everyone who breaks these commandments. Therefore we are to fear God's wrath and not disobey. But God promises grace and every blessing to all those who keep these commandments. Therefore we are to love and trust God and gladly keep these commandments.[92]

It may offend us to hear of the LORD as a jealous God. Yet such an understanding of God is proclaimed throughout the Bible. Over and over again we hear of the jealousy, the jealous wrath, and the jealous concern of God for Jerusalem, for the land, and for the people of Israel.[93] Moreover, in the words of Exodus 34:14, "the LORD's name is Jealous," that is, God's very nature is jealous. But perhaps this is not as offensive as it seems. The Aramaic root of the Hebrew word translated as "jealous" means "to blush," "intensely red," "the ruddy color of cheek caused by deep-seated emotion." The LORD, if you will, is a blushing God, red in the face from deep-seated passion. But the word is positive as well as negative. It is often translated "zealous" as well as "jealous." For example, speaking of the just and peaceful reign of the coming Messiah, Isaiah declares, "The zeal of the LORD of hosts will do this" (Isaiah 9:7). As Luther explains it:

> Jealousy properly is an anger which by nature involves love, as a man feels jealous about his wife. In short, it is a hatred of evil in the object of one's love, a friendly, loving hatred, or anger.[94]

> The verb "to be zealous" . . . is "to be jealous with love" or "to contend and strive out of love for someone."[95]

All this is figurative language to be sure. But the message is clear. The LORD cares. The LORD hates sin, but loves the sinner. Jealous over against our unbelief, compromises, and complacence, the LORD is zealous for our salvation. Indeed, the jealous God of all creation is no mere spectator of our human dilemma. The LORD is actively involved in our lives and in our world, in both judgment and salvation.

God's jealous love and claim is directed first to Israel, God's chosen people. But as the letter to the Ephesians declares, through Christ we who are Gentiles have become "members of the household of God" along with Israel (Ephesians 2:11-22; 3:5-6). Therefore God's jealous love and claim apply to us as well. Luther calls this action of God in Christ, "the great fire of the love of God for us."[96]

God's love is a relentless, jealous love that calls for our trust and faithfulness. When we fail, it is a love that refuses to give up on us, and continually calls us to turn to God in repentance and trust.

Jesus was said to be "consumed by zeal" (John 2:17). As followers of Jesus, we, too, are meant to exhibit zeal. Paul exhorts us to "zealously desire the gifts of the Spirit" (1 Corinthians 14:1); "to never flag in zeal, to be ardent in spirit, to serve the Lord" (Romans 12:11).

The God of Mercy and Justice

But let us recall that after declaring, "I, the LORD your God, am a jealous God," the LORD goes on to say, "I visit the iniquity of the parents upon the children to the third and the fourth generation of those who hate me, but I show steadfast love to thousands of those who love me and keep my commandments" (Exodus 20:5-6).

This declaration reminds us of a formula describing the LORD that occurs a number of times in the narratives and doxologies of the Old Testament (Exodus 34:6-7; Numbers 14:18; Nehemiah 9:17; Psalms 86:15, 103:8, 145:8; Joel 2:13; Jonah 4:2). As we read in Numbers 14:18: "The LORD is slow to anger and abounding in steadfast love, forgiving iniquity and transgression, but by no means absolving the guilty, visiting the iniquity of parents upon the children to the third and the fourth generation."

This formula emphasizes God's steadfast love, but does not neglect God's just and holy judgments. Notice the sequence in the formula:

- What God *is*—"slow to anger and abounding in steadfast love."
- What God *does*—"forgiving iniquity and transgression, but by no means clearing the guilty, visiting the iniquity of the parents upon the children to the third and fourth generation."

What God *does* reveals the wonder of God. As the texts in Exodus 20 and 34 emphasize, God acts with steadfast love and forgiveness for thousands in contrast to judgment upon but the third and fourth generation of those who live in iniquity. These texts use typical Hebrew exaggeration to emphasize the contrast between God's grace and judgment. As Luther writes:

> Terrible as God's threats are, much mightier is the comfort in the promise that assures mercy to those who cling to God alone—sheer goodness and blessing, not only for themselves but also for their children to a thousand and even many thousands of generations. Certainly, if we desire all good things in time and eternity, this ought to

move and impel us to fix our hearts upon God with perfect confidence since the divine Majesty comes to us with so gracious an offer, so cordial an invitation, and so rich a promise.[97]

The Commandments and Jesus

According to Matthew's Gospel, Jesus says, "Do not think that I have come to abolish the law and the prophets; I have come, not to abolish them, but to fulfil them" (Matthew 5:17). "*I have come, not to destroy, but to fulfil. . . .*" This is one of principal themes of Matthew's Gospel. And this is our Lord's way always. He begins with things as they are and goes on from there:

- He takes five loaves and two fish and feeds a multitude.
- He begins with rugged Peter and fiery James and John and slowly but surely builds them into messengers of the gospel.
- He calls despised Matthew and accepts immoral Mary Magdalene, changing their lives from within.
- He encourages women and children, the poor, the confused, and the tainted.

Jesus came, not to abolish, but to fulfil the law and the prophets and to accomplish God's purposes. He did this in three interrelated ways.

First, he fulfilled the law (Torah) *by the way he lived*. A careful reading of the four Gospels makes it clear that his life as a whole was based on living in accord with God's law. True enough, Jesus sometimes *seemed* to disregard the law. For example, on the Sabbath day he walked through the grainfields, allowing his disciples to pick grain to eat (Mark 2:23). On special days of fasting he ate as usual and allowed his disciples to do the same (Mark 2:18). Before eating, he did not practice ceremonial washing and excused his disciples from doing the same (Mark 7:1-3).

However, as the authors of the four Gospels tell it, Jesus acted as he did, not to rescind the law, but for quite positive reasons:

> To live the law as God intends it to be lived—in right relationship to God, others, one's self, and all creation.

> To challenge the misuse of the law we call *legalism*, which perverts the law, turning it into a religion of rigid "dos" and "don'ts."

As Luther argues: "When the example of Christ contradicts any doctrine, that doctrine is undoubtedly neither right nor founded on Scripture."[98]

An example of the way Jesus lived out God's law (Torah) is the way he remembered the Sabbath. As Luke 4:16 states: "When Jesus came to Nazareth, where he had been brought up, he went to the synagogue on the Sabbath day, *as was his custom.*" On the one hand, then, Jesus regularly attended the synagogue on the Sabbath. On the other hand, he healed the sick on the Sabbath, which angered the religious leaders of that day. The scribes and Pharisees interpreted God's Sabbath command in a legalistic way—turning it into a great number of rules. One regulation forbade carrying a burden on the Sabbath. And what was a burden? They said a burden was milk enough for one swallow, ink enough to write two letters of the alphabet, honey enough to put on a wound, oil enough to rub on a finger, food enough to equal one dried fig—and so on and on.[99]

Such practices removed the law (Torah) from the context of God's gracious purposes and turned it into regulations that hampered a person's everyday living. It was such distortions of the law that Jesus challenged. And it was such distortions of the law that Jesus set aside in order to help people in need. By healing and helping people on the Sabbath Jesus was, in principle, fulfilling God's intent to provide *rest* for those, who like slaves, hired hands, and animals, needed relief from their everyday burdens. As Luther declares:

> ... one should maintain the distinction between the outward use of the Sabbath, with regard to time, hour, or place, and the necessary works of love, which God requires at all times and hours and all places wherever there is need; so that we may know, as Jesus says, that the Sabbath was made for human beings, not human beings for the Sabbath.[100]

A second way Jesus fulfilled the law (Torah) was *by teaching it as God intends* that it be taught, both in order to declare God's will for the well being of human beings, and in order to to convict us when we fail to do right in relation to God and others. As Luther says:

> Jesus does not intend to bring another doctrine, as though the former one were no longer in force. He intends, rather, to preach it, to emphasize it, to show its real kernel and meaning, and to teach them what the law is and what it requires, in antithesis to the glosses which the Pharisees have introduced, the shells and husks which they have been preaching.[101]

What we call "The Sermon on the Mount" (Matthew 5:1-7:29) is itself a restatement of God's law (Torah) for the followers of Jesus. Apart from Jesus, the Sermon on the Mount is an impossible ideal. The key to

The Ten Commandments | 51

the Sermon on the Mount is Jesus himself, just as the key to the Torah is God. The Sermon on the Mount (as well as the Torah) is designed for people who already belong to God's kingdom through God's gracious action and who, then, are called to live out their lives in the power of God's Spirit. We see, then, that Jesus fulfilled the law in his life and in his teaching. His actions, his behavior, his teaching, his promises, his encounters with people, his suffering, and his death on the cross—all embody and illustrate the meaning and purpose of the law (Torah). To be more specific, people came first for Jesus as they do for God's law. In his life and ministry the needs of people took precedence over every rule and regulation. For after all, every rule and every regulation of the law was given for the benefit of people.

A third way Jesus fulfilled, and continues to fulfill, the law (Torah) is *by giving us what the law describes and demands*—a right relationship with God and with others. The Torah was never intended to be a way of salvation or a universal moral code. Neither is the Sermon on the Mount. Both the Torah and the Sermon on the Mount are designed for those whom God has already redeemed to God's people. Jesus himself is the key. It is not *primarily* by Jesus' example and teaching that we live. We live, first and foremost, in the gift of a right relationship with God that Jesus accomplished on our behalf through his cross and resurrection. We live and are renewed in this relationship through the work of God's Spirit calling us to faith in Christ. As Martin Luther puts it:

> The chief article and foundation of the gospel is that before you take Christ as an example, you accept and recognize him as a gift, as a present that God has given you and that is your own.
>
> When you have Christ as the foundation and chief blessing of your salvation, then the other part follows: that you take him as your example, giving yourself to your neighbor just as you see that Christ has given himself for you. There faith and love move forward, God's commandment is fulfilled, and a person is happy and fearless to do and to suffer all things.
>
> Therefore make note of this: Christ as a gift nourishes your faith and makes you a Christian. But Christ as an example exercises your works.[102]

Christ—the End of the Law

Paul makes a startling statement in his letter to the Romans: "Christ is the end of the law, so that every one who has faith may be justified [put right with God]" (Romans 10:4). What did Paul mean by this? The Greek word translated as "the end" can mean "the finish" or "the conclusion" of something, in the sense of *completed* or *fulfilled*. It can also mean "the finish" or "the conclusion" of something, in the sense of *over and done with*. Both senses apply to Romans 10:4.

For those in Christ, the law has been fulfilled. This is so because Christ gives us what the law demands—a right relationship with God. And, for those in Christ, the law comes to *an end*. That is, it comes to an end in the sense that the law can no longer threaten or condemn us when we fail to live as it commands. We are set free in Christ; that is, having been put right with God through Christ, we may, when we fail, turn to him for forgiveness and a renewed right relationship with God.

Luther sums it up when he says:

> All those who take hold of Christ in faith will possess the forgiveness of sin, the law will be fulfilled for them, death and the devil will be conquered, and they will obtain the gift of eternal life. In this man, all things are concluded and fulfilled. Whoever accepts him has everything.[103]

Of course this does *not* mean we no longer need to pay any attention to the Ten Commandments or to the Sermon on the Mount. God's law remains in force in two important ways. The first or civic use of the law continues to function to keep order, to restrain evil, and to promote harmony within human society. As long as we live in this world this use or function of the law is needed. The second or theological use of the law continues to function to reveal that we are sinful and to turn us to Christ again and again for the forgiveness and renewal of life God gives us through him.

The Law and the Gospel

The Fourth Gospel also makes a striking statement: "The law was given through Moses; grace and truth came through Jesus Christ" (John 1:17). In his sermon on John 1:17, Martin Luther proclaims to us the all-important distinction between the law and the gospel:

> The law reveals God's will, points to life, and exposes our sin. It must not be discarded. It is indispensable in its task. But it must not be treated as a way of salvation or as a way to win God's approval. That is not its purpose.

> The gospel alone reveals the way of salvation. Only God's redeeming action in Christ can deliver us from our faults and failures, restore us to a right relationship with God, and instill us with the spirit of holiness.

> We need the law to reveal God's will, to point us to right and wholesome living, and to stir and convict us when we act

in selfish, arrogant ways. We need the gospel to proclaim God's redeeming action for us, to assure us of God's love, to call us to faith, and, through the work of the Holy Spirit, to restore us to trust in God when sin defeats us and guilt overwhelms us.[104]

Elsewhere Luther admonishes us:

> Let everyone learn diligently how to distinguish the law from the gospel, not only in words but in feeling and in experience. That is, let us distinguish well between these two in our heart and consciences. For as far as the words are concerned, the distinction is easy. But when it comes to experience, you will find the gospel a rare guest but the law a constant guest in your conscience, which is so accustomed to the law and a sense of sin. . . .[105]

The Commandments and Christians

Quite clearly Luther reveres the Ten Commandments as God's Word. But he does not regard the Ten Commandments *themselves* to be binding for Christians. He writes:

> The law of Moses binds only the Jews, not Gentiles. It was given only to the people of Israel. To be sure, Gentiles have certain laws in common with Jews, such as, there is one God, no one is to do wrong to another, no one is to commit adultery or murder or steal . . . . This is written by nature into their hearts.

> If I were to accept Moses in one commandment, I would have to accept the entire Moses—then I must have myself circumcised, wash my clothes in the Jewish way, eat and drink and dress thus and so, and observe all that stuff. So then, we will neither observe nor accept Moses. Moses is dead. His ruled ended when Christ came.[106]

Why, then, did Luther include the Ten Commandments in his sermons, catechisms, and other discourses? As he himself asked and answered: "Why then keep and teach the Ten Commandments? Because the natural laws were never so orderly and well written as by Moses. And so, it is reasonable to follow the example of Moses."[107]

The Law Written in Our Hearts

Luther writes:

> Thou shalt not kill, commit adultery, steal, etc.," are not Mosaic laws only, but also *the natural law* written in each

person's heart, as Paul teaches (Romans 2:15). Also Christ himself (Matthew 7:12) includes all of the law and the prophets in this natural law: "So whatever you wish that others would do for you, do so to them; for this is the law and the prophets." Paul does the same thing in Romans 13:9, where he sums up all the commandments of Moses in the love that the natural law teaches in the words, "Love your neighbor as yourself."[108]

Furthermore, as Philip Watson points out, Luther teaches that:

> To be a believer is to be no longer under the law, but under grace. It is to stand in a filial [parent-child relationship to God], not a legal [law-based] relationship to God. In this sense the law is abolished by the gospel—and only in this sense. Believers are free from the law, inasmuch as it no longer tyrannizes over their conscience, driving them to despair on account of their sin. It cannot do so, because their sin is forgiven by the Author of the law. But they are not therefore free to do what the law forbids, or to omit what it commands. The "civil" or "political" [or *First*] use of the law . . . must still be maintained.[109]

Jesus' Word as Law and Gospel

We believe our Lord's Word continues to address us as both law and gospel. On the one hand, as we read in Matthew 5:21-22, 27-28:

> You have heard it said, "You shall not kill," but I say to you, "If you are angry with your brother or sister, you are liable to judgment." . . . You have heard it said, "You shall not commit adultery," but I say to you, "If you look upon another in lust, you have already committed adultery in your heart."

On the other hand we read:

> "The Son of man has come to seek and to save the lost" (Luke 19:10).

> "Come to me, all you who labor and are heavy-laden and I will give you rest" (Matthew 11:28).

> "Whoever comes to me I will not cast out" (John 6:37).

> "I have come that you might have life and have it abundantly" (John 10:10).

As persons who have been made God's own through faith in Christ, we are not called to live by rules or regulations that stand by themselves as a standard of human conduct. We are called to live in response to one another in company with the living God, who claims us through a new covenant in Christ and who continues to address us through law and gospel. Our call, then, is to be a people fit to represent God and to live for others in this world.

How the Law Remains Valid for Christians

When we are made right with God through the cross and resurrection of Jesus, our relationship to the law is transformed. Through Christ we are set free from the power of the law to accuse and condemn us. Yet, as Luther points out, the law remains valid for us.

One, the law remains valid for us as the proclamation of God's will to be our Lord, Savior, and Sanctifier.[110] As the LORD affirms in the first of the Ten Words, "I am the LORD your God."

Two, the law remains valid for us in its "civil" or "political" purpose: To restrain evil; to preserve, protect, and promote human welfare; and, in Luther's words, to give us "a pattern for a life of good works."[111]

Three, the law remains valid for us since, as long as we live in this world,[112] we are, in Luther's words, *simul justus et peccator* ("at one and the same time justified and sinners").[113] We are entirely and completely justified (made right with God) through faith in the crucified, risen Christ; yet we remain sinful.

As those who are justified through faith in Christ we are no longer "under the law" in its power to accuse and condemn us. As those who are still sinful we continue to be confronted by the "accusing, condemning" law which "points out" that we are sinful and in need of forgiveness and salvation. In Luther's words:

> For as long as we live in a flesh that is not free of sin, so long the law keeps coming back and performing its function—the daily mortification of the flesh, the reason, and our powers, and the renewal of our mind (2 Corinthians 4:16).[114]

Thus the law summons us to fight against the sin within us through the power of God's Holy Spirit.

PART TWO

THE APOSTLES' CREED

Background of the Apostles' Creed

The Apostles

The word *apostle* comes from a Greek verb meaning "to be sent out." The apostles were twelve men whom Jesus chose from among his many disciples "to be with him, and *to be sent out* to preach and to have authority to cast out demons" (Mark 3:14-15).

In Luke's Gospel (6:12-13), we read:

> In those days Jesus went out to the mountains to pray, and all night he continued in prayer to God. When it was day, he called his disciples and chose from them twelve, whom he named apostles.

In the Book of Acts (1:2-3, 8; 4:33), we read:

> To the apostles whom he had chosen, Jesus presented himself alive after his passion by many proofs, appearing to them during forty days, and speaking of the reign of God. He said to them: "You shall receive power when the Holy Spirit has come upon you; and you shall be my witnesses in Jerusalem and in all Judea and Samaria and to the end of the earth." And with great power the apostles gave their testimony to the resurrection of the Lord Jesus, and great grace was on them all.

These attributes, then, characterized the apostles:

- They were *chosen* by Jesus after night-long prayer to God.
- They were *with* him during his earthly ministry.
- They were *witnesses* to his resurrection from the dead.
- They were *empowered* by the risen Jesus with the gift of his Spirit.
- They were *sent out* to witness, to make disciples, and to lead the young church of Christ in his name.

The resurrected Jesus himself chose Paul, promised to be with him, and empowered him with the Spirit to be Jesus' apostle to the non-Jewish world.

As Luther writes concerning the apostles:

> This is the touchstone by which all doctrine is to be judged. One must take care and see whether it is the same doctrine that was published in Zion through the apostles.[115]
>
> Christians everywhere . . . are to attach themselves to the apostles and cling to their teaching. For these apostles are to be elevated among the Gentiles as sacred stones and battle insignia or as markers in Christendom
>
> All Christians will look to them and will be guided by their teaching, so that unity of doctrine and of faith may be maintained. . . .[116]

The Apostles' Creed

The English word, creed, comes from the Latin word, *credo*, meaning "I believe." A creed, then, is a confession or declaration of faith.

What we call the Apostles' Creed was not written by the apostles of Jesus, but it does represent what they believed and taught. In its present form the Apostles' Creed is probably from the late fourth century, c. 390 BCE, when it appeared in the writings of Ambrose of Milan. But every phrase and sentence in this creed is based on the teachings of the apostles as presented in the New Testament.

Like some earlier creeds, what we call the Apostles' Creed is a baptismal creed. It was originally meant to be used whenever someone was baptized, to indicate that person's faith in God. Today we use it on many occasions, including times when persons are baptized. Luther revered what he called "the Children's Creed" and wrote: "The first symbol (creed), that of the apostles, is truly the finest of all. Briefly, correctly, and in a splendid way it summarizes the articles of faith, and it can easily be learned by children and simple people."[117]

Creeds in the Bible

Creeds have been part of biblical faith in God from early in the history of God's people. These creeds are characterized by their declarations of what God had done. Every Old Testament creed, for example, recalls:

- God's act of delivering the people of Israel out of slavery in Egypt.
- God's gift to them of the land of Canaan.
- God's earlier covenant and promise to their ancestors (Abraham, Isaac, and Jacob). Cf. Deuteronomy 6:20-24;

26:5-9; Joshua 24:2ff.; Nehemiah 9:6ff; Psalms 78; 105; 106; 136; etc.

Certain of these creeds mention other acts of God for the people:

- God's covenant with the people at Sinai (Nehemiah 9:13; cf. Deuteronomy 6:24).
- God's guidance, patience, and provisions for Israel in the wilderness (Nehemiah 9:15, 19-20; Psalms 78:23-29; 105:39-41; 136:16).
- Even God's creation of the universe (Nehemiah 9:6; Psalm 136:5-9).

New Testament creeds declare the Good News of what God has done through Jesus Christ. The earliest creeds were brief:

"Jesus is Lord!" (Romans 10:9; 1 Corinthians 12:3).

"Jesus is the Son of God!" (John 11:27; 20:31; Acts 9:20; Hebrews 4:14; 1 John 4:15; 5:5; cf. Acts 8:37).

"Jesus is the Christ" (1 John 5:1; cf. 1 John 2:2).

A longer New Testament creed is preserved in 1 Corinthians:

For I delivered to you as of first importance what I also received: that Christ died for our sins, in accord with the scriptures, that he was buried, that he was raised on the third day in accord with the scriptures, and that he appeared to Cephas [Peter], then to the twelve; then he appeared to more than five hundred brothers and sisters at one time . . ." (1 Corinthians 15:3-8).

Acts 13:16-40 is a statement of faith which includes key elements of the creeds of both the Old and New Testaments—from God's choice of Israel's ancestors up to the crucifixion and resurrection of Jesus.

We see, then, that the creeds of the Bible are gospel—good news of what God had done to deliver God's people. This is true of the Apostles' Creed as well.

Personal Faith and Public Confession

In his letter to the Christians in Rome, Paul wrote: "If you confess with your lips that Jesus is Lord and believe in your heart that God raised him from the dead, you will be saved" (Romans 10:9). This statement shows what a creed is meant to be:

- It is a *spoken* word; a confession or declaration *with one's lips*. The Greek word translated here as *confess* literally means "to speak out together."

- It is a *specific* word of confession; in this case, "Jesus is Lord," probably the earliest creed of the Christian church.
- It is a word of *faith*: a confession arising out of a heart-felt trust in God. The confession, "Jesus is Lord," expresses trust in God who raised the crucified Jesus from the dead to be the Lord of all creation.
- It is a word of *salvation*: a confession of what God had done to set people free from bondage. "Jesus is Lord" proclaims one's faith in God's action in Jesus to deliver us from bondage to sin, evil, and death.

Martin Luther sums up Paul's words by saying:

> Praise is really a work and fruit of faith, concerning which St. Paul teaches in Romans 10. . . . St. Paul here seems to want to say: to believe in Christ secretly in your heart and to praise him in a private corner is not true faith. You must confess openly with your lips before everyone what you believe in your heart.[118]

As he says on another occasion:

> The true teaching and confession of Christ is impossible without faith; as St. Paul says, "No one can say, 'Jesus is Lord,' except by the Holy Spirit."

> So the most reliable index to a true Christian is this: if from the way a person praises and proclaims Christ people learn that they are nothing and that Christ is everything. In short, it is the kind of work that cannot be done in relation to one or two people, remaining hidden like other works. It has to shine and let itself be seen publicly, in front of the whole world.[119]

Confessing With Heart and Voice

Paul goes on to write: "For a person believes in the heart and so is justified, and confesses with the lips and so is saved" (Romans 10:10). These parallel phrases are inseparable expressions of Christian faith.

Of course, it is possible to confess without believing. As Luther says: "There are many who speak the words, 'I am a Christian,' with their mouth, but do not believe this in their heart."[120] To confess, then, does not necessarily mean to believe. But surely, to believe is to confess.

This reminds us that no one becomes a Christian automatically. There are those who have the idea that we can make Christians of our children without their knowing what has happened to them. But that's not possible. We don't just baptize children and that's that. Jesus said: "Go, make disciples, baptizing them and teaching them." The "faith once delivered to the saints"[121] must become a trust in Christ that is alive in us, and will be, as God's Spirit works in our hearts through the gospel proclaimed.

But what if we question the reality our faith? What if we are not sure that our relationship with God is real and right? Luther wrote:

> The question of justification [being put right with God] is an elusive thing—not in itself, for in itself it is firm and sure, but so far as *we* are concerned. . . . It is an elusive matter because *we* are so unstable. In addition, we are opposed by half of our very selves, namely, by reason and all its powers. Moreover, because the flesh cannot believe for sure that the promises of God are true, it resists the spirit.
>
> This is why we continually teach that the knowledge of Christ and of faith is not a human work but utterly a divine gift. As God creates faith, so God preserves us in faith. And just as God initially gives us faith *through the Word*, so later on God exercises, increases, strengthens, and perfects faith in us *by that Word*.[122]

"I believe *in*. . . ."

The Apostles' Creed begins with the words "*I* believe. . . ." The Nicene Creed begins with the words, "*We* believe. . . ." Why this difference? It is because the Apostles' Creed is a baptismal creed, originally designed to be used as a public confession of faith by an individual who desired to be baptized. The Nicene Creed was designed to be used as a public confession of faith by a community of believers who were already baptized.[123]

Following the words "I believe," the Apostles' Creed immediately adds the preposition "in." This is significant. It is one thing to believe *that* something is true or *that* someone is trustworthy. It is something else again to believe *in* something or *in* someone. When I believe *in* someone or something I am linked to that person or thing in a relationship of trust. Only when I believe *in* someone or something can I join others in a genuine confession of that belief. As Luther writes:

> Faith is exercised in two ways. First, a faith *about* God meaning that I believe that *what is said* about God is true. This kind of believing is more an item of knowledge or an observation than a creed. The second kind of faith means believing *in* God—not just that I believe that what is said about God is true, but that *I put my trust in God*.

> So the little word *in* is well chosen and should be noted carefully. We do not say, I believe *about* the Father, but rather, I believe *in* God the Father, *in* Jesus Christ, *in* the Holy Spirit.[124]

Everyone of us "believes in" any number of persons, concepts, ideas, and activities. So all of us could declare our faith in the persons and things we believe in. In any case, "believing in" someone or something is the essential element in our lives that moves us to declare our faith.

Born to Believe

We are born to believe. Faith is as natural and normal to a new-born baby as breathing, eating and drinking, and responding to love and care. Believing is meant to be, and is, part and parcel of everything we are and do, every day of our lives.

We are also born to sin. Sinning is as natural and normal to a new-born baby as breathing, eating and drinking, and responding to love and care. It wasn't meant to be this way, but sinning, too, is part and parcel of everything we are and do, every day of our lives.

We are born to believe. We are born to sin. In God's design we are meant to live and interact with one another in trust and faithfulness. But as heirs of our mothers, fathers, and grandparents, we live and interact with one another in mistrust and unfaithfulness as well as in trust and loyalty. Our believing, then, is messed up by our sinning. And yet, as little children, we have to learn *not to believe* the hard way—by hard knocks, by being deceived, by being let down by family, friends, and others.

And so, for sinful believers who have learned the hard way not to believe, the question becomes, "Believe in what and in whom?" In ourselves? In others? In luck? In fate? What about God? As sinful believers who have learned to become sinful doubters, how can we believe in God whom we have never seen? Only God can solve that problem and does, by calling us to faith through the Good News of God's gracious action for us in and through Jesus.

The Word of Faith

In his Romans letter, Paul points to God's Word as the key to faith: "The word is near you, on your lips and in your heart—that is, the word of faith that we proclaim" (Romans 10:8).

"The Word is *near* you." —The message of God's merciful action for us is as near as the sound of the Good News in our ears, and the call of God's Spirit in our hearts.

"The Word is near you . . . that is the word of *faith*. . . ."—Faith in God is a possibility for anyone who hears God's Word. Faith is not something we create or stir up within ourselves, and it is certainly not the thing *we* contribute to our salvation. In no sense do we initiate the way of salvation. In no sense do we prepare for a right relationship to God by *our* repentance, by *our* prayers, or by *our* anything.

"The Word is near you . . . that is the word of faith that *we proclaim*." It is through the spoken Word that God's Spirit generates in us faith in God. Without the Word being spoken to us we will not believe. As Paul goes on to say in Romans 10:13-14: "Scripture says, 'Every one who calls on the name of the Lord will be saved.' But how can people call on one in whom they have not believed? And how can they believe in one of whom they have never heard? And how can they hear without preaching?"

And in Romans 10:17 he concludes: "So faith comes from hearing and hearing from the Word of God." As Luther tells us:

> We must learn by all means that forgiveness of sins, Christ, and the Holy Spirit are given—and given freely—only when we hear with faith. . . . so, a person becomes a Christian, not by working but by listening.[125]

> Through the gospel the light (of Christ) is brought to us, not from afar, nor is it necessary to run after it a great distance; it is very near to us and also shines in our heart. Nothing more is necessary but that it be pointed out and preached. And whoever hears it preached and believes, finds it in the heart, for faith can only be in the heart.[126]

Believing is Receiving

According to the Fourth Gospel Jesus said:

> Everyone the Father gives me will come to me, and whoever comes to me I will not cast out. No one can come to me without being drawn to me by the Father who sent me" (John 6:37, 44).

We see, then, that in relationship to God, believing is receiving. Faith in God is not something we decide to do or are able to do. Why? Because, as the authors of the Bible declare, we are by nature selfish and blinded by sin. Luther puts it this way in his explanation of the third article of the creed:

> I believe that I cannot by my own understanding or effort believe in Jesus Christ my Lord, or come to him, but the Holy Spirit has called me through the gospel, enlightened me with spiritual gifts, and sanctified and kept me in true faith.[127]

As Paul writes: "Faith comes through what is heard, and what is heard comes through the word of Christ" (Romans 10:17). When I hear the Good News of God's love and action for me in Jesus, the Holy Spirit stimulates my mind, activates my heart, and calls and inspires me to respond in trust toward God. So it is with everyone. As Luther goes on to say in his explanation of the third article of the creed:

> In the same way the Holy Spirit calls, gathers, enlightens, and sanctifies the whole Christian church on earth, and keeps it united with Jesus Christ in the one true faith.
>
> In this Christian church day after day the Spirit fully forgives my sins and the sins of all believers; and on the last day will raise me and all the dead and give me and all believers in Christ eternal life. This is most certainly true.[128]

Salvation by Grace through Faith

> "Jesus said, 'I have told you that no one can come to me unless it is granted by the Father'" (John 6:65).

Luther writes:

> With the words "No one can come to me," Christ intends to say that faith is God's gift. And God is willing to give it, if only we request it.
>
> It is the Father who draws us and gives us the Word and the Holy Spirit and faith by the Word. It is God's gift, not our work and power. Paul also tells us that in Ephesians, "For by grace you have been saved through faith; and this is not your own doing, it is the gift of God, not because of works, lest any one should boast."
>
> And so, since faith is created in us without our work and power, but solely by the grace of God, it must be esteemed and honored highly.[129]

But what is this grace by which we are saved through faith? As commonly defined, grace is "God's unmerited mercy or favor" toward us. But this mercy or favor should *not* be thought of as some divine commodity or quality that God sends us. As indicated earlier, God's grace is *God's personal action* in our behalf. It is God's favorable, merciful action to be sure, but with the accent on *action* as opposed to some sort of God-sent substance. As Luther writes:

> Grace means the favor by which God accepts us, forgiving sins and freely justifying us through Christ. It belongs to the category of *relationship*. . . . So you should not think it is a quality, as the scholastics dreamed.
>
> Grace is the continuous and perpetual *operation* or *action* through which we are grasped and moved by the Spirit of God.[130]

As a wonderful acrostic on the word defines it, God's grace is: **G**od's **R**edeeming **A**ction **C**oncerning **E**veryone.[131] This sounds like John 3:16—God's loving action for all humanity, giving us the only Son to redeem us from sin and death and to give us eternal life. This sounds like the work of God's Spirit—calling us to faith through the Good News of new life in Christ.

Is Christian Faith Unreasonable?

In his second letter to the Corinthian Christians, Paul writes: "We walk by faith, not by sight" (2 Corinthians 5:7). Does this mean that Christian faith is unreasonable? No. At least not to those of us who are Christians. However, there are some things that God has revealed to us that are *beyond reason*. As Luther writes:

> It does indeed seem ridiculous and absurd to reason that in the Lord's Supper the body and the blood of Christ are presented, that Baptism is "the washing of regeneration and renewal in the Holy Spirit" (Titus 3:5), that Christ the Son of God was conceived and carried in the womb of the Virgin, that he was born, that he suffered the most ignominious of deaths on the cross, that he was raised again, that he is now sitting at the right hand of the Father, and that he now has "authority in heaven and on earth" (Matthew 28:18).[132]

Most disconcerting of all to human reason, as Luther puts it:

> God rules in a manner strange and different from what human beings are able to understand or conceive. Therefore God's wisdom, authority, and power are hidden to all reason. In fact, God will demonstrate these things precisely by the opposite, which is called foolishness, frailty, and nothing everywhere and by all people.[133]

Luther received this understanding from Paul, who wrote:

> God chose what is foolish in the world to shame the wise. God chose what is weak in the world to shame the strong. God chose what is low and despised in the world . . . so that no human being might boast in the presence of God (1 Corinthians 1:27-29).

But as Paul goes on to declare:

> "As it is written, 'What no eye has seen nor ear heard nor the human heart conceived, what God has prepared for those who love God,' God has *revealed* to us through the Spirit" (1 Corinthians 2:9-10).

For believers, then, faith is not unreasonable. But there are promises and actions of God *beyond reason* that can be received only through that faith engendered in us by the Holy Spirit.

Did Luther "Decry Reason"?

Luther writes:

> Reason plays blindman's buff with God. It consistently gropes in the dark and misses the mark. It calls "God" that which is not God and fails to identify the One who really is God.[134]

Such comments upset John Wesley who said that Luther

> decries reason, right or wrong, as an irreconcilable enemy to the gospel of Christ! Whereas, what is reason but the power of apprehending, judging, and discoursing? Which power is no more to be condemned than seeing, hearing, or feeling.[135]

True enough, Luther often points to the failure of reason to grasp God's Word and actions, and goes so far as to call reason "the devil's whore."[136] Yet, he also says:

> God has not given us reason and the counsels and help of reason that we should despise them.[137]

> *In external and worldly matters* let reason be the judge.[138]

> Reason is the most important and the highest in rank among all things and, in comparison with other things of this life, the best and something divine. It is the inventor and mentor of all the arts, medicines, laws, and of whatever wisdom, power, virtue, and glory people possess in this life.[139]

In external and worldly matters, then, Luther understands reason exactly as Wesley does. He writes that "reason illumined by faith"[140] or "by the Holy Spirit" enables us to discern and act rightly in response to God's Word and actions, and then declares, "We must make use of sound and sure reasons especially in theological matters."[141]

To sum up this issue in Luther's own words:

> In heavenly matters and in matters of faith, when a question of salvation is involved, bid reason observe silence and hold still.[142]

> We should use our reason and wisdom for other things, for managing the household, doing our jobs, for buying and selling.[143]

> Christ is grasped, not by the law or by works, but by a reason or an intellect that has been illumined by faith.[144]

The Rule of Faith and the Rule of Love

In his letter to the Galatians congregations Paul writes: "In Christ Jesus neither circumcision nor uncircumcision counts for anything; what counts is faith working through love" (Galatians 5:6). Here, in a nutshell, is Paul's conviction of what Christianity is all about; not religious rituals or traditions, but "faith working through love"—that is, a relationship of trust in Jesus our Lord that *effects* and *is expressed* in a relationship of love for God and for others.

But notice, faith in Christ is first, foremost and creative. Love follows faith, not vice versa. In accord with Paul, Luther makes much of this point, especially in the face of those who seem willingly to set aside "the truth of the gospel" (cf. Galatians 2:5, 14; 4:16; 5:7) in order to promote what they call "love and unity." Luther writes:

> There is a distinction between faith and love. Faith tolerates nothing, love tolerates everything; faith curses, love blesses; faith seeks vengeance and punishment; love seeks reprieve and forgiveness. Therefore *where faith and the Word of God are at stake*, it is not right to love or to be patient but only to be angry, zealous, and reproving. That is how all the prophets behaved; in matters of faith they manifested no patience or kindness.[145]

> As the common saying has it, "A person's reputation, faith, and eye cannot stand being played with." So far as faith is concerned, therefore, a Christian is as proud and firm as can be; and must not relax or yield the least bit.

> Therefore let every Christian follow the example of Paul's pride here [Galatians 2:14]. Let love bear all things, believe all things, hope all things (1 Corinthians 13:7). Let faith, by contrast, bear absolutely nothing; but let it rule, command, triumph, and do everything. For love and faith are exact opposites in their intentions, their tasks, and their values. Love yields even in trifles and says: "I bear everything and yield to everyone." But faith says: "I yield to no one; but everything must yield to me—people, nations, kings, princes, and judges of the earth."[146]

We see then, that in Luther's understanding of Paul, when it comes to matters of God's Word and Christian doctrine, we must apply what Luther calls "the rule of faith," not the "rule of love," simply because the truth and freedom of the gospel are at stake.[147]

"I believe in God the Father... Son... Spirit...."

The first Christians were either Jews or "God-fearers" (Gentiles who accepted the Jewish belief in the one true God). When such believers put their trust in the resurrected Jesus as the Messiah/Son of God, they confessed, "Jesus is Lord," "Jesus is the Son of God" or "Jesus is the Christ." Then they were baptized "in the name of Jesus Christ."[148]

The New Testament as a whole suggests that baptism continued to be carried out "in the name of Jesus Christ" throughout the New Testament era. Only the Gospel of Matthew states that baptism is to be done "in the name of the Father and of the Son and of the Holy Spirit" (Matthew 28:19).

By the beginning of the second century (101-200 CE), however, baptisms were being carried out "in the name of the Father and of the Son and of the Holy Spirit." Why this change? Perhaps because more and more of those who became Christians were neither Jewish nor "God-fearers." Perhaps because such Gentiles were challenged not only to trust in Jesus as their Lord, but to trust in the One who sent him, YHWH, the one true God and Creator of the universe. And so, the question addressed to a candidate for baptism was no longer, "Do you believe in Jesus as Lord?" The question was: "Do you believe in God the Father Almighty? Do you believe in Jesus Christ, God's only Son, our Lord? Do you believe in the Holy Spirit?"

How Do Father, Son and Spirit Relate to One Another?

Christians regularly use the Apostles' Creed to confess: "I believe in God the Father Almighty. I believe in Jesus Christ, God's only Son, our Lord. I believe in the Holy Spirit." But what does this mean? How do we explain our confession of faith in God the Father, God's only Son, and the Holy Spirit? To put it in other words, how are Father, Son and Holy Spirit related to one another?

It all depends: Do we stay with what the New Testament has to say about the Father, the Son and the Spirit? Or do we attempt to explain what the largely Gentile, Greek-oriented church leaders of the fourth century CE had to say. What we do makes a difference, simply because the New Testament arises out of a Jewish or Hebrew understanding of reality, while the later church leaders had more of a Greek understanding of reality. A comparison of the Apostles' Creed and the Nicene Creed illustrates the difference.

The Apostles' Creed is made up of statements based on the Bible. The Nicene Creed is also made up of statements based on the Bible, but adds material that the later Greek-oriented church believed necessary to clarify those statements.

As a prime example, the authors of the Nicene Creed amplify what they believe the New Testament teaches about Jesus by adding that he is *"of one being with the Father."* In other words, the Nicene Creed declares that God the Father and Jesus, the Son of God (as well as the Holy Spirit), have one common divine nature. Many of us are used to such language of course. We sing hymns with phrases such as, "With God, the Three in One," "great One in Three," and "God in three persons, blessed Trinity."[149] However, the authors of the New Testament do not use such language.

But what about the language of the Gospel of John? Jesus said, "The Father and I are one"? (John 10:30) Yes, and he also said, "Holy Father, keep, in your name, those you have given me, that *they* may be one, even as *we* are one" (John 17:11). The point is, the word "one," as used in these passages, does not refer to a common nature or being. It refers to a mutual harmony and unity of purpose.

As for Jesus' statement, "Whoever has seen me has seen the Father," (John 14:9), this is a claim, not of equality with the Father, but of representing and revealing the Father. Indeed, Jesus goes on to say, ". . .the Father is greater than I" (John 14:28). As Raymond Brown writes:

> . . . the Johannine stress on the oneness of Jesus and the Father is primarily related to the Son's mission to humanity and has only secondary metaphysical implications about life within the Godhead. We have also suggested that much of the equivalence between Father and Son is phrased in language that stems from the Jewish concept that the one who is sent (*saliah*) is completely the representative of the one who sends him.[150]

And as Luther points out:

> . . . in many passages in the Gospel of John . . . Christ, in his commission, calls us back to the will of the Father, so that in his words and works we are to look, not at him, but at the Father. For Christ came into the world so that he might take hold of us and so that we, by gazing on Christ, might be drawn and carried directly to the Father.[151]

Father, Son and Spirit as Trinity

The reason that third and fourth century CE church leaders attempted to define God's innermost nature was to combat a variety of false teachings regarding the relationship of God the Father and Christ Jesus. In the end they determined that the innermost nature of God's being is "three distinct persons, Father, Son and Spirit, but of one divine essence, coequal, uncreated and eternal." Or to state it more simply, God is Triune (three in one). As British theologian J. S. Whale writes: "Christian thought, working with the data of the New Testament and *using Greek philosophy as its instrument*, constructed the doctrine of the Trinity."[152]

Interestingly enough, the Apostles' Creed does not use the terms *Triune* or *Trinity*. Neither does the Nicene Creed, nor does Luther's Small Catechism, nor does the Augsburg Confession. As Luther says:

> The title "Trinity" is found nowhere in Holy Scripture. People conceived and invented it, and therefore, it sounds rather cold. It is better that we speak of "God" than "the Trinity."
>
> . . . this, as well as every other article of faith, must not be based on reason or comparisons, but must be understood and established by means of passages from the Scriptures.[153]

For the same reason Luther did not care for the use of the "nonscriptural word" *homoousian* (one being) in the Nicene Creed.[154] He held that "the integrity of scripture must be guarded" and we should rely on what the authors of scripture have to say on these things. Nevertheless Luther accepted the trinitarian doctrine of God as a true expression of the Christian faith, *but* he always interpreted this understanding in the light of scripture.[155] As Leif Grane puts it:

> Luther does not reject trinitarian language that attempts to express the inner being of God, but simply emphasizes that the inner being of God is known *only* through God's *works* in revelation.[156]

The Son and God's Revealing Actions

There are many *triadic* statements in the New Testament that testify to the intrinsic relationship and activity of the Father, the Son and the Holy Spirit.[157] Among the many are:

> The grace of our Lord Jesus Christ and the love of God and the fellowship of the Holy Spirit be with you all (2 Corinthians 13:14).
>
> Through Christ Jesus, Jews and Gentiles alike have access in one Spirit to the Father (Ephesians 2:18).
>
> May God grant you to be strengthened with might through the Spirit in the inner person, that Christ may dwell in your hearts through faith (Ephesians 3:14-17).

But there are no *triunic* statements in the New Testament. That is, the Father, Son and Spirit are never identified as sharing "one divine essence, coequal, uncreated, and eternal." The authors of the New Testament would never have conceived of trying to define the nature of God's innermost being. Such a definition was beyond them and, quite frankly, such a definition remains beyond any human being. Their purpose was rather to proclaim *the actions* of the Father, the Son and the Holy Spirit in our behalf; actions carried out and made known concerning our salvation and eternal well being. As Oscar Cullmann writes: "Here is the key to all New Testament christology. To speak of the Son has meaning *only* in reference to God's *revelatory action*, not in reference to God's being."[158]

Luther expresses it this way:

> We are seeking . . . not a definition of the divine essence, which is incomprehensible, but of God's will and attitude.[159]

> You have often heard from us that it is a rule and principle in the Scriptures, and one that must be scrupulously observed, to refrain from speculation about the majesty of God, which is too much for the human body, and especially for the human mind, to bear.

> True Christian theology, as I often warn you, does not present God to us in majesty . . . but Christ born of a virgin as our Mediator and High Priest. . . . . nothing is more dangerous that to stray into heaven with our idle speculations, there to investigate God's incomprehensible power, wisdom and majesty.[160]

One God and One Mediator

How, then, do the authors of the New Testament understand the relationship between the Father, the Son, and the Spirit?

First of all, in accord with Old Testament teaching, the authors of the New Testament declare, "God is one."[161] That is, the LORD, the God and Father of Christ Jesus, is the *only* One—the one and only true and living God. In describing God, then, the word "one" is more than just a number. It is a word that emphasizes the *uniqueness* as well as the *singleness* of the LORD God. As expressed elsewhere in Scripture:

> The LORD is God, there is no other (Deuteronomy 4:35).

> Only in the LORD are righteousness and strength (Isaiah 45:24).

> . . . Who alone does great wonders . . . (Psalm 136:4).

> . . . Who alone is immortal . . . (1 Timothy 6:16).

Second, there is no question in the minds of the New Testament authors that Jesus is absolutely unique and that the one true God was and is at work in and through him. He was and is God's chosen Messiah/Son. He was crucified, died, and buried, but raised again from the dead by the one true God. He has been exalted by the one true God to be the Lord of heaven and earth.

Passage after passage declares the unique relationship of Jesus to God the Father. For example:

> There is one God and one mediator between God and humanity, the man Christ Jesus, who gave himself a ransom for all (1 Timothy 2:5-6).

> God's love was revealed among us in this way: God sent the only Son of God into the world so that we might live through him (1 John 4:9).

> He is before all things and in him all things hold together. . . . For in him all the fullness of God was pleased to dwell and through him to reconcile all things to God (Colossians 1:17, 19).

> The Word that was "in the beginning with God" and "was God" "became flesh" in Jesus, "the only Son from the Father" (John 1:1, 14).

> He was known before the foundation of the world, but was revealed in these last times for your sake. Through him you have come to trust in God, who raised him from the dead and gave him glory, so that your faith and hope are set on God (1 Peter 1:21).

God the Father and God the Son

The New Testament authors vary in their descriptions of how and when Jesus was designated as God's Messiah/Son.[162] The Gospel of Mark identifies him as "the Son of God" (1:1) and points to the event of his baptism, during which "a voice came from heaven, 'You are my beloved Son, with whom I am well pleased" (1:11).

The Gospels of Matthew and Luke point to his conception (by the Holy Spirit) and birth (of the Virgin Mary). Matthew, in his birth account, identifies Jesus as "Christ" and "Emmanuel," and follows Mark in describing the voice from heaven at his baptism calling him "my beloved son" (Matthew 1:18-25; 3:17). Luke, in his conception account, describes the angel Gabriel telling the Virgin Mary, he will be "called the Son of the Most High;" and in his birth account, again through an angel, Luke calls Jesus "a Savior, who is Christ the Lord" (Luke 1:26-35; 2:1-14).

Paul writes that Jesus was "designated Son of God in power through the Spirit of holiness by his resurrection from the dead" (Romans 1:4).

The Gospel of John declares that the Word that was "in the beginning with God" and "was God" "became flesh" in Jesus, "the only Son from the Father" (John 1:1-2, 14).

The letter to the Colossians calls him " . . . the first-born of all creation, for in him all things were created . . ." (Colossians 1:15-16).

The letter to the Hebrew describes him as the "Son . . . through whom God created the world" (Hebrews 1:3).

But, as we would expect, John's Gospel, the Letter to the Colossians, and the Letter to the Hebrews all make a clear distinction between God the Father and Christ Jesus, the Son of God.

> According to John 17:3, Jesus prays, "This is eternal life, that they know you, the only true God, and Jesus Christ whom you have sent."
>
> Colossians 1:19 tells us, "He is the image of the invisible God—in whom all the fulness of God was pleased to dwell."
>
> The Letter to the Hebrews calls him "a Son who . . . reflects God's glory and bears the very likeness of God's being" (1:2-3).

The Incarnation

The incarnation, *God with us in the humanity of Jesus*, is at the heart of the New Testament revelation of the one true God. As the authors of the New Testament declare:

> God was in Christ, reconciling the world to God . . . (2 Corinthians 5:19).
>
> In Christ the whole fullness of Deity dwells bodily . . . (Colossians 2:9).
>
> Christ also assumed flesh and blood . . . (Hebrews 2:14).
>
> The Word became flesh and dwelt among us . . . (John 1:14).

It would be impossible for us to survive an encounter with the awesome God of majesty and holiness. We would be overwhelmed. We would, as the Old Testament puts it, die of fright. But in the earthly, fully human Jesus it was possible for the great and glorious LORD of the universe to draw near to us, to be revealed and to redeem us from sin and death. And now—in the twenty-first century—through the presence and work of the Holy Spirit we can be touched by the majestic, holy God who came among us two thousand years ago in the humanity of Jesus.

To take it one step further, just as the awesome God of glory drew near to us in the humanity of Jesus; so now, the risen, glorified Jesus draws near to us in the earthly ways of his choosing—the spoken Word of God, the waters of baptism and the bread and wine of the Lord's Supper—all of which are extensions of his humanity and instruments of the Holy Spirit to bring us to Christ. As Luther writes:

> If you take hold of Christ, you have all; you have taken hold of the entire Godhead. . . . This calls for a humble and

helpless, a hungry and thirsty soul that relies on the words and seeks God nowhere but in Christ who lies in a manger or wherever he may be—on the cross, in baptism, in the Lord's Supper, in the ministry of the divine Word, or with my neighbor or brother or sister.[163]

Again Luther writes:

> . . . we could never come to recognize the Father's favor and grace were it not for the Lord Jesus, who is a mirror of the Father's heart. . . . But neither could we know anything of Christ had it not been revealed by the Holy Spirit.[164]

The Creative Activity of Father and Son

One of the common images of God in the Bible is God as Creator. The very first verse of the Bible declares, "In the beginning God created the heavens and the earth." It is a conviction echoed throughout the Bible. But notice how the New Testament describes the Creator God:

> There is one God, the Father, from whom are all things and for whom we exist, and one Lord Jesus Christ, through whom are all things and through whom we exist (1 Corinthians 8:6).

> The Word was in the beginning with God; all things were made through him, and without him was not anything made that was made. In him was life, and the life was the light of all people (John 1:2-3).

> In him (the Son of God) all things in heaven and on earth were created, things visible and invisible, whether thrones or dominions or rulers or powers—all things have been created through him and for him (Colossians 1:16).

> . . . God has spoken to us by a Son, whom God appointed the heir of all things, through whom also God created the universe. He reflects the glory of God and bears the very stamp of God's nature, upholding the universe by his word of power" (Hebrews 1:1-3).

> The words of the Amen, the faithful and true witness, the origin of God's creation (Revelation 3:14).

Clearly these authors portray the creation in terms of Father and Son. And in tandem with Old Testament texts that describe God's creative activity, these authors assume the power of the Spirit in the very life and preservation of what God creates. As Luther writes: "We can never grasp and comprehend this article of our salvation and eternal welfare with our human reason."[165] And referring to the New Testament passages cited here, he writes: "Within these limits our thinking concerning the creation must remain; and we should not go too far afield, because then we shall surely get into darkness and mischief."[166]

The Father, Son and Spirit in Stephen's Vision

Hans Küng points out, "In the New Testament there is probably no better story to illustrate the relationship of Father, Son and Spirit" than the description of Stephen's vision (Acts 7:54-56) before he is put to death.[167] We read:

> When the Jewish council heard what Stephen said, they became enraged and ground their teeth at him. But filled with the Holy Spirit, he gazed into heaven and saw the glory of God and Jesus standing at the right hand of God. "Look," he said, "I see the heavens opened, and the Son of man standing at the right hand of God!" (Acts 7:54-56).

Stephen is described as filled with the Holy Spirit, and so is enabled to see into heaven. Stephen sees, not God, but the *glory* of God. Stephen sees *Jesus* clearly revealed as the Son of man, exalted with power and authority (at the right hand of God). What does this tell us about Father, Son, and Spirit? We might say:

- The Holy Spirit is not seen because the Spirit is God's active power at work in and for and through Stephen.
- God the Father is not seen because God's majesty is too great. Stephen would be overwhelmed by what God truly is. Stephen rather sees the awesome glory that radiates from the one, true holy God.
- Only Jesus is seen because, as Colossians puts it, he is the image of the invisible God, who is exalted as God's representative to us and for us, and as our representative and mediator before God.

As Küng concludes, the relation of Father, Son and Spirit could be described like this:

> God, the awesome Father, *beyond* us,
> Jesus, the Son of man, *with* God the Father *for* us,
> The Holy Spirit, God's powerful presence at work *in* us.[168]

God Manifest in the Spirit through Christ

In Ephesians 2:18 we read: "Through Christ Jesus, Jews and Gentiles alike have access in one Spirit to the Father." Here, again, we are reminded that the New Testament statements about Father, Son, and Spirit are never about God's innermost nature. They are always about

God's activity in creating, revealing, redeeming, calling, preserving, guiding, judging. That is, they are statements about God's self-revealing activity through Jesus Christ; God's dynamic and universal activity in history; God's relationship to human beings. They are about God made manifest in the Spirit through Jesus Christ.

As Hans Küng puts it so well, this means:

> To believe in God the Father is to believe in the one God, creator, preserver and perfecter of the world and humanity.
>
> To believe in God's Son is to believe in the revelation and activity of the one God in the man Jesus, who is God's Word, Image and Son.
>
> To believe in the Holy Spirit is to believe in God's effective and purposeful power in human beings and in the world.[169]

Luther writes:

> To the Father is ascribed power, to the Son, wisdom, and to the Holy Spirit goodness, which we can never attain and of which we must despair. But when we know and consider that Christ came from heaven and loved sinners in obedience to the Father, then there springs up in us a bold approach to and firm hope in Christ.[170]

So then, considering the way the New Testament describes the Father, the Son, and the Holy Spirit in relation to one another, should we abandon the word "Trinity" in reference to God? Not at all. There is a clear *unity* of mission and purpose in the actions of the Father, the Son, and the Holy Spirit. Are, then, the Son of God and the Holy Spirit "of one being with the Father"? So we confess and affirm in the Nicene Creed and in the Augsburg Confession. But it is with much greater assurance that we confess and affirm, along with the authors of the New Testament, the "self revealing action" of the Father, the Son, and the Holy Spirit in our behalf.

Will the Son Be Subject to the Father?

We read in 1 Corinthians 15:24-28:

> After he has destroyed every ruler, authority and power Christ will hand over the kingdom to God the Father. For he must reign until he has put all his enemies under his feet. The last enemy to be destroyed is death. "For God has subjected all things under his feet." But . . . it is plain that this does not include the One who has subjected all things under him. When all things are subjected to him, then

the Son himself will also be subjected to the One who has subjected all things under him, so that God may be all in all.

This seems to be saying that, at the end of time, God's Son will be subordinate to the Father. So how are we to understand this passage? Many theologians simply quote this passage with an emphasis on God being "all in all" and make no further comment. Others call it "uncertain" or "mysterious."

Luther, too, says this passage "seems very obscure," but understands the point to be:

> The messianic lordship of God's Son will come to an end, his mission accomplished, and God the Father (whose presence and awesome majesty is now hidden) will, together with the Son and Spirit, be openly revealed, loved and worshiped.[171]

As William Barclay writes (and I summarize):

> God gave Jesus a task to do: to defeat sin, to vanquish death and to liberate humanity. When that task is finally accomplished, the Son will return to the Father like a victor and the triumph of God will be complete. It is not a case of the Son being subject to the Father as a slave or a servant to a master. It is a case of the Son accomplishing the work given him to do—to redeem the world so that in the end God will receive back a world redeemed, and then there will be nothing in heaven or in earth outside the love and the power of God.[172]

In the meanwhile, we believe and confess: The majestic God of creation, revealed in Christ Jesus, is present and active in the community of faith through the Holy Spirit. In Christ Jesus the one true God has entered the limits of earthly sinful life in order to set us free from sin and death. By the Holy Spirit, the one true God calls us to faith and new life through the Good News of redemption and new life in Christ.

"I believe in God the Father Almighty. . . ."

*"I believe in God **the Father** Almighty*

To call God "Father" can mean several things in the Old Testament. It can refer to God's procreative power in creating all things. "Have we not all one Father? Has not one God created us?" (Malachi 2:10). Cf. Isaiah 64:8. It can refer to God's special relationship to the people of Israel. "Thus says the LORD . . . 'I am a Father to Israel, and Ephraim is my first-born'" (Jeremiah 31:7, 9). Cf. Exodus 4:22. It can refer to God's special relationship to each king of Judah (descendant of David), who was anointed to be king of Judah. "I will tell you the decree of the LORD, who said to me, 'You are my son, today I have begotten you'" (Psalm 2:7). Cf. Psalm 89:26.

In the New Testament God as "Father" refers in particular to God's unique relationship to Jesus, as well as to God's special relationship to those who trust in Jesus as their Lord. Of course, God the Father as Creator is a key feature of New Testament faith (John 1:1ff; 1 Corinthians 8:6; Hebrews 1:1ff; etc.). But calling God "Father" is more often, and perhaps always, a term of love and respect in response to God's grace revealed in Christ.

What, then, does it mean to confess our faith in "God the Father almighty, creator of heaven and earth?" No doubt God's creative power is basic in this confession. But surely, as a confession of faith in God, the Apostles' Creed calls us to declare our trust in the "one God and Father of us all" who, in Christ, has acted for our salvation and who, by the Holy Spirit, empowers us to live as children of a loving heavenly Father.

Luther often calls the Lord God "our Father and Creator," but even more often refers to God as our caring Father.[173] For example: "God wants to be called 'Father' by us and as a father has promised to hear us and help us."[174]

"I believe in God the Father **Almighty**...."

Most New Testament authors do not use the word *almighty* in reference to God. Paul uses the word once. The author of the book of Revelation uses it nine times. No one else uses the word. In the Old Testament as well, *almighty* is not a highly favored word. It is never used as a name or title for God in the Hebrew Bible. It is never used in the liturgical formulas that praise God's qualities (cf. Exodus 34:6f; Numbers 14:18; Psalm 86:15; 103:8; 145:8; Joel 2:13; Jonah 4:2; etc.).

Several English versions of the Bible mistranslate the Hebrew term *Shaddai* or *El Shaddai* as "the Almighty" or "God Almighty." It is not certain what *Shaddai* originally meant. Perhaps it referred to the God of procreation. Luther thought so. He wrote:

> One should note the special name for God in this place [Genesis 28:3]. It is *Shaddai*, from *Shad*, that is "breasts," "teats." It befits God's dignity to be called this name. God wants to be praised for nourishing and cherishing, for God nourishes all creatures. Not only is God the Creator, but also the Sustainer and Nourisher.[175]

But why are the authors of the Bible so reluctant to refer to God as almighty? Perhaps because, for many people, the word almighty suggests a God of absolute power who can (or should) do anything. To be sure, those authors teach and we believe that God is all-powerful. But to focus primarily on that quality, or to separate it from God's will and purpose for human beings and the universe, is misleading. Clearly God does not use power to force people to do this or that. God's way is much more gracious. When we remember that God is, first and foremost, "gracious and merciful, slow to anger and abounding in steadfast love " we might say, as Leslie Weatherhead has suggested, *Almighty means God's ability to achieve God's purposes in a godly way.*[176]

We might say the words "Father almighty" stand together in the Apostles' Creed to remind us that God the Almighty is our Father, whose power is tempered by a gracious purpose, and whose ways are active with loving care. It also reminds us that God the Father is almighty, whose will is made known and whose purposes are achieved in a godly way.

In his explanation of the First Article of the Creed, Luther writes:

> I believe that God has created me and all that exists. God has given me and still preserves my body and soul with all their powers. God provides me with food and clothing, home and family, daily work, and all I need from day to day. God also protects me in time of danger and guards me from every evil. All this God does out of fatherly and divine goodness and mercy, though I do not deserve it. Therefore I surely ought to thank and praise, serve and obey God. This is most certainly true.[177]

The word "all" occurs three times in this English version of Luther's explanation. In the original German version the word (*alle*) occurs nine times.[178] Luther wants to emphasize that God the Father almighty is completely involved and fully committed to us within this created world. But as Luther writes on another occasion:

> Although we are sure that God provides and cares for us, we should nevertheless know that *we must use* the things and means supplied by God. . . . For God's way of ruling does not want us to be idle. God gives us food and clothing, but in such a way that we should plow, sow, reap, and cook. Then when we have done what is in us, we should entrust the rest to God, for God will act.[179]

The Caring Creator

We who live in a scientific era tend to think the determining factors in our lives are things such as heredity, environment, circumstances, luck and accidents. In contrast to such thinking, Luther, in his explanation of the First Article of the Creed, points to God as the caring Creator of "me and all that exists." Luther is not saying that everything that happens to us is God's will.

God is no cosmic chess-player who makes this move and that, causing everything that happens. And in no way are things such as heredity and environment simply tools of God's will and action.

Neither is God a cosmic architect or divine watchmaker who created the universe and now lets it run on its own. Luther is saying that within the wonder of creation in all its mystery, God is involved for my good and for the good of all creation. Of course there are other factors to be considered in the things that happen in our lives; factors such as our humanity, our sinfulness, and the flexibility that God has built into the universe.

God has put wonderful resources and possibilities at our disposal and called us (made in God's image) to be stewards of the earth. At the same time, God has placed limitations on us. We are not gods, but creatures who are limited in space, time, and ability. Because we rebel against being creatures with limitations and desire to be our own little gods, we often mess up ourselves and our world.

Therefore God's wrath against our sinful rebellion and God's sentence of death upon us are very real indeed. Nevertheless, God does not simply reject us. Nor does God force us to be what God wishes us to be. Rather, God continues to bless us with great good and opens to us the way of salvation in Christ.

The LORD Reigns

James Luther Mays asks the question: "Is there in the psalms some one central, organic characterization of God out of which all the rest unfolds and to which all the variety can be related?" Mays proposes as an answer: *"The LORD reigns."*[180] One might propose other answers, especially "the steadfast love of the LORD," but surely "the LORD reigns" is one of the key affirmations of the Psalms and of the Bible as a whole. As Psalm 96 puts it, the LORD reigns in the dual action of continual creation and ongoing salvation.

But if the LORD reigns, why is the earth such a mess? Why do we experience suffering, pain, and evil? Why are war, disease, and broken lives everywhere we turn? Because, as Psalm 2 declares, nations rage against the LORD; because industrial corporations exploit the earth; because we who are human ignore and abuse God's kingship. In part, then, because of human sin.

But why does God put up with such a mess? In the words of Mr. Britling, in H. G. Wells' novel of that title: "Why, if I thought there was an omnipotent God who looked down on battles and death and all the waste and horror of war—able to prevent these things, I would spit in his empty face."[181] But that's just it. God is *not able* to prevent these things; that is, out of love for us and love for all creation God *refuses* to eliminate sin and evil by sheer force. God's power is never sheer force, but as we have seen, "the ability to achieve godly purposes in a godly way."

The LORD has created the universe with a grand purpose and with a capacity for flexibility, expansion, and change. And the LORD has created human beings with the purpose and capacity to relate to each other, to God, and to the universe as a whole; as well as with a capacity to learn, to adapt, to love, and to be stewards of the earth. Therefore God is determined to deal with human rebellion and the mess we make of creation, not with sheer force, but in ways that restore our humanity and redeem the universe. At the heart of these ways is Christ, his cross and resurrection; and the Holy Spirit's activity in our lives through the gospel.

God Works Within Creation

William Temple says: "The capacity to love and the capacity to sin are the same capacity."[182] This means we can misuse our gifts, and we do. And this, too, is from God, for God has created a universe that makes sin possible. In addition, God's high purposes for us could not be achieved if we lived in a world isolated from any possibility of sin or rebellion or suffering. And sin, rebel, and suffer we do.

But that's not the end of the story. As Psalm 96 puts it, *the LORD reigns* and is at work to change things by the double activity of creation and redemption. However, God is not a two-bit dictator or a fairy tale magician who turns everything around just because it doesn't meet with God's approval. God acts *within* the universe, not over against it. God's way is to take no short cuts, to achieve nothing by violence. God's way is to continually create and to save again and again. This has been God's way down through history, and supremely so through the cross and resurrection of Jesus

Make no mistake about it. The promise is, the LORD will judge the earth with equity and truth. All things will be made right. Until that day we walk by faith. Until that day, the ultimate victory over disappointment, decay, and death is not given directly into our hands. It is promised.

What God the Father Almighty Cannot Do

"Nothing is too hard for you," prayed Jeremiah (32:17). "With God, nothing is impossible," said the angel Gabriel, and so said Jesus as well (Luke 1:37; 18:27). In the sense they meant it, it's true. God's purposes and power are sure and certain. And yet, God is not perfectly free to do anything, any time, any where simply because of who and what God is.

First, as the Letter to Titus (1:2) says, "God cannot lie." Or as the Letter to the Hebrews (6:18) puts it, "It is impossible for God to be false." The words "lie" and "false" in these texts are based on the same Greek word, meaning "empty" or "barren." This word is not so much "the opposite of the truth" as it is "empty of truth," "without substance," "lacking reality." In the picture language of the Old Testament, a lie is "a cloud without rain," "a fleeing vapor," "an empty nothing."[183]

In his book, *The Great Divorce*, C. S. Lewis expresses the biblical understanding of "a lie" as opposed to "the truth" by his imaginary portraits of hell and heaven. Hell he calls "grey town." The residents of hell he calls "ghosts," that is, people of no substance. Life in hell he describes as dismal, dingy, quarrelsome, lonely, empty. Heaven he pictures as a land of brilliant colors and enormous quality—bright blue, emerald green; fresh, spacious; the grass, tender and fragrant, yet as hard as diamonds. The residents of heaven he calls "solid people," made of real, vigorous stuff. Life in heaven he describes as wholesome, lively, full of joy, love, and delightful surprises. The point is, it is impossible for God to lie or to be false. God's promises are full of reality. God's purposes are sound and solid. God's actions are vital and God's ways are wholesome, fresh, surprising.[184]

A second thing God cannot do, as 2 Timothy puts it, "God cannot deny God's self" (2:13). There is a childish idea which believes that whatever God pleases God can do. If God wished to do so. God could turn an apple into an orange and back again in a flash. God could give a zebra spots and a leopard stripes. God could make a bad person good, eradicate Dutch elm disease, and eliminate floods, earthquakes, and tornadoes from the earth. But God's power never contradicts God's character, it is always at the service of God's wisdom, holiness, and love. God will not intrude on the freedom we have been given as human beings and will not overwhelm us with force. God will not interfere with the created order of things, no matter how much we distort it and disturb it.

Dr. Crichton-Miller tells about a woman who rushed into a London train depot and begged the trainmaster to postpone the next train. "My son has been in a serious accident," she said. "He's not expected to live. My husband is on his way, but he can't possibly get here before the next train leaves. Please hold the train so we can see our son alive." The trainmaster responded: "I'm deeply sorry madam, but I cannot. This train makes many important connections which would be lost if I delayed it. Who knows who would be injured if I held the train. I sympathize with you, but it is my duty to maintain the most trustworthy railway service possible, for the good of all."[185]

This is the way it is with God. God cannot suspend the law of gravity for one person or violate the created order for a few. As Leslie Weatherhead says, "God cannot do all things because God must not do all things."[186] God's way is to endure what must be; to wait; to achieve godly purposes in ways that fit God's character.

A third thing God cannot do, as the Letter of James tells us: "God cannot be tempted with evil" (James 1:13). This means God is never arbitrary or capricious, but always reliable and trustworthy. The "gods" of the nations may be fickle, self-centered, and erratic, simply because they are the creatures of human imagination. Not so with the one true God.

Again, as the Letter of James puts it: ". . . with God there is no variation or shadow due to change" (1:17). This doesn't mean God is static and predictable. God is God after all: free to act, free to change direction, and free to "repent," as Scripture puts it. That is, God is free to back away from an intended course of action because of changing circumstances or out of sheer mercy.

Neither is God beyond human influence. God invites us to pray freely, to ask what we will, to boldly approach God with any and every request. And we are assured that God hears and graciously responds. In response to our confession of sin, for example, God turns aside from judgment, forgives, and cleanses us.

On the other hand, God cannot be bribed. God is not swayed by our piety, our vows, our offerings, or our good intentions, but always responds to us justly, mercifully, out of concern for our best interests. The apocryphal book of Judith (8:16-17) expresses it well:

> Do not try to bind the purposes of the Lord our God; for God is not like a man, to be threatened, nor like a mere mortal, to be won over by pleading. Therefore, while we wait for divine deliverance, let us call upon God to help us, and our voices will be heard, if it pleases God.

A fourth thing God cannot do, according to the prophet Hosea: God cannot and will not give up on those whom God has chosen. We read:

> How can I give you up, O Ephraim!
>   How can I hand you over, O Israel!
> My heart turns over within me;
>   it is kindled with tender compassion.
> I will not execute my fierce anger,
>   I will not destroy Ephraim again;
> For I am God and not mortal, the Holy One in your midst,
>   and I will not come in wrath" (Hosea 11:8, 9).

In this passage from Hosea, God's heart is laid bare. The LORD is a God of great compassion—"afflicted in all our afflictions," pained by our sinfulness.[187] God calls us into question, yes. God chastises and corrects us, but, true to the covenant, God will not give up on us. True enough, when we rebel and insist on going our own way, God lets us go. Still, God does not give up on us.

Notice the difference, then, between God letting us go and God refusing to give up on us. As we read again in Hosea (5:5-6):

> The arrogance of the people of Israel cries out against them.
>   Their sins make them stumble.
> They take sheep and cattle to sacrifice to the LORD,
>   But it does them no good.
> They cannot find the LORD, who has withdrawn from them.

Here is God's fierce compassion at its deepest—withdrawing from God's sinful people. This is *God's* wrath in action—not thunderbolts from heaven, but God letting us go—letting us run the course of our sin; letting us mess up, so that perhaps we might realize our need and turn back again. In the words of Psalm 81:11-12, "My people would not listen to me; Israel would not obey me. So I left them to their stubborn selves, to follow their own counsels."

But though God let's us go, God will not give up on us. As Psalm 81 goes on to declare: "O that my people would listen to me, that Israel would walk in my ways" (Psalm 81:13).

What God the Father Almighty Will Not Do

First, in tandem with God's refusal to give up on the chosen people, God has promised never to forsake these chosen ones. Moses declares: "The LORD your God is a merciful God, who will not fail you or destroy you or forget the covenant with your forebears which the LORD swore to them" (Deuteronomy 4:31). The psalmist asserts: "The LORD will not forsake the chosen people; the LORD will not abandon this heritage" (Psalm 94:14).

Such assurances continue throughout the generations of God's people, right on up to Jesus, who declared, "All that the Father gives me will come to me, and whoever comes to me I will not cast out" (John 6:37).

Second, according to Isaiah, the LORD makes a double promise to the chosen people: "I will not remember your sins. I will not forget you." (43:25; 49:15)

As Paul Tournier has said, real forgiveness is "always difficult, always miraculous, always productive of good. . . . Genuine forgiveness is a spiritual victory which frees the heart of all resentment."[188]

But what if a once-forgiven incident rears its ugly head in our memory? Then we say to ourselves, "No! I'm not going to let that incident afflict my life. It's over!" Forgetting a once-forgiven sin is not a matter of suppressing it or of refusing to deal with it. It is just the opposite.

But the primary issue here is what God will not do, and according to Isaiah 43:25, the LORD emphatically affirms: "I, I am the One who blots out your transgressions for my own sake, and I will not remember your sins."

Third, God will not do for us what we can and should do for ourselves. In particular, God will not do for us what God has required us to do. As we read in Micah 6:8: "The LORD has showed you, O people, what is good; and what does the LORD require of you but to do justice, and to love kindness, and to walk humbly with your God?"

We sometimes hear public prayers that ask God to do what is clearly our responsibility—to help the poor, to feed the hungry, to care for the sick, and the like. Praying for the poor, the hungry, and the sick is good, but only if we act to alleviate the difficulties of such persons. As the Epistle of James (2:15-16) expresses it: "If a sister or brother is poorly clothed and lacks daily food, and one of you says to them, *'Go in peace, be warmed and fed,'* but you do not supply his or her bodily needs, what is the good of that?" Such a "blessing" is vain, empty, worthless. And prayers for such persons, without appropriate action, are vain as well. For the LORD has *shown* us what is good and *requires* that we act.

So too, when it comes to issues of disease, famine, war, and natural disasters, we *know* what is good and we are *required* to act. Prayer has a vital place as we strive to solve such problems, but only as we strive. We need God's guidance and strength in our efforts, but the striving is our responsibility. In God's design it is a vital part of our development as human beings. As a prayer by Sister Marilyn Kane puts it:

> We cannot pray to you, O God, to banish war, for you have filled the world with paths to peace, if only we would take them.
>
> We cannot pray to you to end starvation, for there is food enough for all, if only we would share it.
>
> We cannot merely pray for prejudice to cease, for the good in all people lies open to our eyes, if only we will use them.
>
> We cannot merely pray, "root out disease," for you have given us the resources of life and health, to discover and use for the benefit of all.
>
> And so we pray, O God, for the wisdom and the will, and for the courage and the strength to act for the benefit of humanity, earth, and all its creatures.[189]

"I believe in God . . . creator of heaven and earth."

The first sentence of the Bible declares: "In the beginning God created the heavens and the earth." This, like the first sentence of the Apostles' Creed, is a confession of faith. As with all creation accounts of the Bible, the first chapter of Genesis is a confession of faith arising out of praise to the LORD God of Israel.

Creation Accounts in the Bible
1. Genesis 1:1-2:4a
2. Genesis 2:4b-25
3. Psalms of Creation
   a. Psalm 8
   b. Psalm 19:1-6
   c. Psalm 33:4-9
   d. Psalm 104
   e. Psalm 136:4-9
   f. Psalm 148
   g. Psalm 95
4. Second Isaiah (Isaiah 40-55)
   a. Isaiah 40:27-31 (28)
   b. Isaiah 42:5
   c. Isaiah 44:24-28
   d. Isaiah 45:9-13 (12)
   e. Isaiah 45:18-19
   f. Isaiah 48:12-13
   g. Isaiah 51:9-16
5. Proverbs 8:22-31
6. Job 9:4-10; 38:1—39:30; 40:15—41:34
7. New Testament
   a. John 1:1-10; 5:1
   b. Colossians 1:15-17
   c. Hebrews 1:1-4; 11:3
   d. Cf. Romans 4:17b

Both the Old Testament and the New Testament contain many more references to God as Creator.

"In the beginning **God**. . . ." is a confession of faith. God's existence cannot be proven, of course. "God is spirit" (John 4:24), which, in part, means God cannot be discovered, seen, or controlled. And yet, creation itself provides some evidence that God exists. As Paul writes: "Ever since the creation of the world, God's eternal power and divine nature, invisible though they are, have been clearly perceived and seen in the things God has made" (Romans 1:20).

Albert Einstein said the world is like a well-constructed crossword puzzle. You can suggest any number of words, but only one word will fit all the facts. Evidently Einstein meant the word, "God."[190]

Charles Darwin said: "I cannot believe with my mind that all this was produced by chance."[191]

Scientist Murray Eden of MIT used high-speed computers to determine whether or not this complex universe could have come into being by chance. His conclusion was negative. The universe cannot be the product of chance. A superior Mind is behind it all.[192]

It is true, then, that creation provides evidence that God exists. But evidence is not proof. It is, rather, a challenge to faith. Of course there are people today who question the existence of God. As Luther writes: "Even the greatest minds have stumbled and fallen, denying the existence of God and imagining that all things are moved at random by blind chance or fortune."[193]

As authors in both the Old Testament and the New Testament declare, "No one has ever seen God" (John 1:18; Exodus 33:20). It is impossible to discover God and there is no way from human beings to God. Creation is evidence that God exists, but creation does not contain God. Neither does creation tell us what God is like. If God exists, and if we are to know of God's existence, God must personally make it known.

The authors of the Bible tell us this is what has happened. They tell us that God has been at work in events of human experience down through the ages—events that indicate who God is and what God is like. In particular, God has acted in and spoken through the lives of specific persons such as Abraham, Sarah, Moses, Hannah, and the prophets, as well as through the nation of Israel as a whole. Supremely, God has personally acted and spoken in and through a particular heir of Abraham—Jesus of Nazareth. In the words of John's Gospel (1:18): "No one has ever seen God; but God's only Son, who is nearest to the Father's heart, has made God known."

But notice, God's self-revelation in Jesus doesn't *prove* God's existence. It is *evidence* that calls us to respond in faith. This is why we read in John 1:10-12: "He was in the world, and the world was made through him, yet the world knew him not. He came to his own home, and his own people received him not. But to all who received him, who believed in his name, he gave power to become children of God."

And, in fact, to believe in Christ is itself the result of God's personal action. As Luther writes:

> The Holy Spirit must be the Master here and inscribe this knowledge and faith deep in our hearts, must bear witness to our spirit, and say yea and amen to the fact that we have become and eternally remain children of God through faith in Christ.[194]

"In the beginning God **created** the heavens and the earth." This is a confession of faith. Because it is a confession of faith, the primary purpose of Genesis 1, is not to give an account of *how* creation took place, but to proclaim *who* created the universe and *why*.

Who and *why* are primarily "religious" questions—questions which can neither be proved nor disproved by modern science. In fact, genuine science does not address the question *who* or the question *why* as it relates to purpose. What, then, is the relationship between a scientific knowledge of creation and the biblical knowledge of creation? It has been said:

> The scientific account of creation has been written by the finger of God upon the crust of the earth [and throughout the universe], and human beings are slowly spelling it out; but the religious account of creation is written in the first chapters of Genesis [and other biblical accounts], in letters that all can read. Both accounts are from God, and should be received accordingly.[195]

When all is said and done, it is a fruitless effort to attempt to harmonize scientific accounts of creation with the biblical accounts. The purposes and functions of each are quite different.

In science the key is *observable data,* and the primary questions are what, how, when, where, and why. In the Bible the key is God's revelation, and the primary questions are who and why.

"*In the beginning* God created. . . ." This is a confession of faith. Some scientists contend that the stuff of the universe has always existed, and therefore is without beginning or ending. Other scientists believe that the world had a beginning, coinciding with a gigantic cosmic explosion some fourteen billion years ago—a cosmic explosion commonly known as the Big Bang. Recent scientific observations seem to give added support to the Big Bang theory. Of course, a beginning out of a cosmic explosion doesn't prove that the universe is anything other than a fantastic accident. But, as Hans Küng says, it raises some key questions: Why is it that the cosmos appears to have begun in a state of amazing order, rather than in chaos? Why is it that specific laws of nature seem to have been in place from the very beginning? Why is it that the cosmos isn't lapsing into chaos, in accordance with the physical law of entropy?[196]

Some even more crucial questions: What was before the Big Bang? That is, what made it possible for the Big Bang to occur—in terms of energy, matter, space, and time? Why is there anything instead of nothing?

But, of course, with this last question, we move into the world of the Bible rather than the world of science—a world which declares its faith in the God who not only has created, but who continues to create and to care for all creatures great and small. As Luther comments in his study of Genesis, chapter one: "God has left with us this general knowledge: that the world had a beginning and that it was created by God out of nothing."[197]

Luther goes on to say: "God is personally revealed to us as the Speaker, who through the uncreated Word, has created the world and all things with the greatest ease, namely, by speaking."[198]

In Genesis, chapter one we read: "God said, 'Let there be light'; and there was light. God said, 'Let there be a firmament. . . .' And it was so. God said, 'Let the waters be gathered together. . . .' And it was so. God said, 'Let the earth put forth vegetation. . . .' And it was so" (Genesis 1:3, 6-7, 9, 11).

"**God said**. . . ."This is a confession of faith, a confession that is at the very heart of Genesis 1 and of the Bible as a whole. First, this confession declares that the universe is a product of God's personal will. The world didn't just happen. It is not the result of chance or the product of a cosmic accident. God decided to create the universe and did. God said, "Let it be," and it was. In addition, there is a design, meaning, and purpose to it all.

Second, this confession declares that God is distinct from creation. God said, "Let it be," and *it* was. Creation is not part of God, nor God part of creation. God is transcendent—before creation, beyond creation, greater than creation. At the same time, in Luther's striking words: "God is within, without, and above all creatures; that is, God is incomprehensible."[199]

The universe, say the psalm writers, bears the mark of its Creator. That is, by its very grandeur and order the universe bears witness to God's creative power. But God cannot be discovered in nature or be known through nature. And certainly God is not restricted or limited by nature. Indeed, we believe God is involved in the universe as its source and its most dynamic reality. Yet God remains distinct from and sovereign over all creation.

Third, this confession declares that God created the universe out of nothing. This declaration distinguishes the witness of the Bible from every other account of creation. Luther writes: "This expression is indeed remarkable and unknown to the writers of all other languages, that through speaking God makes something out of nothing."[200] Nonbiblical creation stories always begin with pre-existing material, usually tainted or chaotic material, which is then fashioned by the gods into the universe. The Bible insists that God begins with nothing and creates out of nothing. God said, "Let it be," and it was so.

According to this confession, then, God is not confined to nor restricted by the material at hand. More importantly, all things that are —light, energy, space, time, creatures, and human beings—owe their existence to God alone and to no other cause.

Furthermore, just as God was there at the beginning, and just as God continues to be present and active in the universe now, so God will be there at the end—present, alive, and active when the graves of the world are opened for the last time. In the words of Paul: "The LORD is the God . . . who gives life to the dead and calls into existence things that do not exist" (Romans 4:17). As Luther writes:

> Whoever believes that God is the Creator, who makes all things out of nothing, must of necessity conclude that therefore God can raise the dead. 'Why is it thought incredible by any of you that God raises the dead?' asks Paul (Acts 26:8).[201]

Elsewhere Luther makes a beautiful twist on what God can create, saying: "It is God's nature to make something out of nothing; and so, God cannot make anything out of someone who is not yet nothing."[202]

Fourth, this confession declares God's special relationship with human beings. We are, of course, creatures of the earth. We are affected by the same sort of instincts, urges, needs, and desires as the birds and the beasts. The struggle of nature is part of human experience. And yet human beings are uniquely different. Human beings are different, first of all, because, according to the first account of creation (Genesis 1:26-28), we have been created in the image of God. As Martin Buber writes: "The gift of the *zelem* (God's image) and the delegation of power to govern the earth belong together."[203]

In other words, to be created in God's image goes hand and hand with God's commission to us to have dominion over all the earth. As Gerhard von Rad writes: "God set human beings in the world as the sign of God's own sovereign authority, in order that they should uphold and enforce God's claims as Lord."[204] This means we are given the responsibility of acting as God's regents on earth and we are accountable for carrying out that responsibility. We are different, too, because, according to the second account of creation (Genesis 2:4b-25) and the rest of scripture, we are addressed by God, "I to you," and thus called into relationship with God.

Of course, many important things make up our lives: family heritage, race, work, education, etc. But when all is said and done, it is our relationship with and responsibility to God that makes us human.

"I believe in Jesus Christ, God's only Son, our Lord."

In this brief phrase is a name and three titles:

- The name "Jesus" [in Hebrew *Jeshua*] meaning "the LORD saves."
- The title "Christ" [in Hebrew *Messiah*] meaning "the Anointed." For generations this title was used to designate each descendant of David who became the king of Judah. After the fall of that kingdom (587 BC), this title was used to refer to the king whom God promised to restore to the Jewish people.
- The title "God's only Son," that is, *God's one and only Son*, which refers to the unique relationship of Jesus to God the Father.
- The title "Lord" which means God has exalted Jesus to reign over all creation. In the Old Testament the title "Lord" [in Hebrew *adonai*] is used to refer to earthly kings, but most often it is a title applied to God; not to be confused with the word "LORD" (four capital letters), the usual English translation of God's name (in Hebrew *YHWH*).

The Genealogy of Jesus

> An account of the genealogy of Jesus Christ, the son of David, the son of Abraham. Abraham was the father of Isaac; Isaac the father of Jacob; Jacob the father of Judah . . ." (Matthew 1:1ff).

It is no surprise that Matthew begins the story of Jesus with a genealogy. To a first-century Jew, a genealogy was the most natural, the most interesting, and most important way to begin the story of a person's life. However, Matthew's genealogy is quite unusual in that the names of five women are listed there, including Mary, the mother of Jesus. We read:

> Judah was the father of Perez and Zerah by *Tamar*. . . . Salmon the father of Boaz by *Rahab*; Boaz the father of Obed by *Ruth* . . . . David the father of Solomon by *the wife of Uriah*. . . . Jacob the father of Joseph, the husband of *Mary*, of whom Jesus was born, who is called Christ (Matthew 1:3, 5, 6, 16).

The thing is, the names of women are not normal in Jewish genealogies, especially women such as these: Tamar, a temptress who seduced her father-in-law and bore him twin sons; Rahab, a prostitute who earned her money by selling her body; Ruth, a pagan who became a believer, but who gained her husband in a rather enticing way; Bathsheba, the wife of Uriah, who had an adulterous affair with King David and bore him a son. We see, then, that not only does God work in the common course of everyday life, as represented by the repetitious rhythm of a genealogy. God works in irregular ways as well, through a Tamar, a Rahab, a Ruth, a Bathsheba, and through the holy irregularity of a virgin named Mary. The message is:

1. The barrier between male and female has been taken down. Women are prominent in the Messiah's genealogy. *"In Christ there is no longer male and female."*

2. The barrier between Jew and Gentile is down. Tamar of Canaan, Rahab of Jericho, and Ruth of Moab are accepted into God's people. *"In Christ there is no longer Jew nor Greek."*

3. The barrier between saint and sinner is down. Tamar, Rahab, Bathsheba, yes, and Judah, David, and Ahaz are in the royal line. *"In Christ there is no longer slave nor free."*[205]

Luther makes much of the fact that Tamar of Canaan, Rahab of Jericho, and Ruth of Moab, as well as Bathsheba, are mothers within the royal line of David. Luther draws three conclusions from this fact. First, referring to the story of Judah and Tamar, he writes:

> Examples of this kind are told to us for the purpose of teaching and consolation, as well as for the strengthening of our faith, so that we may consider the immeasurable mercy of God, who has saved not only the righteous—namely, Abraham, Isaac, and Jacob—but also the unrighteous—namely, Judah, Tamar, Reuben, Simeon, and Levi, who were outstanding sinners. Consequently, no one should be presumptuous about his or her own righteousness or wisdom, and no one should despair on account of his or her sins.
>
> God wants to console sinners with these examples and to say, "If you have fallen, return; for the door of mercy is open to you."
>
> This is the real reason why narratives of the most disgraceful scandals are intermingled with the legends and histories of the saintly patriarchs.[206]

Second, Luther points out that the Son of God entered into a birth line that was "outstandingly sinful and contaminated."[207] He did so in order to overcome that very contamination and provide for us a way out of sin and death through his death and resurrection.

Third, Luther emphasizes that the Gentiles, too, are included in the Messiah's birthline, through Tamar, Rahab, and Ruth, and their sons and daughters. He writes:

> By this avenue the Gentiles come into communion and fellowship with the people of Israel, not only in the matter of religion but also in the matter of the same flesh.
>
> By this God wanted to point out that the Messiah would be a brother and a cousin of both the Jews and the Gentiles, if not according to their paternal genealogy, at least according to their maternal nature.
>
> The LORD is the God not only of the Jews but also of the Gentiles.[208]

"He was conceived by the Holy Spirit and born of the virgin Mary."

The teaching that Jesus "was conceived by the Holy Spirit and born of the virgin Mary" occurs only in the opening chapters of Matthew and Luke. There is no hint of this particular teaching in the writings of Mark, Paul, John, or any other New Testament author, although all these authors proclaim Jesus to be God's Son, the Messiah.

How literally, then, are we to take the virgin birth of Jesus? Is it simply a symbol of his unique relationship with God? Or was Jesus truly born without benefit of an earthly father?

This much is certain, the accounts of Jesus' birth emphasize the initiative and power of God in Jesus' life and ministry. It is a familiar theme in the Bible. Again and again the biblical authors tell of God initiating a new era, beginning with a woman and the birth of her child. Often the woman is barren, but God enables her to bear a child—Sarah bearing Isaac, Rachel bearing Joseph, Hannah bearing Samuel, etc.

But according to Matthew and Luke, Mary's situation is unique. She is not barren, but a virgin. Here is a uniquely new thing—not simply God working in and through human beings, but God becoming a human being; not simply God beginning a new era, but God beginning a new creation.

Must we, then, believe that Jesus was born without benefit of an earthly father? Perhaps this belief is not essential to the story of salvation. Yet, isn't this just the sort of thing we have come to expect from God?

The Apostles' Creed | 93

To do something completely different? To begin a new creation by being born the child of a virgin? It is.

But, believe in the virgin birth or not, the underlying message of this birth is startling. Clearly Jesus was born into a male dominated society, but according to Matthew and Luke, in this birth males are set aside. The message is, where God reigns, woman and children move to the forefront and no one dominates any one else. In the words of Mary's song:

> The Lord has brought down the powerful from their thrones,
>   and lifted up the lowly;
> The Lord has filled the hungry with good things,
>   and sent the rich away empty (Luke 1:52-53).

And yes, where God reigns, men are "brought down" from dominance and women and children are "lifted up" to a vital and valued place.

The Announcement of the Birth of Christ

> In that region there were shepherds out in the field, keeping watch over their flock by night. And an angel of the Lord appeared to them, and the glory of the Lord shone around them, and they were filled with fear. And the angel said to them, "Be not afraid; for behold, I bring you good news of a great joy which will come to all the people; for to you is born this day in the city of David a Savior, who is Christ the Lord. And this will be a sign for you: you will find a babe wrapped in swaddling cloths and lying in a manger" (Luke 2:8-12).

First, it was to *shepherds* that the message came, and at *night*. Wouldn't you think such astounding news would have come to kings and queens, prime ministers and governors, prophets and priests, all in broad daylight? But no. Everything is turned around and upside down where God is at work.

It is good news for *"all the people,"* as the angel puts it—a child born, not to royalty, but to commoners from the country; a child born, not in a palace, but in a stable, wrapped in bands of cloth, lying in a manger. And quite fittingly, the message is announced to people of the country, to the most ordinary of the ordinary, to shepherds, and at night.

Why at night? Perhaps because the LORD is a *hidden* God, awesome in majesty, terrifying in purity, whom no human being can see and live. Or perhaps because of the mysterious grandeur of it all; a message completely beyond what any one would expect; an action stunning in its design and astonishing in its purpose.

But then, maybe we shouldn't be surprised that this birth and this message came at *night*. According to the Old Testament this is God's way.

We read that God came to Abraham by night, also to Jacob, Solomon, Daniel, Balaam, and Abimelech by night. And quite significantly, we recall that God saved Israel out of slavery, by bringing them out of Egypt by night.

Here, then, is God at work, in God's way—initiating salvation by night and sending the good news of that salvation to the most ordinary of people, because it is for just such people that the Messiah comes.

Second, Luke tells us that the message came to shepherds by night, proclaimed by *an angel*. It is proclaimed by an angel *because* such an action by God could not have been conceived by prophet, oracle, or seer. It is a *revelation* straight from heaven, beyond expectation, beyond human reason, beyond the way we human beings might have wished.

It is like the resurrection of this same Jesus from the dead. It took an angel to bring the message because it was God's action alone—beyond human ability, power, or reason. As Luther writes:

> There must be a revelation from heaven. The light that shone around the shepherds is meant to teach them that here a light is needed that is entirely different from any natural reason.
>
> The gospel must be heard, and one must believe the appearance and the voice of the angel. Had the shepherds not heard from the angels that Christ was lying there, they might have looked at him a thousand and another thousand times and yet they would not have found out from that, that the child was Christ.[209]

And yet, as Luke tells it, once the angel's message is delivered, it is human beings who spread the good news—the shepherds at Messiah's birth, the women at his resurrection, and now we, who are called upon to tell our neighbors, friends, family, and everyone around us.

In Luther's words:

> The shepherds [as well as the angels] became messengers, telling everyone what they had heard about this infant. They rush to the innkeeper's building and to other places, telling everyone what they had heard and seen. We should follow their example: seek Christ in the Word, believe in him, and publicly confess him before all people.[210]

Third, Luke tells us that when the message came to shepherds by night, proclaimed by an angel, "the glory of the LORD shone round about them."

Glory, as we recall, literally means "weight" or "heaviness." It refers to "what a person really is"—his or her "substance" or "character." So then, to say that "the glory of the LORD *shone* round about them" is to say that "the very substance of God's fiery splendor" was reflected there; the aura of God's awesome majesty was shining round about them.

And immediately, we are told, the shepherds were filled with fear. How could it be otherwise? They were overwhelmed by the brilliant reflection of God's awesome presence. But the angel said to them: "Do not be afraid. Behold, I bring *you* good news of a great joy." Good news indeed! Filled with fear by the radiance of God's glory, the shepherds were comforted by God's gracious Word, "For *to you* is born this day in the city of David a Savior who is Christ the Lord."

Shepherds, an angel of the LORD, the glory of the LORD—the familiar stuff of the Christmas story. Where are the shepherds today? Gone, of course, these two thousand years. And the Christmas angel? Unknown to us, even by name. As for the glory of God's awesome presence, it is hidden, concealed beyond our sight and grasp, but not beyond our hearing, minds, and souls. For the Word remains: "*To you* is born this day a Savior, who is Christ the Lord." As Luther says: "We must write the words 'to you' with letters of fire in our hearts and welcome the Savior's birth gladly."[211] It is a Word as real, effective, and alive for us as for the shepherds who first heard it two thousand years ago. For in this Word, "to you," is revealed, though concealed, the very "weight," the very glory of God.

Jesus' Ministry

The Apostle's Creed says nothing about the earthly life and ministry of Jesus. In fact, we know only a few things about his early years: He grew up in Nazareth in Galilee (Luke 4:16). His parents were practicing Jewish believers (Luke 2:21, 22ff, 41). He had brothers and sisters (Mark 6:3). He worked as a carpenter (Mark 6:3). He was baptized by John the Baptist (Mark 1:9). He began his public ministry at about thirty years old (Luke 3:23), soon after John the Baptist was imprisoned (Mark 1:14).

We know more about Jesus' ministry. People were at the heart of his ministry. He called disciples to follow him (Mark 1:16ff). He involved himself in the lives of people of every rank and station, from the best and most important to the despised and least important (Mark 1-3).

Matthew summarizes his ministry, saying: "Jesus went about all Galilee, *teaching* in their synagogues, *preaching* the gospel of the kingdom, and *healing* every disease and every infirmity among the people" (Matthew 4:23).

"The gospel of the kingdom of God" was the theme of his teaching, his preaching, his healing, and his daily encounters with people. And what was that gospel? It was the good news that the LORD, the faithful God of Abraham, Isaac, and Jacob, reigns, that God the King was and is active and at work in order to redeem the world. Moreover, the authors of the four Gospels portray Jesus himself as the Messiah, God's Son, the agent of God's kingly activity. In Jesus' entire ministry, then—in his parables, miracles, and contacts with people—we see God at work, for the sake of all humanity.

Jesus' Teaching Ministry

> In his hometown, on the Sabbath, Jesus began to teach in the synagogue. Many who heard him were astonished, saying, "Where did he get all this? What is the wisdom given to him? What mighty works are done by his hands! Is not this the carpenter, the son of Mary and brother of James and Joses and Simon; and are not his sisters with us?" And they took offense at him (Mark 6:1-3).

They were *astonished*. The word literally means "to be struck sharply." That is, the people were not simply surprised, but stunned. He wasn't just another custodian of the truth, like the scribes. God's Word was alive in him. His teaching went straight from the depths of his being to theirs. Because his word to them was so direct, so heart-felt, he, in turn, was amazed at their unbelief (Mark 6:6).

But this old story is more than just old. It is meant for us. In and through this old story the straight-on, astounding Jesus comes, not simply to teach us, but to encounter and invigorate us with the power of his word. You might say, he still doesn't know his place.

The people of Nazareth felt he was out of place talking to them in such a direct, heart-to-heart way. Today we tend to think of him in terms of religion, church, and spiritual things, and feel he is out of place in our offices, workshops, neighborhoods, and places of pleasure. But here he is and there he will be. And how often he must be amazed at our practical unbelief when it comes to our response to him.

As we define it, he still does not know his place. When we desire his powerful presence to meet our needs in our way, with our timing, he seems to be absent or impotent and unconcerned. But when we have no desire to have him around, at inconvenient places or embarrassing times, there he often is, present with us in a friend, or in a neighbor, or in some other disconcerting way. As Luther says: "It is God's nature to do contradictory things when things are contradictory."[212]

Why? To bring us up short perhaps? To call us to faith, faithfulness, and commitment? But, surely, for our good and for our salvation. As Luther writes of Jesus' teaching:

> The Jews were astonished that Jesus, a plain, simple layman, should be a better preacher than all the chief priests and scribes.[213]
>
> Jesus makes this teaching penetrate and strike the heart as none other can. Christ's Word breaks through and wounds. It is more effective and penetrating than any sword.[214]

Jesus' whole ministry was designed to "penetrate and strike the heart." This was true of the on-the-job-training he gave his disciples to prepare them to bring the good news of God's kingly reign to all the world. This was and *is* true of the way he has challenged his followers to live.

Jesus' Preaching Ministry

> Now after John was arrested, Jesus came into Galilee, preaching the gospel of God, and saying, 'The time is fulfilled, and the kingdom of God is at hand; repent and believe in the gospel (Mark 1:14-15).

With these words, Mark's Gospel introduces and summarizes the preaching ministry of Jesus. It is a proclamation of good news. It is a call to be different. It is an invitation to trust. It is a challenge to be involved. And it all depends on the nearness of God. In biblical language, "the kingdom of God" is, first and foremost, God's royal action. It is God the King at work in and among people. As Mark tells it, it is God the King at work in and through Jesus.

This is a startling word because the kingdoms of humanity clash with God's kingly reign. We prefer to be kings and queens of our own realms. And so, Jesus' message is a sharp challenge to us. It is the proclamation of a new order of things, a new age—God's age.

The rest of the Gospel of Mark spells out what this age and order are all about. It is a Kingdom of grace, not of privilege or rank. It is a Realm of care and concern, not of self-indulgence or personal prestige. It is a society of service, not superiority or patronage.

The *strategy* of this kingdom is a plan of action carried out through love, invitation, and promise. But the *tactics* of this kingdom are anything but soft or easygoing. This kingdom stands against the status quo. It challenges the elite, proclaims woe to the self-righteous, condemns injustice, and rolls up its sleeves to eradicate laziness, pride, exclusiveness, discord, pain, and disease. Everything is topsy-turvy in this kingdom. The first are last and the last first. The greatest are those who wait on others. The most important take a back seat to the least important. And little children are at the center of things.

All this we hear and see in the words and actions of Jesus. He is God's kingly reign in the flesh. His word today is as fresh, challenging, and, yes, as offensive as ever. Here and now he calls to us: "The kingdom is at hand! Turn around! Believe the Good News!"

Jesus' Healing Ministry

> When Jesus entered Peter's house, he saw Peter's mother-in-law lying sick with a fever; he touched her hand, and the fever left her, and she rose and served him. That evening they brought to him many who were possessed with demons; and he cast out the spirits with a word, and healed all who were sick (Matthew 8:14-16).

Like his preaching and teaching, the healing ministry of Jesus reveals who and what he is. It's not that his miracles *prove* anything about him. In fact his miracles don't *prove* anything. As the authors of the Four Gospels point out, a miracle, in itself, never convinced any one to believe in Jesus. Most people who witnessed his miracles were simply astonished. Others thought he was practicing black magic in league with the devil. Only some of the people recognized him for what he was, the Messiah of God. What, then, were the miracles of Jesus?

First, as Dietrich Bonhoeffer suggests, Jesus' miracles exceeded normal everyday happenings, but took place, not in opposition to, but in accord with God's created order, only on another level of reality.[215] To put it another way, they were actions of what might be expected of one who was in perfect harmony with God the Creator.

Second, according to the four evangelists, the miracles of Jesus were *signs* of God's presence, *witnesses* to the God's purposes, *signals* of God's dominion over the chaotic disorder that threatens humanity. Perhaps this is why the most common Greek word for *miracle* is not used in the New Testament to refer to the miracles of Jesus (or to the miracles of the apostles).[216] Jesus' miracles were never merely wonders. They were signs, and at the same time, challenges to see what and who Jesus was and is.

Third, it is a striking fact that miracles were part of Jesus' ministry from beginning to end. They were so much a part of who he was and *is* that, in the face of suffering and misfortunate, he simply had to act. He was and *is* the compassionate, caring Lord of heaven and earth.

"True God and True Man"

The authors of the New Testament are quite clear about Jesus' identity. Luther, too, is quite clear. He writes: "I believe that Jesus Christ, true God, Son of the Father from eternity, and true man, born of the Virgin Mary, is my Lord."[217]

"True God" and "true man!" Here is a concept beyond explanation, outside of all human experience, and, for many, quite unbelievable. How could one person be both human and divine? This concept and question led to great controversy and heresy in the early church. Some taught he was fully divine, but in the "form" of humanity. Others taught that he was simply human, but chosen and specially blessed by God.

The authors of the New Testament say straight out that he is the Christ, the Son of God. Which means, what? Weren't Adam, David, the people of Israel, and others called "God's Son"?[218] Yes, and in that sense the authors of the New Testament present Jesus as *the* true man (Adam), *the* Messiah (true descendant of David), and *the* son that Israel was meant to be.[219] But more, these authors proclaim him to be "God with us," "the only Son from the Father," and "indwelt by the fullness of God."[220]

Luther never attempts to explain how Jesus could be both human and divine. He says, "Reason cannot fathom this."[221] On the basis of Scripture and personal belief, he simply declares:

> If this foundation stands and is ours by faith—that Christ is both God's Son and the Virgin's Son in one Person, though of two different natures . . . then I have all that is necessary, and it is superfluous for me to let my thoughts flit heavenward and explore God's will and plan. Then I am spared all the disputations . . . about how God is to be sought and encountered, served and pleased. I am also relieved of the anxiety and fear of my own heart.[222]

"He suffered under Pontius Pilate, was crucified, died. . . ."

As the Gospel of Matthew tells it: "Jesus began to show his disciples that he must go to Jerusalem and suffer many things from the elders, the chief priests, and the scribes, and be killed, and on the third day be raised. But Peter took him and began to rebuke him . . ." (Matthew 16:21-22).

This short text introduces us to two bedrock facts of our faith, the *scandal* of the cross and the *failure* of Jesus' followers to understand and accept it. The unthinkable disgrace of the cross is decisively pictured by Peter's rebuke of Jesus. And the crucial necessity of the cross is decisively dramatized by Jesus' rebuke of Peter. Matthew's Gospel describes this drama and its scandal in two scenes.

Scene One

Jesus asks his disciples, "Who do you say that I am?"

Peter replies, "You are the Christ, the Son of the living God."

Jesus says, "Blessed are you, Simon Bar-Jona! For flesh and

blood has not revealed this to you, but my heavenly Father. And, I tell you, you are Peter, the Rock, and on this rock I will build my church and the powers of death shall not prevail against it"(Matthew 16:13-20).

Scene Two

Jesus announces that he must suffer and be killed.

Peter rebukes him, saying, "God forbid, Lord! This shall not happen!"

Jesus rebukes Peter, saying, "Get behind me Satan! To me you are a stumbling-block. You are not on God's side, but men's" (Matthew 16:21-23).

Isn't this something? The chief spokesman among the disciples goes from *Peter the Rock* to *Satan the Stumbling-block* as quick that! Such is the scandal of the cross in the lives of believers and non-believers alike, then and now. For who can imagine the necessity of suffering, shame, and death for the Messiah of God? As Luther writes:

> It is very difficult to recognize as King one who has died such a desperate, shameful death. The senses strongly repel such a notion, reason abhors it, experience denies it, and a precedent is lacking. Plainly this will be folly to the Gentiles and a stumbling block to the Jews (1 Corinthians 1:23). . . .
>
> What then? Let the apostle Paul decide, who says, "For since in the wisdom of God the world did not know God through wisdom, it pleased God through the folly of what we preach to save those who believe."[223]

The Scandal of the Cross

Johann Wolfgang von Goethe, the great German poet, once said: "There are four things I hate like poison—lice, garlic, tobacco smoke, and the cross."[224] Goethe was quite right. There is something appalling about the cross. It was a slow, painful, hellish death by dehydration. Among Roman citizens, it was considered bad manners to talk about crucifixion. It was a death reserved for the rabble of Roman society—for slaves, rebels, and political criminals.

There is a surviving graffito on the Palatine hill in Rome, with the inscription, "Alexamenos worships his god." The graffito shows a man kneeling before a cross, and on the cross is a human figure with the head of a donkey.[225] As Jürgen Moltmann writes: "The cross is the truly irreligious thing about Christian faith."[226]

If we are not repelled by the cross, we probably do not understand what it is all about. The cross of Jesus is a scandal, at the very least, because it stands for rejection. To suffer is one thing. Suffering can be a courageous, admirable thing. But to be rejected is a humiliating thing. The cross of Jesus is both suffering and rejection. It is shameful, dishonorable suffering and rejection. He was rejected by the religious leaders, condemned by Jewish law; repudiated by government officials, sentenced to death as a blasphemer and rebel, abandoned by his followers, cut off from the covenant people.

The Suffering Servant

Isaiah speaks of God's suffering servant—"who was despised and rejected by men," who was considered by people to be "stricken, smitten by God and afflicted," but who "was wounded for *our* transgressions" and "by whose stripes *we* are healed." And who, at last, "will see his offspring and will prolong his days" (Isaiah 53:3-5, 10).

For Matthew, Luke, and the authors of 1 Peter and the Book of Revelation the description of the suffering servant of Isaiah prefigures the rejection, shame, suffering, death and saving sacrifice of Jesus in our behalf. Luther declares:

> To believe that Christ, so exceedingly disgraced and dying between robbers, is the Savior—no reason can believe.[227]
>
> Is it really possible or ought a person to believe that God would be mindful of such a wretched and miserable man and care for a son of man who dies so miserably, executed on a cross? Is he supposed to be the dearest child and the chosen one of God, he whom everyone spits upon, mocks, and blasphemes? How foolishly God acts! Is he supposed to be God's Son, the Lord, our Ruler, whose name is glorious in all the lands and to whom thanks are given in heaven— he who hangs on the cross and is regarded as a mockery and curse of the people?
>
> The whole world thinks God has forgotten this man and does not care for this Son of man. But "the stone which the builders rejected has become the chief cornerstone. This is the Lord's doing; it is marvelous in our eyes" (Psalm 118:22, 23).[228]

Why the Cross?

> Jesus said to his disciples, "Let these words sink into your ears; for the Son of man is to be delivered into human hands." But they did not understand this saying. It was concealed from them (Luke 9:43-45).

Why should the Son of man be delivered into human hands? Why the cross? The authors of the New Testament give several reasons why:

He gave his life as a ransom for many;[229] as a sacrifice for sin;[230] to redeem us from sin;[231] to free us from the curse of the law;[232] to deliver us from this evil age;[233] to destroy the devil;[234] to abolish death;[235] to reconcile us to God.[236]

But when all these reasons are spelled out, one primary fact remains. He died. He *had* to die.[237] Born as one of us, with "the very nature of sinful flesh," as Paul puts it, what could he expect but death? And so he died. But the Good News is, he died *for us*.

As Roy Harrisville points out, the apostle Paul, in particular, emphasizes the deliberate action of God's Son in *identifying* himself with us.[238] That is, by identifying himself with us (by his birth, by his baptism, and in his ministry) and by going to the cross in our behalf, Jesus opened to us the possibility of redemption from bondage to sin and death—as we respond by identifying ourselves with him, that is, by trusting in him.

Take note then! Jesus did not die to appease God or to balance the books of heavenly justice. He did not die to pay the penalty for our sins or as a substitute instead of us, as we so often hear. He became one of us, in order to die for us, on our behalf.

Of course, we, too, must die some day, sinful flesh that we are. For death is the only way to abolish sin. But God raised Jesus to life again, and through him God has opened the way to freedom from sin and to life out of death for all of us who trust in him. In Luther's words:

> It was Christ's true and proper function to struggle with the law and with the sin and death of the whole world in such a way that, having undergone them, he conquered and abolished them in himself, in order to liberate us from the law and from every evil.[239]

Watching the Messiah of the Cross

> When the soldiers had crucified Jesus, they divided his clothing among themselves by casting lots. Then they sat down and kept watch over him there (Matthew 27:35-36).

In keeping watch over Jesus that day, the soldiers saw something quite different from the usual crucifixion. Here was a man who refused the anesthetic cup of wine and gall and remained clear in mind and spirit to the bitter end. He didn't curse like most crucified victims. When mocked and ridiculed, he made no reply. He didn't linger on like most, slowly dying of dehydration. It was almost as if he decided when to die. This is what the soldiers saw. And this is what they heard: "Father, forgive them, for they know not what they do."[240]

Others watched Jesus that day. Priests, scribes, elders, two robbers crucified with him, some people passing by—all watched; some mocked him. And what did they see? They saw a would-be king, nailed to a tree. How ironic! Here was a man who said, "The kingdom of God is at hand!" Here was a man who had power to win disciples, to heal the sick, and to revive the dead, yet here he was, naked, humiliated, and helpless, nailed to a tree. This is what these others saw. And this is what they heard: "My God, my God, why have you forsaken me?"[241]

One other group of people saw him that day: Mary his mother, Mary Magdalene, a few other women, his friend John, Joseph of Arimathea, and perhaps Nicodemus. And what did they see? They saw their loved one and friend, condemned, insulted, shamed. They saw their faith, hopes and dreams smashed to bits. And this is what they heard: "Father, into your hands I commit my spirit."[242]

And what do we see? In the words of Paul, we see "Christ Jesus openly displayed before us on the cross." We see his shame. We see his nobility. We see his acceptance of death. This is what we see. And this is what we hear: "It is finished!"[243] And in that cry, we hear the echo of his sure and certain word: "The Son of man came not to be served but to serve, and to give his life as a ransom for many."[244]

We Preach Christ Crucified

Paul makes a straight-out, astounding declaration regarding Jesus and the cross in his first letter to the Christian in Corinth: "We preach Christ crucified, a stumbling block to Jews and folly to Gentiles, but to those who are called, both Jews and Greeks, Christ the power of God and the wisdom of God" (1 Corinthians 1:23 24).

Today we too preach Christ crucified—not simply "Christ died for us," but Christ crucified; not simply a heroic, sacrificial death, like a soldier throwing himself on a grenade to save his comrades, or like a lifeguard losing her life to save a drowning swimmer, but Christ crucified. As Hebrews 13 tells it, Jesus died outside the city limits, outside the limits of sacred ground, in a place fit for little more than the disposal of waste products. His was not simply a humiliating death then, but a God-forsaken death, cursed by Jewish law.

But why? If Jesus is truly God's Son as we say he is, why such a scandalous death? Could it be to shock us, perhaps? To shatter our illusions about ourselves and God? For to speak of the Holy God and a Roman cross in the same breath is as outrageous as to speak of your mother and the electric chair, or your spouse and skid row; or your daughter and the street-walkers of downtown Chicago.

This is the sort of shock the Corinthian Christians must have felt about Paul's word of the cross. They had been carried away by their enthusiasm. Their message was the victorious, resurrected Christ. They believed in an appealing, triumphant Christianity, complete with signs and wonders, wisdom and knowledge.

How all-too-modern all this is! How all-too-tempting it is to set aside the cross as something over-and-done with, set aside by the resurrection. But, of course, the message of the resurrection does not announce the raising up of just any human being. It is announces the raising up of the rejected, God-forsaken Jesus. His resurrection does not cancel out his crucifixion, but glorifies it.

The heart-and-soul of the gospel remains Jesus Christ and him crucified. Like the Corinthians of old, we need that message. Like them, we misunderstand God. Like them, we want God to inspire us; to fulfil our desires, to satisfy our hungers, to approve our decisions, and to undergird our efforts. We need the word of the cross to bring us to our senses so that we acknowledge God as God and not our idol.

Death to the Power of Death

> The Son of God took upon himself human nature, so that through death he might destroy him who has the power of death, that is, the devil, and deliver all those who through fear of death were subject to lifelong bondage (Hebrews 2:14-15).

Charles Ryberg was a brilliant young man, an "honors" graduate of Harvard University who became an officer in the Marine Corps and died from enemy mortar fire in Viet Nam. And to what purpose? What difference did his death make? Certainly not to help win a war which in fact we lost. Certainly not to rescue Viet Nam or Indo-China from Communism which we did not. Such a promising life! And such a wasteful, senseless death!

And right here is where Jesus comes in; Jesus with his brilliant, promising life and his tragic, outwardly senseless death. The point is, we have a God who cares about every promising life and every wasteful, senseless death. We have a God, who in Christ, has experienced it all—the shame, the waste, the rejection, the loneliness, and, yes, the empty senselessness of death.

He became obedience unto death, even death on a cross, and as Paul writes to the Philippians, "Therefore God has highly exalted him and given him the name which is above every name." *Therefore*, through that cross, we are assured that we have a God who is personally involved in *every* hurtful situation, *every* harmful incident, *every* senseless event, *every* shameful circumstance, and *every* sinful life.

As Henrich Bornkamm writes:

> For those who believe, the cross of Christ is the assurance that God's work really begins where, from the human point of view, everything in the life of the individual, the church, and the world is lost.[245]

This is the straight-on, honest, and, for many, the *offensive* message of the gospel—the horror and weakness of his death on the cross now enables the risen Christ to enter with grace and power into the sins, the failures, and the frustrations of our lives, yes, and into the emptiness of our deaths.

The God of the Crucified Messiah

> In all the affliction of the house of Israel, the LORD was afflicted, and the angel of God's presence saved them. Out of love and pity the LORD redeemed them, lifted them up, and carried them (Isaiah 63:9).

What? Can the LORD, our heavenly Father, be afflicted? Human wisdom would say no. For example, Aristotle's "god" cannot suffer and, in fact, cannot love. Aristotle's "god" is too transcendent, too perfect, too self-contained and self-sufficient to suffer or to love.

But according to Isaiah not only is God afflicted in all afflictions of the people, but God grieves, cares, and cries out like a woman in travail.[246] And according to Hosea, God is like a husband who suffers the pain of a lost love and seeks to restore that love whatever the cost. Jürgen Moltmann writes: "A God who cannot suffer is poorer by far than any human being."[247] Luther would agree, and writes:

> We never suffer injustice without God suffering it first and more than we. God the Father's solicitude for us is so great that God feels our suffering before we do and bears it with greater resentment than we ourselves.[248]

Perhaps we would prefer a God who would not put up with sin, rebellion, or evil, a God who would eliminate greed, bitterness, envy, malice, spite, pride, war, and every injustice. However, the true God is not, first and foremost, a God of sheer power and perfect justice, but rather, a God of pure and holy love.

What, then, if God were to react by crushing sin and evil? That is, what if God were to stop loving just long enough to crush sin and evil once and for all? As Leslie Weatherhead points out, wouldn't God, then, have failed?[249] Wouldn't God cease to be God? Yes, for God's true nature, which is caring and self-giving, is made most clear when God acts in ways that are the opposite of what we would expect. God fights the forces of sin and evil by the way of suffering and self-sacrifice, in short, by the way of the cross. Nothing, not even God's hatred of sin, will force

God to use methods that run contrary to divine justice and grace, what ever the cost may be to God, be it suffering, shame, rejection, or death.

"He . . . died, and was buried."

"Marley was dead, to begin with. There is no doubt about that."[250] So writes Charles Dickens in the opening lines of his immortal *Christmas Carol*. "The register of his burial was signed by the clergyman, the clerk, the undertaker, and the chief mourner. Scrooge signed it. And Scrooge's name was good for anything he chose to put his hand to. Old Marley was as dead as a door-nail."

Jesus of Nazareth, too, was dead, to begin with. There is no doubt about that. The Roman soldiers saw him die, he was buried, and his tomb fastened with the imperial seal signed by Pontius Pilate. Yes, Pilate signed the seal. And Pilate's name was good for anything he chose to put his hand to. Jesus of Nazareth was as dead as a door-nail.

This is a vital point. "He was buried," declares Paul, as does the Creed. In Luther's words: "They put him under the ground, and they thought he was buried so deep that no one would ever sing or speak his name again."[251] This is a vital point because over the centuries there have been theories that his death was a fake, that he was simply unconscious and later recovered to appear again. But the actions of the Jewish and Roman authorities and the demeanor of the disciples give the lie to such theories.

There was no doubt in the minds of the two Marys and Salome that he was dead. That's why they went to anoint his body. But they were in for a shock. The stone door of the tomb was rolled away, the tomb empty, his body gone. Then a young man in a white robe said to them: "Do not be alarmed. You seek Jesus of Nazareth, who was crucified. He is not here. He has risen!" Luther's words strike home to those of us who believe:

> I believe that Christ died and was buried to put my sin to death and bury it and do the same for all believers and, moreover, that he slew human death, transforming it into something that does no harm, but is beneficial and salutary.[252]

"He descended into hell."

The phrase, "He descended into hell," was not part of the oldest forms of the Creed. It first appeared in creeds of Eastern churches about 360 CE We are not sure why. Three possibilities are:

1. It was a way to emphasize that Jesus truly died and was buried.
2. As 1 Peter 3:19-20 states, "He went and preached to the spirits in prison, who disobeyed long ago when

God waited patiently in the days of Noah." That is, he proclaimed the gospel to people of an earlier age who had not heard the good news.

3. To quote Ephesians 4:8, "he led a host of captives." That is, he overcame the powers of hell. In the words of the New Revised Standard Version, "he made captivity itself a captive."

Some medieval theologians taught that Jesus descended into hell *to suffer* the tortures of the damned as a part of his victory over the devil. Others taught that he descended *to proclaim* his victory over the devil and the demons.

Luther accepted the validity of the phrase, but wrote: "What the manner of this descent was we, of course, do not know."[253]

Yet he also wrote:

> I believe that for me and all his believers Christ descended into hell to subdue the devil and take him captive along with all his power, cunning, and malice so that the devil can no longer harm me, and that he redeemed me from the pains of hell, transforming them into something nondestructive and beneficial.[254]

The Latin original of the phrase is *descendit ad inferna*. *Inferna* refers to Hades, the abode of the dead, not to Gehenna, a place of torment. Perhaps, then, we should interpret this phrase as a way to emphasize Jesus' death and burial.

"On the third day he rose again."

The Resurrection of Jesus According to Luke's Gospel

> Two men stood before the women in dazzling array, and said to them, "Why seek the living among the dead? Remember how he told you, while he was still in Galilee, that the Son of man must be delivered into the hands of sinners, and be crucified, and on the third day rise" (Luke 24:4-7).

Notice the testimony of "the two men." Their testimony is to the crucified, risen Jesus himself and to his words: "The Son of man must be delivered into the hands of sinners, and be crucified, and on the third day rise."

The suffering, crucifixion, and resurrection of Jesus belong together. They belong together, not simply in sequence—first suffering, then crucifixion, and finally resurrection, though that is true. Rather, his suffering, crucifixion, and resurrection are bound together permanently.

The resurrected Christ *is* the crucified Jesus. His resurrection does not cancel out his crucifixion, but glorifies it.

The cross is the permanent emblem of the living Christ. The cross distinguishes the resurrected Jesus from all the so-called "risen gods" of every mystery cult and religion. The cross is exalted by the resurrection as the foundation our faith and remains before us to *proclaim* "God so loved the world that God gave the only Son;" to *assure* us of forgiveness and new life offered to us in Christ; to *remind* us that we are not alone in our struggles, but that God is involved in our battles with sin, evil, and death in this world; to *call* us to follow the risen, crucified One in the way of discipleship.

It is the risen, crucified Jesus himself who calls us. He offers us, not immortality of the soul, naturally, automatically, but new life out of death. He gives us, not the same old dreary existence going on and on forever, but *eternal* life, ever new and expanding, wholesome and rich—a life that begins now, ahead of time, through faith in him.

> Returning from the tomb the women told all this to the eleven and to the rest; but these words seemed to them an idle tale, and they did not believe them (Luke 24:9, 11).

The apostles couldn't believe it. Who could blame them? Jesus, risen from the dead? "These words seemed to them an idle tale." This initial unbelief by the apostles is a vital point. It assures us that Christian faith is not a valiant carrying-on of the message of Jesus in spite of his shameful death. Such valiant discipleship may be true of the followers of Mohammed, Confucius, Lenin, or Gandhi. It is not the case with Christianity.

Our faith is not a matter of the cause of Jesus living on in his disciples. The apostles were not great heros who decided to keep up their dead Master's work. They were a discouraged, beaten lot who refused to be convinced by an empty tomb or women's words or an angel's message. Then the resurrected Jesus himself appeared to them. And suddenly these heart-broken, disillusioned disciples were changed, and in the years to come they showed their willingness to suffer and die for their faith in him.

This, surely, is the most convincing evidence for the resurrection of Jesus—that the fearful disciples were suddenly courageous, dedicated, and faithful to their Lord no matter what. And from that small band of disciples has grown the millions of persons who have followed Christ down through the centuries.

Jesus lives, God's victor over death! And though death shall surely claim us in due time, it cannot hold us captive. In the words of Paul: "If the Spirit of God who raised Jesus from the dead dwells in you, God who raised Christ Jesus from the dead will give life to your mortal bodies also through God's Spirit that dwells in you" (Romans 8:11).

The Presence of the Risen Lord

> That very day two of the disciples were going to a village named Emmaus about seven miles from Jerusalem. And while they were talking and reasoning together about the things that had happened, Jesus himself drew near and went with them. But they did not recognize him (Luke 24:13-16).

"They did not recognize him." How often that was the case! Mary Magdalene, Peter, the apostles in the upper room, these two on the Emmaus road—none of them recognized the risen Jesus, *until* he made himself known. There was more to knowing the Risen One than a previous relationship with him. "Jesus himself," as Luke puts it—but an unrecognizable Jesus until he made himself known.

He was different now—no longer subject to death; no longer subject to the limits of time and space; exalted now, transformed, transfigured. But make himself known he did. He said to the pair from Emmaus: "O foolish ones and slow of heart to believe all that the prophets have spoken! Was it not necessary that the Messiah should suffer these things and enter into his glory?"

And beginning with Moses and the prophets, he interpreted to them in all the scriptures the things concerning himself. Then, later on, in their home, "When he was at table with them, he took bread, blessed it, and broke and gave it to them. And their eyes were opened and they recognized him." Those were familiar actions to the pair from Emmaus—actions reminiscent of the feeding of the five thousand (Luke 9:16) and other meals in which Jesus was the host; and to readers of Luke's Gospel, reminiscent of the actions of Jesus at the Last Supper.

And so, by opening the scriptures concerning his passion, together with the breaking of bread, Jesus made himself known. Here, to be sure, is that *dual ministry* presented all through the Gospel of Luke—Jesus preaching and Jesus at table, a dual ministry carried on by the apostles in the Book of Acts, and carried on by Christians to this very day—through the gospel proclaimed and the sacrament given.

The Resurrection of Jesus According to the Gospel of Mark

> The women said to one another, "Who will roll away the stone for us from the entrance to the tomb?" But when they arrived at the tomb, the stone was already rolled back.

Entering the tomb, the women were amazed to see a young man sitting there. He said to them, "Do not be amazed; you seek Jesus of Nazareth, who was crucified. He has risen. He is not here. See the place where they laid him. But go, tell his disciples and Peter that he is going before you to Galilee; there you will see him, as he told you" (Mark 16:3-7).

Irony is a feature of the brief resurrection account in Mark's Gospel. There is the irony of the stone. What the women considered to be their primary problem, "Who will roll away the stone for us," turned out to be the least of their problems.

There is the irony of speaking and silence. Throughout Mark's Gospel Jesus is pictured commanding silence regarding his identity and his miracles, but the more he urges silence, the more people speak out. Here, at the resurrection scene, the white robed messenger urges the women, "Go! Tell his disciples and Peter!" But we read, "They said nothing to any one, for they were afraid" (Mark 16:8).

Finally, there is the cryptic word of the angel: "He is going before you into Galilee, there *you will see him.*" These are words, which in Mark's Gospel, focus on the coming again of Christ (cf. Mark 9:1; 13:26; 14:62).

Of course we believe these women and the disciples saw Jesus face-to-face. That's the message of the other three Gospel writers. But as Mark presents it, for his first readers and for us, only at his coming again will we see him. Until then, the risen Jesus is among us as the hidden One. As Luther writes:

> To be sure, in this life we cannot see the Lord face to face. Instead we have the kingdom of faith here until we die. Then we are going to know the Lord face to face.[255]

> Here on earth we shall not perceive God with our senses and our thoughts. Here we see God, as Paul states, 'in a mirror dimly,' enveloped in an image, namely, in the Word and the sacraments.[256]

The Hiddenness of the Risen Christ

> The three women fled from the tomb, for terror and amazement had seized them, They said nothing to anyone, for they were afraid (Mark 16:8).

So ends Mark's Gospel. And a most peculiar ending it is: obscure and incomplete, with no encounter with the risen Christ; only the evidence of the empty tomb, the presence of the white robed young man, and the message: "Jesus who was crucified is risen."

So peculiar is this ending that some scholars have thought the original ending has been lost. In fact, at least two or three endings have been created down through the centuries and added to the Gospel. But the best ancient manuscripts have no such endings. And the evidence of Mark's Gospel as a whole suggests that this obscure, ambiguous ending is just what the author had in mind.

Why? What would be Mark's purpose in ending his Gospel in this way? Perhaps because it is so realistic. *Christ is risen!* That is Mark's clear message. But, in reality, the Risen One remains concealed, hidden to this very day. The evidence of his resurrection is with us, but it cannot be proven. We walk by faith, not by sight.

Moreover, the primary event for Mark is the cross. One-fifth of this Gospel deals directly with the crucifixion. One-third of it describes the events of Holy Week. Over one-half of it explicitly leads from the day Jesus declares that he must die to the day of crucifixion itself. And the entire Gospel falls under the shadow of the cross.

Why? No doubt because the cross gives us the key to a proper understanding of Jesus' life and resurrection. Only the cross reveals the heart, the truth, and the way of the Son of God as he truly is. In Luther's astounding statement:

> True Christian religion begins, not at the highest as other religions do, but at the lowest. So, whenever you are occupied in the matter of your salvation, set aside all speculation regarding God's unsearchable majesty—and run straight to the manger to see the child there: born, sucking, growing up, involved with human beings, teaching, dying, rising again, and ascending on high, with authority over all things.[257]

Proclaiming the Resurrection

In spite of the evidence of Scripture and the experience of modern men and women whose lives have been changed by their encounter with the living Christ Jesus, many among us consider the resurrection of Jesus and belief in a life to come to be nonsense. Luther knew how hard it is to believe in the resurrection. He wrote:

> This article has suffered and continues to suffer the most opposition and is very difficult to believe. No article so contradicts experience as this one does. For our eyes see that all the world is swept away by death and dies. Emperors and kings, high and low, young and old, one after another, are laid in the grave. Wild animals devour one person, the sword another; this man leaves a leg in Hungary, fire

consumes that one; worms eat this person in the earth, fish eat that person in the water, while birds under the sky eat yet another. And so it is difficult to believe that people who die in so many different ways can live again.[258]

In a seminary class not long ago, a middle-aged student declared, "It wouldn't matter to me if it could be shown that Jesus never rose from the dead. It's the idea of the resurrection that I find so beautiful." The professor noticed a young student scowling at this remark and asked, "Karl, what do you think about that?" The young man answered, "If Jesus isn't raised from the dead, I'm out of here."

That young man was in harmony with Paul and the early church. Luther, too, would have approved of his response. He wrote:

> Everything depends on our retaining a firm hold on this article in particular. If this one totters and no longer counts, all the others will lose their value and validity. For Christ has come and has established his kingdom in the world for the sake of the resurrection and the life to come. If, then, the article that is the foundation, cause, and end of all articles of faith is overthrown and taken away, all the rest must fall and go with it. Therefore it is certainly necessary diligently to stress and confirm this article.[259]

"He ascended into heaven. . . ."

The proclamation of the ascension of Jesus permeates the whole New Testament, but only the author of Luke-Acts presents it as a separate event. Matthew, Paul, and the author of Hebrews present what we call the ascension as part and parcel of the resurrection of Jesus. John's Gospel presents the resurrection, the ascension, and the gift of the Spirit (Pentecost) as a single event on the first Easter day.

Luke presents the ascension as a special event separated from the resurrection by some forty days, observed and experienced by the disciples (Luke 24:50-51; Acts 1:1-11). Why is that? We can't really say. Perhaps Luke felt a need to de-emphasize the coming again of Christ Jesus and to stress his present Lordship. Evidently the congregations to whom Luke wrote were confused about the delay of Christ's return.

It was about 85 CE when the author we know as Luke wrote his two volumes (Luke/Acts). Many of the early Christians had expected Jesus to return before then. Persecuted as many of them were, they longed for freedom from this world and its troubles and they counted on the return of Jesus as the solution to their sufferings. Luke could not agree. Who could say when the Lord would return? According to Luke, Jesus said:

> It is not for you to know times and seasons fixed by the Father's authority. But you shall receive power when the Holy Spirit has come upon you, and you shall be my witnesses in Jerusalem, in all Judea and Samaria and to the ends of the earth (Acts 1:7-8).

Luke sees the solution to the sufferings of Christians, not in rescue out of the world through the return of Jesus, but in the power given by the ascended Lord here and now. Not that Luke denies the reality of the Jesus' coming again, but he stresses the *present* lordship of Jesus.

The Hidden Authority of the Ascended Lord

Luke presents Jesus' ascension as a lifting up into heaven. He writes: "As the apostles looked on, Jesus was lifted up, and a cloud took him out of their sight" (Acts 1:9-11). We, in turn, confess week by week:

> He descended into hell (or to the dead). On the third day he rose again. He ascended into heaven, and is seated at the right hand of the Father.

But surely we, of the twenty-first century, no longer believe in a universe of three levels—with heaven above, hell below, and earth in between. That is way first century people understood the universe. Yet the authors of the New Testament may not be as naive as we think. We may be the naive ones if we judge them too quickly. How, then, are we to understand this first-century language of "lifting up," "clouds," "heaven," and "seated at the right hand of the Father?" We begin by remembering that this is picture language.

When Luke tells us, "Jesus was lifted up and *a cloud* took him out of their sight," we recall that in the Old Testament a cloud is not only a symbol for God's presence, but also a symbol for the hidden quality of God's presence and power.[260] The phrase "at the right hand of the Father" is something like today's "right hand man or woman."[261] It refers, not primarily to a place, but to the God-given power and authority of Jesus.

This, then, is the message of Luke and the Apostles' Creed:

> Jesus, taken up in a cloud, is in the presence of God.
>
> At God's right hand, Jesus is in the realm of power and authority.
>
> For now his power is hidden. It will become clear only when he comes again. Meanwhile, it is a very real power for those who trust in him.

Why hidden? Because as Luther writes, Christ's kingdom is "a kingdom of faith."[262] The Lord will not compel, force, or overwhelm anyone, but promises, invites, and calls people to respond to him in faith.[263]

"The Beyond in Our Midst"

The authors of the Bible use the word "heaven(s)" in three ways: One, to refer to the atmosphere: the clouds, wind, and rain;[264] two, to refer to the sky or the stars and planets above;[265] three, to refer to the super-natural realm of God, which is also called "the heaven of heavens," or spoken of as "above the heavens."[266]

Since we no longer believe in a three-story universe with heaven above, hell below, and earth in between, must we give up a belief in a super-natural heaven? No. But we should not think of heaven as a far off place, somewhere in space, beyond the stars.

As we have seen, the authors of the Bible proclaim that God is *distinct* from creation. That is, God is *transcendent*—before, beyond and greater than creation. But, as we have also seen, this does not mean God is disengaged from creation. On the contrary, we believe God is involved in the universe as its source and its most dynamic reality.

Since heaven, then, is where God is and since God is involved in the universe here and now as its dynamic source and reality; heaven must be among us—invisible, incomprehensible and unlimited by space or time. Indeed, heaven is eternal—beyond us, and yet very near us. Heaven is "the beyond in our midst." As Luther illustrates:

> Paul says, "God is not far from each one of us, for in him we live and move and have our being" (Acts 17:27-28); and "From and through and to God are all things" (Romans 11:36). Jeremiah 23:23 f., "Am I not a God at hand, and not a God afar off? Do I not fill heaven and earth?"
>
> ... God, in essence, is present everywhere, in and through the whole creation, in all its parts and in all places, and so the whole world is filled by God, and yet God is not limited or circumscribed by it, but is at the same time beyond and above the whole creation. [267]

It is into this "heaven" of God's dynamic presence and power that Jesus has entered, and in which and from which he lives and moves and exercises his lordship among us.

"He . . . is seated at the right hand of the Father."

It is the rejected, crucified Jesus who has been raised from death and exalted to God's right hand as Lord. In the words of Acts 2:36: "Let all the house of Israel be assured of this, that God has made this Jesus, whom you crucified, both Lord and Christ" (Acts 2:36).

And because it is *the Crucified One* who is elevated by God to exercise authority in all creation, we are given to understand how he rules and functions as Lord in the world today. He rules now, just as he lived, taught, encountered people, suffered, and died two thousand years ago. His principles are respect for all creation, respect for our humanity, and respect for the responsibility each of us is given as a human being.

As Martin Luther put it, our Lord's methods include two kingdoms or governments: On the one hand, he governs by the gospel, as proclaimed and practiced by those who believe and follow him. On the other hand, he governs through the law—both the laws of human society and the natural ways of the universe.[268]

In Luther's words:

> . . . one must carefully distinguish between these two governments. Both must be permitted to remain; the one to produce righteousness, the other to bring about external peace and prevent evil deeds. Neither one is sufficient in the world without the other.[269]

This means our Lord is not the great dictator of everything that happens. He does not order this particular event or that, causing this to happen or that to take place. The great Muslim poet, Omar Khayyam, wrote:

> This all a chequer-board of nights and days,
> Where destiny with men-for-pieces plays.[270]

But that's a far cry from the biblical understanding of God and life. The biblical view is this—because God respects creation and its ways; because God reveres our humanity and will not force us to obey; because each of us is given responsibility—therefore a great many things that take place in this world are quite the opposite of God's will. But in no case does the Lord abandon us to our fate. Rather, the Lord is active among us, ruling through law and through gospel.

"He will come again to judge the living and the dead."

In spite of all that is contrary to God's will in this world, God does not abandon us. Though we abuse and misuse creation, and things go haywire; though we sin and innocent people are hurt; though human government falters through corruption or stupidity; though nation rises against nation, and the result is chaos—God does not abandon us. On the contrary! God is powerfully at work among us, even working through evil for the good of all. When we count on Christ Jesus, God's powerful love equips us, whatever comes our way.

We believe the day is comng when Christ will make all things right. In the mean time, our Lord is present and powerful even when he seems absent and weak. As Luther emphasizes, our Lord's rule over heaven and earth is not *imperium*, but *dominium*. That is, the Lord Jesus is not a coercive emperor, but a gracious overseer. His method is not compulsion, but call; not demand, but command; not submission, but commission; not dictation, but invitation. He is a Lord whose power is made perfect through weakness, goodness, and grace (cf. 2 Corinthians 12:9). To quote Luther directly:

> Christ does not want his rule to rest on force and violence, because then it would not stand firm. He wants to be served willingly and with the heart and the affections. In this way his kingdom is eternal and will not be destroyed, since it does not rest on force.[271]

Luther's Explanation

Luther's explanation to the Second Article of the Creed is centered on the cross and resurrection of Jesus.

> I believe that Jesus Christ, true God, Son of the Father from eternity, and true man, born of the Virgin Mary, is my Lord.
>
> At great cost he has saved and redeemed me, a lost and condemned person. He has freed me from sin, death, and the power of the devil, not with silver and gold, but with his holy and precious blood and his innocent suffering and death.
>
> All this he has done that I may be his own, live under him in his kingdom, and serve him in everlasting righteousness, innocence, and blessedness, just as he is risen from the dead and lives and rules eternally. This is most certainly true.[272]

Luther's explanation is true to his faith and ministry as "a theologian of the cross." He is convinced that, dependent on our own resources and abilities, we are "lost and condemned." We need to be rescued from sin, death, and the devil. This is why the Son of God became "truly human," to do battle with these powers that hold us captive. Something had to give, either him or them. They seemed to win, of course. Working through the forces of human society, they conspired to reject and condemn him, bringing him to an end on the cross. It seemed that even God joined in, abandoning him in that awful hour.

Then came the resurrection. Suddenly the Crucified One was alive, triumphant over sin, death, and evil and exalted to be Lord over all things! Today, through "the word of the cross," he acts to overcome sin and evil in our lives, so that we might receive the new and abundant life he alone can give.

A Summary of the Gospel Message

The gospel of Christ was first proclaimed by word of mouth; and word of mouth is still the chief way of spreading the gospel. In fact, the earliest part of the New Testament was not written until twenty years after the resurrection of Jesus.

The Apostles' Creed might be said to be patterned after the gospel message proclaimed by the first Christians. As C. H. Dodd has shown, that message can be summarized as follows:

1. Prophecy is fulfilled; the New Age has begun.
2. God has accomplished this by Jesus' ministry, death and resurrection.
3. Jesus is Lord—exalted to God's right hand by the resurrection.
4. Jesus is powerfully present in the church by the Holy Spirit.
5. Jesus will come again as Savior and Judge to complete the New Age.
6. Therefore: repent, believe, receive forgiveness, follow Jesus.[273]

Like the gospel message first proclaimed by the disciples, the Creed says little or nothing about the life, words, and actions of Jesus, but emphasizes his cross, resurrection, and exaltation as Lord of all things.

In the striking words of Gerhard Forde: "The life and teachings [of Jesus] are of no significance apart from the death and resurrection. Indeed, they had to be transformed in the light of the cross and resurrection."[274]

Indeed, the four Gospels are not biographies of Jesus. Neither are they collections of as many of his words and deeds as his followers could remember. Rather, they are chronicles of the Good News of God at work in the life, death, and resurrection of Jesus. As Luther writes:

> None of the four major Gospels includes all the words and works of Christ; nor is it necessary. . . . In short, the gospel is a discourse about Christ, that he is the Son of God and became human for us, that he died and was raised, and that he has been established as Lord of all things.[275]

"I believe in the Holy Spirit. . . ."

Both the Old and New Testaments speak of the Spirit as God's energetic power, active in and through and for human beings. In fact, God's Spirit is seldom described apart from God's dynamic activity in and for human beings.

The Old Testament describes God's Spirit as empowering *leaders* such as Joseph, Moses, and Joshua to guide and strengthen the people;

energizing *the judges* (military leaders) of the Twelve Tribes to lead their tribes to victory over enemies who oppress them; inspiring *the prophets* to proclaim God's Word to the people; invigorating *skilled artists and craftsmen* such as Bezalel and Ohaliab; wholly enlivening and empowering *King David* as ruler of a United Kingdom of Judah and Israel.[276]

The New Testament describes God's Spirit as inspiring particular persons such as Elizabeth, Zechariah, and Simeon before the birth of Jesus; empowering John the Baptist in his ministry; wholly indwelling and empowering *Jesus* in his ministry; inspiring and indwelling *all those who believe* in Jesus as Lord after the resurrection of Jesus.[277] In Luther's words: "The Holy Spirit has always been in the devout from the beginning of the world . . . but has not been publicly manifested."[278]

The Day of Pentecost

> When the day of Pentecost had come, they were all together in one place. Suddenly a sound like the rush of a mighty wind came from heaven and filled the whole house where they were seated. And there appeared to them tongues as of fire, distributed and resting on each of them. And they were all filled with the Holy Spirit and began to speak in other tongues, as the Spirit enabled them to speak (Acts 2:1-4).

As he does with the ascension of Jesus (in contrast to other New Testament writers), the author of Luke–Acts presents the giving of the Spirit as a separate special event, which he describes as taking place at the Jewish festival of Pentecost, fifty days after Jesus' resurrection.

As Luke tells it, the Spirit *arrived* with the sound of rushing wind; the Spirit *appeared* as tongues of fire distributed and resting on each disciple of Jesus; and the Spirit *indwelt* the disciples, enabling them to speak in languages other than their own.

It was a spectacular display of power, energy, and wonders. Yet, when Peter offered the Spirit to others that very day, he said: "Repent, and be baptized every one of you in the name of Jesus Christ for the forgiveness of your sins; and you shall receive the gift of the Holy Spirit" (Acts 2:38). And we read that: "Those who received Peter's word were baptized and there were added that day about three thousand persons" (Acts 2:41).

It is quite a contrast. The Spirit's arrival, appearance, and indwelling of the original disciples in such a spectacular way! Then the giving of the Spirit to new disciples of Jesus, that very day, through the rather unspectacular means of the waters of baptism. As Luther says:

> The Holy Spirit does wonderful things that cannot be grasped by the senses, so that the weakness of the water .

. . has in baptism so much power that it drives out demons and yet seems so weak. But it shows its power through weakness . . . and now makes alive contrary to all grasp of wisdom and reason.[279]

As Luke tells it, then, the Spirit of God is given, not just to those closest to Jesus (Peter, James, and John), not just to the apostles, but to *all* the disciples. And the promise is extended to everyone who turns to Christ Jesus in faith (Acts 2:38-39). Moreover, unlike previous days, when the Spirit would inspire selected leaders and prophets for a time, then depart from them when their missions were over; the Spirit is here to stay. This lasting gift of the Spirit is symbolized by tongues of fire *resting* on each believer (Acts 2:3), which means *remaining* on each one and continuing to be active in and through each one. God's Spirit, Word, and action, then, is no longer restricted to the particular persons alone, as God's chosen instruments. All who are baptized into Christ Jesus receive the gift of the Spirit. All who receive the message of God's saving work in Christ are chosen and sent out, in turn, to bring the Good News to others.

The Varied Gifts of the Spirit

There are those who consider the gift of the Spirit as "something more," as a blessing above and beyond what is given through faith in Jesus. But the New Testament supports no such idea. There are, of course, "varieties of gifts" that God gives to the community of faith; gifts that are meant to be used "for the common good" of all (1 Corinthians 12:7). These are not gifts designed to exalt some believers over others. As the Letter of 1 Peter puts it: "As good stewards of God's varied grace, serve one another with whatever gift each of you has received" (4:10).

The giving of the Spirit, then, is God's action creating a new people—an action that cuts across all differences of culture and status, an action designed to appeal to every tongue and temperament, an action that is conveyed through Word and Sacrament. As Martin Luther puts it:

> In sending forth the holy gospel God deals with us in a twofold manner, first outwardly, then inwardly. Outwardly God deals with us through the spoken word of the gospel and through materials signs, that is, baptism and the sacrament of the altar. Inwardly God deals with us through the Holy Spirit, faith, and other gifts. But whatever their measure or order the outward factors should and must precede. The inward experience follows and is effected by the outward. God has determined to give the inward to no one except through the outward. For God wants to give no one the Spirit

or faith outside of the outward Word and sign. . . . My friends, carefully observe this order. Everything depends on it.[280]

The Spirit's Work

> Jesus said to them, "I will pray the Father, who will give you another Counselor, to be with you for ever, even the Spirit of truth, whom the world cannot receive, whom it neither sees nor knows. You know the Spirit, who dwells with you and will be in you" (John 14:16-17).

The Fourth Gospel describes the activity of God's Spirit with the Greek title *Paraclete*. Today, this title is translated most often as "Counselor," sometimes as "Advocate," occasionally as "Comforter." Three hundred years ago "Comforter" was quite a good translation. In those days, *to comfort* meant to strengthen or to fortify. For example, in those days parents would *comfort* their children by giving them good food, by teaching them well, by introducing them to new things, and when they needed it, by disciplining them. In that sense the Holy Spirit is our Comforter, with the emphasis on *fort*. In Luther's words: "Christ promises to send his disciples and the Christians the Holy Spirit, whom he calls the Comforter; for through the Spirit, he wants *to fortify* and keep his followers."[281]

This understanding of the Spirit's work is a fulfilment of God's promises of solid comfort to Israel (Isaiah 40:1; 51:12; 66:13); promises long expected by the faithful (Luke 2:25, 38). But the Spirit's work is also to *discomfort* us—to point out our sins, to convict us of guilt, and to turn us to Christ for forgiveness, cleansing, and renewal (cf. John 16:7-11).

Call the Spirit what we will—comforter, counselor, advocate—the Spirit's work is clear: to call us to faith in Christ through the gospel; to renew us in that faith through word and sacrament; to enlighten us; to fortify us in our struggle against sin; to bring us up short and convict us when necessary; to guide and counsel us as we follow Christ Jesus our Lord.

The Spirit's Primary Work—Justification

The Galatian Christians were being led astray by people who insisted that *to be right with God* they had to be circumcised, practice Jewish food laws, and follow all Old Covenant laws. Paul asks these Christians how they were first put right with God and received God's Spirit. Was it by their obedience to the law or was it through hearing the faith-creating gospel of Christ? He writes: "Does God give you the Spirit . . . because you observe the works of the law or because you believe what you hear?"(Galatians 3:5). Clearly, in Paul's mind, it is through the spoken

Word of the gospel alone that God's Spirit is given and that justifying faith in God is engendered by the Spirit (cf. Romans 10:13-17).

Commenting on the text of Joel 2:32 ("Everyone who calls on the name of the LORD shall be saved"), Luther writes:

> In this passage we have the sum of our salvation. We must understand it simply, just as the words sound, without adding any strange glosses. ". . . *shall be saved*," that is, redeemed from sin, death, and hell. . . . This deliverance is derived from no other source except from the Holy Spirit, . . . who sees to it that people call on the name of the Lord. In short, what Joel is saying here is the same as what Paul emphasizes everywhere—that a person is justified by faith, without the works of the law.
>
> You see, "*to call on the name*" is to believe, as Paul has interpreted it with very beautiful steps in Romans 10:14: 'How can people call on one in whom they have not believed? And how can they believe, etc.' With these steps Paul has very beautifully included the entire progression of our salvation. First people must be sent to announce the gospel. Hearing follows this sending, faith follows hearing, calling on Lord's the name follows faith, and salvation follows this invocation.
>
> Thus the Christian kingdom is nothing else than the kingdom of faith in God's Word, namely that salvation comes to us not by our strength, not by our own merits or righteousnesses, but out of the gracious mercy of God, who, as Paul says in Romans (5:10), loved us even when we were still God's enemies, who sent the Holy Spirit into our heart to be the effective Cause of our calling on the name of the Lord, in whom alone we must be saved.[282]

Washed, Sanctified, Justified in the Spirit

> You were washed, sanctified, and justified in the name of the Lord Jesus Christ and in the Spirit of our God (1 Corinthians 6:11).

What does Paul mean by this verse? Isn't justification the result of Jesus' sacrificial death on the cross? In his own words: "Since all have sinned and fall short of the glory of God, they are put right with God by the gift of God's grace, through the redemption that is in Christ Jesus, whom God put forward as a sacrifice of atonement by his blood, to be received by faith" (Romans 3:23-25).

So, yes, believers are put right with God (justified) because of Jesus' death for us on the cross. But we need to *hear* about it and *believe in* him for his sacrificial death to do us any good. As we read in Luke's Gospel: "Thus it is written, that the Christ should suffer and on the third day rise from the dead, *and* that repentance and forgiveness of sins should be *preached* in his name" (Luke 24:46-47). In Luther's words:

> The passion of Christ occurred but once on the cross. But whom would it benefit if it were not distributed, applied, and put to use? And how could it be put to use and distributed except through Word and sacrament?[283]
>
> Even if Christ were given for us and crucified a thousand times, it would all be in vain if God's Word were absent and were not distributed and given to me with the bidding: this is for you, take what is yours.[284]

So it is through the proclamation of the Word and through the promise proclaimed and conveyed to us in the sacraments that Christ's work of redemption becomes real for us. And this is because the Holy Spirit is at work in and through Word and sacrament calling us to faith in Christ. In Luther's words: "The Holy Spirit alone enlightens hearts and kindles faith, but does not do so without the outward ministry [of the Word] and without the outward use of the sacraments."[285]

The Spirit's Work of Sanctification

"To be sanctified" means "to be made holy" or "to be set apart." The authors of the New Testament have several things to say about this.

First, to be sanctified is the work of God in our lives. It is never our achievement. We are sanctified *in* Christ Jesus (1 Corinthians 1:2); *by* the Holy Spirit (Romans 15:16; 1 Peter 1:2; 2 Thessalonians 2:13); *through* faith in Christ (Acts 26:18) who gave himself for us that we might be sanctified (Ephesians 5:25-26).

All this is from God the Father who is the source of our life in Christ—our righteousness, sanctification, and redemption (1 Corinthians 1:30). Luther puts it this way:

> Working through the Spirit, Father and Son stir, awaken, call, and beget new life in me and in all who are God's. Thus the Spirit in and through Christ quickens, sanctifies, and awakens out spirits and brings us to the Father, by whom the Spirit is active and life-giving everywhere.[286]

Second, to be sanctified is never an end in itself, but always "sets us apart" for a purpose, mission, and ministry beyond ourselves—*for* God (1 Thessalonians 4:1; 1 Peter 1:2; etc.) and *for* others (1 Thessalonians 4:9; Galatians 6:10; etc.). In Luther's words:

> Christians live not in themselves, but in Christ and in their neighbor. Otherwise they are not Christians. They live in Christ through faith, in the neighbor through love. By faith they are caught up beyond themselves into God. By love they descend beneath themselves into their neighbor. Yet they always remain in God and in God's love.[287]

Third, to be sanctified is a *given* that is in the process of being realized. That is, in Christ we *are* sanctified, but in ourselves we *are* being sanctified. On the one hand, "We have been sanctified through the offering of the body of Jesus Christ once for all" (Hebrews 10:10; cf. 1 Corinthians 6:11). On the other hand, we read:

> May the Lord enable you increase and abound in love to one another and to all people, just as we abound in love for you; so that he may establish your hearts *unblamable in holiness* before our God and Father, at the coming of our Lord Jesus with all his saints. . . . May the God of peace personally sanctify you fully; and may your spirit, soul and body be kept sound and blameless at the coming of our Lord Jesus Christ (1 Thessalonians 3:12-13; 5:23).

Fourth, to be sanctified is a lifelong struggle by God's Spirit with the old nature within us. It is not a matter of our becoming wholly sanctified in this lifetime. As Luther writes:

> A Christian who has become righteous by faith and has accepted the forgiveness of sins, should not be so smug, as though pure of all sins. For only then does one face the constant battle with the remnants of sin. . . .
>
> A Christian is righteous and holy by an alien or foreign holiness . . . that is, made righteous by God's mercy and grace. This mercy and grace is not something human. It is not some sort of disposition or quality in the heart. It is a divine blessing, given us through the true knowledge of the gospel, when we know or believe that our sin has been forgiven us through the grace and merit of Christ and when we hope for steadfast love and abundant mercy for Christ's sake. . . . Is not this righteousness an alien righteousness?[288]

Fifth, to be sanctified requires that we continually turn to God for the forgiveness of our sins and to be renewed in the righteousness that comes through Christ alone. Paul writes about receiving "the righteousness from God that depends on faith" and of his desire to "know Christ, the power of his resurrection, and the fellowship of his suffering," and so to "attain the resurrection from the dead" (Philippians 3:9-11). He goes on to say:

> Not that I have already attained this or am already perfect; but I press on to grasp that for which Christ Jesus has already grasped me. I do not consider that I have made it my own; but one thing I do, forgetting what lies behind and straining forward to what lies ahead, I eagerly forge ahead toward the goal for the prize of the upward call of God in Christ Jesus. Let those of us who are mature be thus minded; and if in anything you are otherwise minded, God will reveal that also to you. Only let us hold true to what we have attained" Philippians 3:12-16).

Along with Paul, Luther is convinced that we never "arrive" in this life. Because sin remains strong within us, the Spirit's work of sanctification in our lives is not perfected in this lifetime, but is *in process*. It is an activity in which God's Spirit is involved in a lifelong struggle with our sinful natures. In Luther's words:

> We are not in a state of perfection. No, we are in a state of becoming and transition, or in a state of movement from virtue to virtue, from day to day, from cleansing to cleansing. After being sanctified we are still being sanctified."[289]

> We have been redeemed and we are being redeemed continually. We have received adoption and are still receiving it. We have been made children of God and we are and shall be children. The Spirit has been sent, is being sent and will be sent. We learn and we shall learn.[290]

Sanctification and Striving for Holiness

If to be sanctified is the work of God, why are Christians urged to "strive for holiness" (Hebrews 12:14), to "aim at righteousness" (1 Timothy 6:11; 2 Timothy 2:22; Hebrews 12:14), to "fight the good fight of the faith" (1 Timothy 6:12), to "put off the old nature and to put on the new nature" (Ephesians 4:22, 24) to "lay aside every weight and sin which clings so closely" (Hebrews 12:1)?

It is not a matter of attaining holiness on our own. That is impossible. These exhortations are given to those who have *already* been sanctified in Christ and who now have access to the resources of sanctification—the gift of God's Spirit, the power of the gospel in word and sacrament, and the communion of saints. In the words of Adolf Köberle: "Without the reality of the presence of the Holy Spirit such commands would be utterly meaningless." But, as Köberle goes on to say: "While we can neither create nor maintain the new life, we can always lose it."[291] We can "drift away" and "neglect such a great salvation" (Hebrews 2:1, 3). Luther writes:

> When by mercy we are free of guilt, we still need the gift of the Holy Spirit to clean out the remnants of sin in us or at least to help us lest we succumb to sin and to the lusts of the flesh. As Paul says, it is by the Spirit that we 'put to death the deeds of the body' (Romans 8:13). What happens is most of us are so smug we live as though we were all spirit and nothing of the flesh were left at all. Therefore we must learn that the flesh still remains and that the task of the Spirit is to war against the flesh, lest the flesh accomplish that for which it lusts.
>
> Unless we oppose and fight this with great effort, there is danger that these vices will grow stronger and drag us back into our old wickedness.[292]

The word "flesh," as used here by Luther and as used in the New Testament (*sarx* in Greek), does not to refer to our bodily tissues and tendons, but refers to our whole being—body, mind, and soul. That is, the word refers to everything we are by nature, apart from the Lord; a nature that Paul describes as sinful, self-centered, and displeasing to God. As Luther puts it:

> Paul calls everything "flesh" that is born of the flesh—the whole person, with body and soul, mind and senses.
>
> Whatever is best and most outstanding in people Paul calls "flesh."[293]

Of course, we who are Christians desire to be free from sin and to live holy lives, but as Paul writes: "The desires of the flesh are against the Spirit and the desires of the Spirit are against the flesh; for these are opposed to one another, to prevent you from doing what you would" (Galatians 5:17). As Luther points out so graphically:

> It is true that there is no one passion ceaselessly driving us to distraction. Anger does not always burn, evil desire does not always rage, we are not constantly tormented with envy, but one of these succeeds the other. When they all sleep, then languor and sloth do not sleep. If you are strenuously active, then pride awakens. As I have most truly said, just as we are not without the flesh, so we do not work without the flesh. So we are neither free of carnal faults, nor do we act without them. . . . Sin is a living thing in constant movement, changing as its objects change.[294]

Sanctification and Becoming New in Christ

The Pauline letters to the Ephesians and Colossians urge believers to "put off your old nature" and "put on the new nature." But we should not misunderstand these terms. They are not meant to suggest that a Christian is endowed with two natures, one lower and one higher. No, no. Each of us who is a Christian continues to be "the old me" as long as we live.

But something is happening to a believer's "old nature." That something is the work of God's Holy Spirit within each believer—what Paul calls "the new creation" (2 Corinthians 5:17; Galatians 6:15) or "the new life of the Spirit" (Romans 7:6).

Because of a newborn faith in Christ engendered in this "old me" by God's Spirit, not only am I put right with God, freely, by God's grace alone; I am no longer content with the "old me" that I am. And yet, even though I now desire to be a "new self," the "old me" resists. I am now *simul justus et peccator* (justified before God in Christ, and at the same time, sinful in myself).[295] And so, as Paul describes it in Romans 7:14-25, and Galatians 5:17, I face a life-long battle.

The Christian life, then, is not a struggle between two natures within us, but a conflict between what we are personally and God's Spirit at work in us (Romans 8:4-13; Galatians 5:16-17). Following Paul's thinking, Luther would say that since we, as Christians, continue to be sinners in ourselves, and since our only hope is in the righteousness that Christ alone can give us, progress in sanctification is a continual turning to Christ again and again, day by day.[296] He writes:

> As long as there is life there must be repentance and renewal so that sin may be expelled. . . . Although God has justified us through the gift of faith and is favorable to us through grace, God desires that we rely on Christ so that we will not waver in ourselves and in these gifts, nor be satisfied with the righteousness that has begun in us, . . . so that no fool, having once accepted the gift, will become contented and secure. God does not want us to halt in what has been received, but rather to draw near from day to day so that we may be fully transformed into Christ.[297]

Sanctification and Always Beginning Again

This, then, is Luther's teaching on sanctification:

1. It is God's work in our lives, never our achievement.
2. Its purpose is to set us apart for God and for others.
3. It is a *given* (in Christ) in the *process* of being realized (in us).
4. It is a lifelong struggle of God's Spirit with our "fleshly" nature.

> 5. It requires that we daily turn to God for forgiveness and renewal.

Again and again Luther speaks of sanctification as "movement" and "beginning again." He writes, for example:

> To make progress is nothing else than always to begin. And to begin without making progress is to fail.[298]

> To stand still on the way to God is to retrogress, and to advance is always a matter of beginning anew.[299]

> There is always something left where you may increase, and therefore you are always in motion and at the beginning.[300]

Begin again how? Begin again with Christ. Hear again the Word. Count again on his grace. Turn again in faith. Confess again our sins. Receive again his forgiveness. Live out again our baptism. To move ahead in Christian faith and life is to fall back on Christ again and again.

This reminds us, as Regin Prenter writes, that sanctification for Luther does not mean that, with God's help, we grow better and better. It means that we come daily into the sphere of the Spirit to rely more and more on *Christ* as *our only righteousness*; and, in turn, to be used by him in behalf of our neighbors.[301] Luther writes:

> The whole life of the new, faithful, spiritual people is nothing else but prayer . . . always seeking and striving to be made righteous, even to the hour of death, never standing still, never possessing, never in any work putting an end to the achievement of righteousness, but always awaiting it as something which still dwells beyond them, and always as people who still live and exist in their sins.[302]

Again, as Luther writes:

> As long as we live here on earth, believing in God's Word, we are a work that God has begun, but not yet completed. But after death we shall be perfect, a divine work without sin or fault. This life, therefore, is not godliness but the process of becoming godly, not health but getting well, not being but becoming, not rest but exercise.

> We are not now what we shall be, but we are on the way. The process is not yet finished, but it is actively going on. This is not the goal but it is the right road. At present, everything does not gleam and sparkle, but everything is being cleansed.[303]

"I believe in . . . the holy, catholic church. . . ."

Paul's salutation to the Christians at Corinth defines the "holy, catholic church, the communion of saints" beautifully. He writes: "To the church (assembly) of God that is at Corinth, to those sanctified in Christ Jesus, called to be saints together with all those everywhere who call on the name of our Lord Jesus Christ. . . ."

It is, then, the *assembly* (from the Greek word *ecclesia*) of God, that is at Corinth (a gathering of believers in a particular place), *sanctified* (made holy or set apart) in Christ Jesus, called to be *saints together* (the communion of saints), *with all those everywhere* (catholic or world-wide) who call on the name of our Lord Jesus Christ.

As Luther points out, it is unfortunate that the Greek word *ecclesia* has been translated into German as "*kirche*" (and into English as "church").[304] These translations derive from an abbreviation of the Latin *kyriakos doma*, meaning "the Lord's house." But *ecclesia* simply means "assembly" or "gathering." This is its consistent meaning in the New Testament whether it refers to a secular gathering or to the assembly of believers. Even when used to refer to the whole people of God throughout the world, the word has the connotation of "gathering." In Luther's own words:

> The word *ecclesia* properly means an assembly. . . . In our mother tongue therefore it ought to be called "a Christian congregation or assembly," or best and most clearly of all, "a holy Christian people."[305]

> If the words, "I believe that there is a holy Christian people," had been used in the Children's Creed, all the misery connected with this meaningless and obscure word (church) might easily have been avoided. For the words 'Christian holy people' would have brought with them, dearly and powerfully, the proper understanding and judgment of what is, and what is not, church.[306]

> I believe that throughout the whole wide world there is only one holy, universal, Christian church, which is nothing other than the gathering or congregation of saints—pious believers on earth. This church is gathered, preserved, and governed by the same Holy Spirit and is given daily increase by means of the sacraments and God's word.[307]

The Assembly of Believers

The authors of the New Testament use a host of other terms to describe the assembly of believers, including:

"The body of Christ" (Romans 12:5; 1 Corinthians 12:12ff).

"The company of believers" (Acts 4:323; cf. Acts 1:15; 11:24, 26).

"The household of God" (Ephesians 2:19; 1 Timothy 3:15).

"The children of God" (John 1:12; 11:32; Romans 8:16).

"The people of God" (Hebrews. 4:9; 11:25; cf. Titus 2:14; 1 Peter 2:9-10).

"The flock of God" (1 Peter 5:2-3; cf. Acts 20:28).

"The fellowship of God's Son" (1 Corinthians 1:9; cf. Acts 2:42).

Each of these terms is inclusive in the sense of a gathered community. In the New Testament, then, the believing community is *always* a gathered community. In fact, every assembly of believers, no matter how small, is understood to be, not simply one unit of the universal church, but the whole community of Christ in that place. Just as each synagogue back then was regarded as a microcosm of all of Judaism, so each Christian assembly was considered to be the whole people of God in that place, *because* the Spirit of God was at work there, calling people to faith in Christ through the gospel.

As New Testament scholar Paul Minear writes: "Because the ecclesai [plural] belong to Christ, and to God, they constitute together a single reality—a world-wide covenant community, which is embodied in localized form wherever a congregation exists (Colossians 4:15-16; 1 Thessalonians 1:1; etc.)."[308]

The Hiddenness of the Church

Luther writes:

> This article, "*I believe in the holy Christian Church*," is as much an article of faith as the rest. This is why natural reason cannot recognize it, even if it puts on all its glasses. Christendom will not be known by sight, but by faith.[309]

Though visible, the church remains "hidden," except to the "eyes" of faith. Luther, however, points to certain God-given "signs" that mark the presence of a genuine Christian assembly: the gospel proclaimed, Baptism and Holy Communion rightly administered, God being praised, forgiveness in Christ's name being declared, good lives being lived and good deeds done, suffering for the faith taking place.[310]

Luther particularly emphasizes the all important "mark" of the Word:

> Wherever you hear or see this word preached, believed, professed, and lived, do not doubt that the true "holy catholic church" . . . must be there, even though their number is very small. For God's word "shall not return empty" (Isaiah 55:11). Even if there were no other sign than this alone, it would still suffice to prove that a Christian, holy people must exist

there, for God's word cannot be without God's people, and conversely, God's people cannot be without God's word.[311]

The Daughter of the Word

As New Testament authors make clear, it is God's Spirit, working through the proclamation of the Word, who gives birth to the church. And it is the Spirit, at work through the proclaimed Word, who preserves, sanctifies, and enriches the fellowship of believers. In Luther's language:

> The church was born by the word of promise through faith, and by this same word is nourished and preserved. That is, it is the promises of God that make the church, and not the church that makes the promise of God. For the Word of God is incomparably superior to the church, and in this Word the church, being a creature, has nothing to decree, ordain, or make, but only to be decreed, ordained, and made.[312]

> Christians, or children of God, are made—not by the power or intellectual capacity of human beings but only by the heavenly operation of the Holy Spirit, and yet through the Word, the preaching of the gospel, and Baptism.[313]

> The church is the daughter, born from the Word, not the mother of the Word. Whoever gives up the Word and hastens to rely on persons ceases to be the church and is completely blinded.[314]

> Where the Word is, there the church is, there the Spirit is, there Christ is, and everything. . . . The fathers [Abraham, Isaac, Jacob] had a physical succession, just as later on in the law there was a physical succession to the priesthood. But in the New Testament there is no such physical succession. Christ did not beget sons or daughters according to the flesh. Therefore the church is not confined to a place or to persons but is only where the Word is. Where the Word is not, even though the titles and the office are there, the church is not, because God is not there either.[315]

The Priesthood of All Believers

The term "the priesthood of all believers," from the late Reformation era, depicts a characteristic that is integral to the nature of the church (the assembly of believers) as taught by Paul and other authors of the New Testament. They teach that:

- Believers are "one in Christ," without distinction as to status or worth in their relationship to Christ and without distinction as to status or worth in their call to discipleship and responsibility;[316]

- Every believer is indwelt by the Holy Spirit and endowed with "spiritual gifts" (*charismata*) to be used for the common good;[317]
- Every believer is called to take part in "the work of the ministry;" making use of the gifts that God has given "for the good of all";[318]
- Certain believers are themselves "gifts" (*domata*) to the church, called "to equip others for the work of the ministry."[319]

Luther's first written reference to what is later called "the priesthood of all believers" appears in a letter to George Spalatin, dated December 18, 1519:

> 1 Peter 2 says we are all priests; as does John in the Apocalypse. So the type of priesthood to which we [clergy] belong actually does not seem to differ from the laity, except for the ministerial office through which the Word and sacraments are administered. If you remove the ceremonies and human statutes [of the clergy], all else is equal.[320]

Elsewhere and often in the early 1520s, Luther declared:

> Let everyone . . . who is aware of being a Christian, be assured of this, that we are all equally priests. . . .[321]

> We are all priests before God if we are Christians. . . . For priests, the baptized, and Christians are all one and the same.[322]

> Christ has crowned, ordained, and anointed us all with the Holy Spirit so that all of us together are priests in Christ and exercise a priestly office. . . .[323]

What, according to the New Testament and to Luther, does it mean to say that all Christians are priests? To begin with, it means that each and every believer may, with confidence, stand before God through Christ Jesus our Lord and Mediator.

Jesus promised his followers: "Truly, truly, I say to you, if you ask anything of the Father, it will be given to you in my name" (John 16:23). The author of Hebrews writes: "Since then we have a great high priest who has passed through the heavens, Jesus, the Son of God . . . let us with confidence draw near to the throne of grace, that we may receive mercy and find grace to help in time of need" (Hebrews 4:14, 16; cf. 10:19-22). And Luther declares:

> This is a spiritual priesthood, held in common by all Christians, through which we are all priests with Christ. That is, we

are children of Christ, the high priest. We need no priest or mediator other than Christ. . . . Thus *every* Christian *on his own* or *on her own* may pray in Christ and have access to God.[324]

But as Paul Althaus points out, Luther *never* understood the priesthood of all believers in an individualistic, "protestant" way. It is the priesthood of *all* believers after all. It is an understanding of the church in which each believer is responsible, as a priest, to and for others.[325]

Our Priestly Purpose

In Luther's interpretation of the New Testament, the meaning and purpose of the priesthood of all believers is five-fold:

First of all, in the words of 1 Peter 2:9, our purpose as "priests" is "to declare the wonderful deeds of the One who called you out of darkness into God's marvelous light." Jesus himself calls us to this work: "Go into all the world and proclaim the gospel. . . . You shall be my witnesses in Jerusalem, in Judea, in Samaria, and to the ends of the earth. . . . As the Father has sent me, even so I send you."[326]

In Luther's strong words:

> The first and foremost duty we Christians should perform is to proclaim the wonderful deeds of God.
>
> Let it be your chief work to proclaim this publicly and to call everyone into the light into which you have been called. Where you find people who do not know this, you should . . . teach them as you have learned . . . how one must be saved through the power and strength of God.[327]

Christ Jesus himself commissioned his followers to be his witnesses throughout the world. And that commission is extended to every follower of Christ. It is not intended for the apostles only or for persons especially selected by Christ, such as Paul of Tarsus. As the letter of 1 Peter emphasizes, each and every believer has been redeemed and chosen to declare the wonderful deeds of God in Christ (1 Peter 2:9); and every believer is urged to be ready always to give an answer to everyone who asks for the reason for the hope that is in her or him (1 Peter 3:15-16).

In Luther's mind, how could it be otherwise? In his mind and heart, to know Christ Jesus as one's Redeemer and Lord is such an amazing treasure that a believer is eager to make him known, so that others will have that wondrous treasure in their lives. In his own words:

> Once a Christian begins to know Christ as Lord and Savior, through whom he or she is redeemed from death and brought into Christ's dominion and inheritance, God

completely permeates that person's heart. Now a Christian is eager to help everyone acquire the same benefits. For his or her greatest delight is in this treasure, the knowledge of Christ. Therefore a Christian steps forth boldly, teaches and admonishes others, praises and confesses this treasure before everybody, prays and yearns that they, too, may obtain such mercy. There is a spirit of restlessness amid the greatest calm, that is, in God's grace and peace. A Christian cannot be still or idle, but constantly strives and struggles mightily, as one who has no other object in life than to disseminate God's honor and glory among the people, that others may also receive such a spirit of grace and through this spirit also help him or her pray. For wherever the spirit of grace resides, there we can and dare, yes, must begin to pray.[328]

A second meaning and purpose of the priesthood of all believers is to pray for others. The authors of the New Testament exhort us: "Pray for one another."[329] In Luther's words:

As priests we are worthy to appear before God to pray for others and to teach one another divine things. Therefore we may come boldly into the presence of God in the spirit of faith and cry "Abba, Father!" praying for one another.[330]

Luther calls prayer for others an essential part of "a Christian's true office and function,"[331] and he declares that:

Christ will achieve and produce two things in all Christians: first, he will persuade and assure their hearts that they have a compassionate God; secondly, he will enable them to help others by their supplication. The result of the first is that they will be reconciled to God and have all they need for themselves. Then, since they have this, they will become helpers and saviors of humanity by their supplication.[332]

A third meaning and purpose of the priesthood of all believers is the believer's capacity to judge the things of faith, life, and doctrine. As the New Testament puts it: "Test everything and hold fast to what is good." And again, "test the spirits to see whether they are of God."[333]

As Luther argues, within the assembly of believers no one has a right to lord it over others in matters of faith, life, and doctrine.[334] He writes:

If we are all priests . . . and all have one faith, one gospel, one sacrament [baptism], why should we not also have the power to test and judge what is right or wrong in matters of faith? What becomes of Paul's words in 1 Corinthians 2 [:15], "A spiritual person judges all things, yet is judged by no one"? And 2 Corinthians 4 [:13], "We all have one spirit of faith'? Why, then, should we not perceive what is consistent with faith and what is not?"[335]

Again he writes:

> Scripture gives every Christian the power to judge teaching . . . to know and avoid the wolves. . . . So do *not* depend on the conclusions of other people, even if they be angels. . . . Depend rather on your own conscience, for each of us must have a personal faith and must know the difference between true and false teaching.[336]

A fourth meaning and purpose of the priesthood of all believers is to sacrifice. Paul urges us "to present our bodies as a living sacrifice." The author of Hebrews exhorts us to "continually offer up a sacrifice of praise to God" and "to do good and to share what you have, for *such sacrifices* are pleasing to God" (Hebrews 13:15-16). 1 Peter 2 counsels us *"to offer spiritual sacrifices* acceptable to God through Jesus Christ."

Luther writes:

> We are to offer up ourselves *for our neighbors' benefit* and for the honor of God. This offering is the exercise of our love—distributing our works for the benefit of our neighbors.[337]

And, quite strikingly, he writes:

> Of all the sacrifices the one most acceptable to God is this: to kill sin, to live in righteousness, holiness, obedience, and mortification of the flesh. This is indeed painful and difficult for us; but one must learn to accustom oneself, as Paul says, to "what is the good will of God."[338]

> Just as Christ sacrificed his body, so we, too, must sacrifice ourselves. . . . The true priestly office is practiced when we sacrifice that villainous rogue [our sinful self] to God. If the world does not do this [to us], we must do it ourselves; for in the end we must put aside every vestige of the old Adam. . . .[339]

A fifth and crucial meaning of the priesthood of all believers is the place and purpose of *the office of the ministry* within that priesthood. This office is also known as "the ministry of the Word," "the ministry of Word and sacrament," and "the office of preaching." Of course, these are Reformation era terms, not New Testament terms. As Ernst Käsemann writes: "There is no real equivalent in the New Testament for our present day conception of 'office.'"[340]

Only in the late New Testament era, well after the lifetimes of Paul and the other apostles, do we find what might be called "offices" in congregations. As indicated in Acts, 1 and 2 Timothy, and Titus, these late first century churches established presbyteries and pastoral "offices" to lead and safeguard the believers in the face of heresy from within and of opposition from without. Thus began a distinction between "clergy" and "laity" that grew through the centuries.

As an heir of the medieval church Luther accepted the office of the ministry as a divine institution, but he interpreted it in the light of the priesthood of all believers. That is, he understood this office primarily in terms of "the first and foremost duty we Christians should perform—to proclaim the wonderful deeds of God."[341] He was certain it is the whole church that comes to faith through the Word preached and that every believer, in turn, is called upon to proclaim the Word to all the world. And so he declares that the office of the ministry *belongs* to, *resides* in, and *is the responsibility* of all believers;[342] or more accurately, that the office belongs to our Lord, who has given it into the care of the whole community of faith.[343] Luther writes:

> The one true, genuine office of preaching . . . is common to *all* Christians.[344]

> The ministry of the Word . . . is unique and belongs to *all* Christians, not only by right but by command.[345]

Not only does Luther declare that the ministry of the Word belongs to all Christians; he has the same thing to say about baptism, communion, absolution, teaching, and the other functions of the office of the ministry. He believes and teaches that every one of these functions is held in common by, and belongs to all of us who are Christians.[346] Luther drives this point home when he declares:

> There is no other Word of God than that which is given *all* Christians to proclaim. There is no other baptism than the one which *any* Christian can bestow. There is no other remembrance of the Lord's Supper than that which *any* Christian is able to do. . . . There is no other kind of sin than that which *any* Christian can bind or loose. There is no other sacrifice than of the body of *every* Christian. . . . a Christian may pray. . . . a Christian may judge doctrine. All these make up the priestly, royal office . . . which resides in the community of believers.[347]

But if any Christian may preach, baptize, celebrate the Lord's Supper, and absolve others from sin, why do we call and ordain certain persons to carry out these functions in our congregations? We do so for reasons of good order (cf. 1 Corinthians 14:40).[348] As Luther writes:

> No one may make use of this power except by the consent of the community. . . . For what is the common property

of all, no individual may abrogate to herself or himself, without being called.[349]

The people as a whole cannot do these things, but must entrust or have them entrusted to one person. Otherwise, what would happen if everyone wanted to speak or administer, and no one wanted to give way to the other? It must be entrusted to one person, who alone should be allowed to preach, to baptize, to absolve, and to administer the sacraments.[350]

In Luther's understanding, then, the person who is called to the office of the ministry exercises that office "in the name of," "in the place of," "by the command of," and "on behalf of" the priesthood of all believers.[351] As for the office itself, it remains in the care and keeping of the congregation (the priesthood of all believers); with the office-holder as the primary steward of that office for a time. As Luther writes:

That [the office of ministry] needs nurture is not only the responsibility of the office holder, but of the whole congregation. The whole congregation must be alert through prayer and witness so the shepherd does not run when the wolf comes.[352]

On the day the office-holder [pastor] moves on, the office remains with the congregation, to be filled again by another person called by them. In Luther's words: "Offices and sacraments always remain in the church; persons are daily subject to change."[353]

Implications of the Priesthood of All Believers

What conclusions should we draw from the New Testament doctrine of the priesthood of all believers as applied to our lives today?

A first implication is that *the Word of God* is primary in the life and ministry of Christ and his church. It is the Word that gives birth to the church, the priesthood of all believers. It is the Word that energizes the office of the ministry. It is the Word, which through the ministry of the priesthood of all believers, goes out into the world—calling, challenging, promising—and does not return empty, but accomplishes what God purposes and desires. As Luther writes:

A real Christian knows that the church never ordains or institutes anything apart from the Word of God. Any church that does is no church except in name only. It is not a word from God just because the church speaks it; rather, the church comes into being because God's Word is spoken. The church does not constitute the Word, but is constituted by the Word. A sure sign, by which we know where the church is, is the Word of God, as Paul writes in 1 Corinthians 14.[354]

A second implication is that the priesthood of all believers mandates *an active congregation*, with each and every member called to proclaim the Good News, to pray for fellow believers and others, to evaluate and judge matters of faith, life, and doctrine, and to sacrifice herself or himself in behalf of others in the service and mission of Christ. As Luther writes:

> Since Christ is the Priest and we are his brothers and sisters, all Christians have the authority, the command, and the obligation to preach, to come before God, to pray for one another, and to offer themselves as a sacrifice to God.[355]

A third implication is that the followers of Jesus are called to *a common ministry*. We are equal in status and responsibility. Of course we differ in personal abilities, education, spiritual gifts and the offices we fill, but these abilities, gifts, and offices are to be used for the common good. Luther writes:

> It is enough now that we know that a Christian people is undivided, without distinctions of sects or persons, a people among whom there is to be no layperson, no cleric, no monk, no nun, no differences at all.[356]

Again he writes:

> There is no true, basic difference between lay people and priests, princes and bishops, between religious and secular, except for the sake of office and work, but not for the sake of status.
>
> A cobbler, a smith, a peasant—each has the work and office of a trade, and yet they are all alike consecrated priests and bishops. And each must benefit and serve others by means of each one's work or office so that a variety of works are done for the bodily and spiritual welfare of the community. . . .[357]

A fourth implication is that *the congregation calls and ordains* those who fill the office of ministry in the congregation. Following the authors of Acts and the later Pauline epistles, Luther teaches that the congregation alone has the authority to call and ordain persons to fill the office of the ministry. He writes:

> We should have no doubt that the congregation that has the gospel may and should elect and call from among its members someone to teach the word in its place.
>
> No bishop should institute anyone without the election, will, and call of the congregation, but should confirm the person whom the congregation chose and called. If [the bishop] does not do so, [that person] is confirmed anyway by virtue of the congregation's call.[358]

A fifth implication is that, as the primary steward of the office of the ministry, it is the responsibility of the called and ordained minister(s) to *strengthen the "priesthood" of each member* of the congregation—so that each member will be better equipped to proclaim the Good News, to pray, to minister to others, to learn to judge matters of faith, life, and doctrine, and to offer herself or himself as a sacrifice to God. Luther comments:

> Out of the multitude of Christians some must be selected who shall *lead* the others by virtue of the special gifts and aptitude which God gives them for this office.
>
> For although we are all priests, this does not mean that all of us can preach, teach, and lead. Certain ones of the multitude must be selected and separated for such an office.[359]

A sixth implication is that those who are called to the office of ministry should be *properly prepared*—through faith, personal conviction, study, commitment, and character—to fill that office. Luther writes:

> We must act according to Scripture and call and institute from among ourselves those who are found to be qualified and whom God has enlightened with reason and endowed with gifts to do so.[360]

In Luther's mind, *to be qualified*, a pastor must be a person who is "pious," "faithful," "capable," "worthy and able," must have a knowledge of the biblical languages, and (as in the days of the New Testament) should be "well-tried, learned, fit, and experienced."[361]

Our Ministry and Our Vocations

Not only does God give us a *ministry* to others, but also *vocations* (callings) to exercise in their behalf as well. That is, having been put right with God through faith in Christ we are given *the ministry* of declaring the good news of God's redeeming activity to others. And as part of God's creative activity in the world we are given *vocations* to carry out for the earthly benefit of others.

All of us have a number of vocations during our lives—as daughters or sons, as students, as spouses, as parents, as neighbors, as workers, as citizens. We exercise our vocations in our occupations and in everyday activities (in our families, neighborhoods, schools, work places, and communities). Our several callings will change over a lifetime, but in every circumstance we are called to do what we can for the benefit of others. As Luther says:

> If we want to practice godliness . . . let us first receive the Word of God and believe in Christ. Then let us walk in our simple calling: let the husband support his family; let the maid obey her mistress; let the mother wash, dress, and

teach the children. Because these works are done in one's calling and in faith in the Son of God, they shine in the sight of God, of the angels, and of the entire church of God.[362]

Ministry and vocation are both essential in the fellowship of believers. If either is neglected, God's redemptive and creative activity in the world is hampered. In Marc Kolden's powerful words:

> If we (wrongly) think that faith means only correct "belief" and does not involve us in works of love, then we do not have faith—because faith is trusting God with all our heart and soul and mind and strength. Faith is a total rearrangement of life that occurs when Christ comes to us and calls us to follow. Faith without works is not faith! The gospel without vocation is not gospel because it simply leaves us at ease in our old sinful self—which Christ does not do. He loves us more than that, so he forgives us and gives us callings in daily life—both for the good of others and for our own eternal good.[363]

As we might expect, Luther, too, emphasizes:

> Works cannot be set aside even where faith, which alone justifies, is present, since they are the fruits of a justifying faith. For faith without works is dead and worth nothing.[364]

> Faith without love is not enough; it is not faith at all, but rather a counterfeit of faith, just as a face in a mirror is not a real face but merely a reflection of a face.[365]

"I believe in . . . the forgiveness of sins. . . ."

Someone once said the church is the Society of the Forgiven—not the society of the good or the do-gooders or the religious. At the heart of our faith and life in Christ is the forgiveness of sins.

But isn't forgiveness a cheap way out of our wrong doing? Isn't it only right that we pay for our sins? No. Real forgiveness does not treat sin lightly. None of us would be helped if God simply overlooked our sins. God's forgiveness is straight-on and true. It confronts our sin. As the same time, it proclaims God's grace, promises God's mercy, and calls us to turn to receive what God so readily gives. Moreover, God's forgiveness acts to eradicate our sin, to neutralize its power, to cleanse its stains, to replace the wrong with something good and powerful, and to revitalize our lives.

Forgiveness is exactly what we need in our lives and in human society as a whole. In this world so caught up in the vicious cycle of cause and effect, where we reap what we sow—paying the price for our wrongs and for our stupidity—we need the power of forgiveness to break the cycle, to erase the cause, and to transform the effect.

We need both God's forgiveness and the practice of forgiveness toward one another. In fact the two go together. This is why Jesus taught us to pray, "Forgive us our sins as we forgive those who sin against us." As Luther says, "Forgiving those who sin against us is the sign that we have actually received God's forgiveness.[366] "In his words:

> God has promised the forgiveness of sins. Of that you must be sure and certain, in so far as you also forgive your neighbor. If you have someone whom you do not forgive, you pray in vain. . . . Not that you are forgiven *on account of* your forgiveness. For your sins are forgiven, quite freely, apart your forgiveness. But the Lord enjoins it on you as a sign, so you may be assured that, if you forgive, you too will be forgiven.[367]

"I believe in . . . the resurrection of the body. . . ."

The Apostles' Creed declares its faith in "the resurrection of the body" (a Jewish belief), not faith in the immortality of the soul (a Greek belief). In ancient Greek thinking this material world is inferior; a human being is an immortal soul trapped in a mortal body; life in this world is an exile; salvation is to be set free, by death, from one's mortal body, to return, as an immortal soul, to the spirit world.

However, in ancient Hebrew thinking this world is God's creation and therefore good; a human being is a whole person—body, soul, mind, spirit; life in this world is a pilgrimage; the human problem is sin—rebellion against God, and the desire to be our own little gods; and salvation is to be set free, by God, from bondage to sin and death.[368]

There seems to be a commonly held belief today (an aspect of the theology of glory) that death is simply the gateway for an undying soul to enter heaven. This belief sometimes includes the superstitious idea that that undying soul now sees and knows what is happening on earth.

The cross of Jesus is God's witness to the contrary. Death is not an escape from sin or from an inferior world; it is the consequence of sin. In theological terms, there is simply no hope for the survival of "the old self-centered me." The crucified, risen Jesus *alone* is our Savior from sin and death. Through him, God promises to raise all believers out of the death brought about by our sin to eternal life. In Luther's words:

> . . . you should be different from the other people, who have no hope, simply because you believe that Christ rose from the dead and that through him death has been conquered. . . . because he has overcome death, he will also snatch us from death and bring us with him. For he rose again in order that

he take us with him out of death into life and eternal glory.[369]

We believe that the Savior arose from the dead for the purpose of raising us, too, on the last day and presenting us as glorious and resplendent as he himself is.[370]

"I believe in . . . the life everlasting."

The Christian faith stands or falls with Jesus Christ. As the authors of the New Testament express it: "God's free gift is eternal life in Christ Jesus our Lord" (Romans 6:23); "The God of all grace has called you to eternal glory in Christ. . . ." (1 Peter 5:10); "God gave us eternal life, and this life is in God's Son." (1 John 5:11).

The life God gives us in Jesus is more than everlasting. It is not just an existence that goes on and on forever. It is *eternal* life—a radically new life out of death, ever-expanding, wholesome, and abundant. As Paul writes (1 Corinthians 2:9): "What no eye has seen, nor ear heard, nor any human heart conceived . . . God has prepared for those who love God."

When does eternal life in Christ begin? According to John's Gospel (5:24), it begins now, ahead of time. That is, because the Spirit of Christ is present in our lives now, we begin to experience something of the joy and richness of eternal life to come.

But when will the *fullness* of that life begin? Immediately after death, as some believe? At the end of the world, when all people shall be raised from the dead? Who can say? Perhaps it is immediately after death, since eternity is a dimension beyond here and now.

For a Christian this much is sure: we shall all die the death brought about by our sins. But through our Lord Jesus Christ, God will raise us out of death to eternal life . Exactly when and how, we cannot say, but: "We believe in the resurrection of the body and the life everlasting."

PART THREE

THE LORD'S PRAYER

Background of the Lord's Prayer

What is prayer? What is its purpose? Does it make any difference? When a doctoral student asked Albert Einstein for suggestions for an original dissertation project, Einstein responded: "Find out about prayer. Somebody must find out about prayer."[371]

Examples of persons who pray abound in the Bible—from Abraham to Hannah to Hezekiah to Anna to Jesus himself. Examples of a variety of kinds of prayer abound in the Bible as well, as do God's responses to these prayers.

The author of Luke–Acts, in particular, emphasizes prayer throughout his two volumes. He especially depicts the importance of prayer for Jesus, whom the author pictures at prayer a dozen times.[372] Most notably, Jesus is shown at prayer at crucial times in his ministry: at his baptism, after a day of working miracles, prior to calling the twelve apostles, prior to Peter's confession of faith and the first announcement of his passion to come, on the mount of transfiguration, following the successful mission of the apostles, in the Garden of Gethsemane, and on the cross.

Jesus is also portrayed teaching his disciples regarding prayer. He teaches them what we know as the Lord's Prayer.[373] He tells them a parable describing two men at prayer.[374] He tells them another two parables and a simile on prayer.[375] He gives them specific suggestions and challenges about prayer.[376]

Luke also depicts a number of others at prayer: Zechariah, Elizabeth, Mary, Simeon, and Anna.[377] And in his second volume, Acts, Luke pictures the importance of prayer in the life of the people of the early church.[378] As Luke presents it, then, there is no question about the vital place of prayer in the life of our Lord and of his followers. And there is no question about God's eagerness to hear our prayers and to strengthen and guide us in faith. In particular, Jesus' example and teaching on prayer reveal that we can pray to God, as Luther puts it, ". . . in complete confidence, just as children speak to their loving father."[379]

The Bible records other encouraging calls to prayer. For example:

> Call on me in the day of trouble; I will deliver you, and you shall glorify me (Psalm 50:15).

> If two of you agree on earth about anything they ask, it will be done for them by my Father in heaven (Matthew 18:19).

> The Lord is generous to all who call on the Lord (Romans 10:12).

But we should be aware that the authors of the Bible also record a number of stipulations with regard to prayer. For example:

> The LORD is near to all who call on the LORD *in truth* (Psalm 145:18).

> If my people who are called by my name *humble themselves, pray, seek my face, and turn from their wicked ways*, then will I hear from heaven, forgive their sin and heal their land (2 Chronicles 7:14).

> Whatever you ask in prayer, you will receive, *if you have faith*. And whenever you stand praying, *forgive*, if you have anything against any one, so that your heavenly Father may also forgive you your trespasses (Mark 11:24-25).

> *If you abide in me, and my words abide in you*, ask whatever you will, and it shall be done for you (John 15:7).

> Whatever you ask *in my name*, I will do it, *that the Father may be glorified in the Son* (John 14:13).

Luther comments on Christ's invitation to pray in his name, saying:

> Christians do not pray in their own name. They pray in the name of the Son of God, in whose name they have been baptized.[380]

> From these words, "in my name," we gather that we should not be concerned or worried about our own worthiness but should forget about both our worthiness and unworthiness and base our prayer on Christ and in his name.[381]

Some Reasons We May Not Pray

Prayer isn't easy. Not only is it work, as Luther puts it; at times it seems uncertain, unnecessary, or useless.[382] A number of things may cause us to neglect our prayers or not to pray at all. For example, we pray, but our prayers seem to go unanswered. Or we sin, and consider ourselves unworthy of coming to the Lord. Or we don't pray because we don't wish to be faced with our sin.

To those who wonder if their prayers are heard, Luther writes:

> What kind of a prayer is it when you don't know what you are doing or what God says about it? A Christian doesn't look at prayer this way, but strives to pray to comply with God's command and to rely on God's promise, and offers it to God in Christ's name, knowing that what is asked will not be denied. A Christian actually experiences God's help in every need, even if not immediately delivered from distress, knowing nonetheless that prayer is pleasing to God and is heard and knowing that God enables him or her to bear and overcome the distress.[383]

Knowing How to Pray

Perhaps you remember the experience of Huckleberry Finn.

> Miss Watson she took me in the closet and prayed, but nothing come of it. She told me to pray every day, and whatever I asked for I would get. But it warn't so. I tried it.
>
> Once I got a fish line, but no hooks. It warn't any good to me without hooks. I tried for the hooks three or four times. But somehow I couldn't make it work.
>
> By and by, one day, I asked Miss Watson to try for me, but she said I was a fool. She never told me why. And I couldn't make it out no way.
>
> I set down one time back in the woods, and had a long think about it.
>
> I says to myself, if a body can get anything they pray for, why don't Deacon Winn get back the money he lost in pork? Why can't the widow get back her silver snuff box that was stole? Why can't Miss Watson fat up? No, says I to myself, there ain't nothing in it.[384]

A lot of people would agree with Huck Finn. There ain't nothing in it. Prayer doesn't really work. But the key to Huck Finn's account on prayer is what he says about Miss Watson: ". . . one day, I asked Miss Watson to try for me, but she said I was a fool. She never told me why." That was the flaw in Huck Finn's experience with prayer. Miss Watson was eager to get Huck to pray. But she didn't teach him how. She didn't tell him why. Luther addresses this issue by saying:

> We have a God who is able to give more than we understand or ask for. Even though we do not know what we should ask for and how, nevertheless the Spirit of God, who dwells in the hearts of the godly, sighs and groans for us

within us with inexpressible groanings and also procures inexpressible and incomprehensible things.[385]

God-given Limits to Prayer

Quite frankly, most of the prayers we pray are not granted. So, too, many of the prayers of believers in the Bible were not granted. Why? Because, as Paul says, "We do not know how to pray as we ought" (Romans 8:26). Because there are some sensible *God-given limits* beyond which God will not and cannot grant our prayers.

First, there are the God-given limits of the world as it is—you might call them natural limits or natural laws. We cannot, by prayer, eliminate mosquitoes, control pine needle blight, or turn harsh winter into sudden springtime. Also, it would be sheer chaos for everybody else if God were to suspend the law of gravity for two minutes because a window washer on the 65th floor got dizzy and fell off the ledge.

God has created a faithful world, with natural laws and principles we can count on. Prayers that ask God to contradict the very world God has made are foolish prayers. The girl who prayed that the torn page of her geography book be made whole needed some explanation about what prayer is and what it is not. We don't blame her. We fault the person who, without qualification, told her, "God can do anything."

Yes, Jesus said, "Even if your faith were the size of a mustard seed, you could say to this mountain, 'Move from here to there,' and it would move" (Matthew 17:20). But certainly he was not referring literally to mountains such as Ranier or Fujiyama or Everest. He was speaking like a Hebrew, urging his followers to expect great things from God. And yes, God can and does act within this world. God has created it after all. This is a free and flexible world as well as an ordered, faithful world. So, let us pray, asking God to act, to guide, to heal, to change things, trusting God to do everything possible for our good, within the limits God has established within this flexible, faithful world.

The second limit on our prayers is our God-given responsibility to think and act. God simply will not do for us what we can do for ourselves. God has made us a free and responsible people. We have been set within an unfinished earth. Its fields are infested with weeds. Its gold is held in mountain ore. Its building materials are rough and unprepared.

Perhaps you remember the old story of the man who took over a run-down orchard and labored long and hard to bring it back to its former beauty and fruitfulness. One day, when the orchard was looking great, the man's pastor stopped by, admired the orchard and said: "My, but the Lord has done wonderful things here!" To which the farmer replied, "Yes, but the Lord wasn't doing so well before I came along."

Exactly right! There is a great deal that won't do so well without our efforts. We are stewards of the earth, as Genesis puts it, and prayer was never meant to be a substitute for good, honest, hard work. A faithful world does not spare us the pain of thinking through its problems. And a faithful God does not spare us the pain of hard work in overcoming these problems. Leslie Weatherhead puts it well: "When a fire breaks out, prayer is not relevant; water is."[386] Our prayers are limited by our human responsibilities.

The third limit on our prayers is our sin. This is not to suggest that God doesn't hear the prayers of sinners. On the contrary! If not, whom would God hear? However, God will not allow us to pass over our faults and failures as if they did not matter. The moment we approach God in prayer, our prejudices, resentments, and ill-mannered behavior come to the forefront. We simply will not be able to pray about anything else until these shortcomings are confessed to God and squared away with those whom we have offended. Two examples from the Bible come to mind.

First, the experience of the Psalm writer:

> When I declared not my sin, my body wasted away
>   through my groaning all day long.
> For day and night your hand was heavy upon me,
>   my strength dried up as by the heat of summer.
> Then I acknowledged my sin to you,
>   and I did not hide my iniquity;
> I said, "I will confess my transgressions to the LORD."
>   Then you forgave the guilt of my sin (Psalm 32:3-5).

Second, the words of Jesus:

> If you are offering your gift at the altar, and there remember that your brother or sister has something against you, leave your gift there before the altar and go; first be reconciled to your brother or sister, and then come and offer your gift (Matthew 5:23-24).

It is probably true to say that our reluctance to confess our sins to God and to be reconciled with others is a basic reason many of us pray as little as we do. Our sinful behavior causes problems for others, that only we, not God, can set right.

A fourth limitation to God's granting our prayers is the limit set by God's love for us. There are prayers God does not answer simply because God loves us too much to grant such requests. God has something greater in mind, something that would not be possible if we received what we prayed for. This was true of Paul who prayed, "Lord, let this thorn in the flesh leave me" (2 Corinthians 12:7). This was true of Jesus who prayed, "Father, if it be possible, let this cup pass from me" (Mark 14:26). This was true of Augustine's mother who spent a whole night in prayer, begging the Lord to keep her son from sailing to Italy. She wanted her son to become a Christian. She was afraid of what he might become, far away from her, in Italy. But his ship sailed, and it was in Italy that Augustine became a Christian.[387]

God always responds to our prayers, in one way or another. We are certain of this. And always, God acts with our best interests in mind. As George Buttrick writes: "Prayer's greatest healing may very well go beyond healing itself."[388] It may be the grace to accept things as they are: to face trouble, to endure pain, to grow in patience, courage, and insight, to come to know the healing presence of God in and though trouble and pain. In Luther's words:

> Whatever God gives us is something beyond our understanding or hopes. Sometimes we are allowed to go on asking for something that God does not give right away, or perhaps does not give at all, for God knows very well what is necessary and useful for us and what is not. We ourselves may not see this, but finally we have to admit that it would not have been good for us if God had responded to us on the basis of our petition.[389]

"The Spirit Intercedes for Us. . . ."

Paul writes:

> The Spirit helps us in our weakness; for we do not know how to pray as we ought, but the Spirit intercedes for us with sighs too deep for words. For God, who searches human hearts, knows what is the mind of the Spirit, because the Spirit intercedes for the saints according to the will of God (Romans 8:26-27).

"We do not know how to pray as we ought." That is, "We do not know *what we ought to pray for*," as the New International Version puts it, or *"how to pray worthily"* as J. B. Phillips' translation puts it: But "the Spirit helps us in our weakness" and "intercedes for us with sighs too deep for words . . . according to the will of God." Or as a parallel passage in Psalm 38:9 declares: "LORD, all my longing is known to you, my sighing is not hidden from you."[390]

What great news! Whatever be the limits to our prayers, we are heard. Not just our words or thoughts are heard, but *we* are heard. Though our prayers batter against the barriers of good order, good sense, sin, or love, *we* are heard. The psalms make this point over and over again.

The psalmists boldly complain to the LORD about their troubles. But again and again, even the most pointed psalms of lament or complaint ring with affirmations of faith and praise. Why? Because they are convinced that *God has heard* their prayers. Even though their troubles continue, the psalmists trust and praise the LORD, simply because they are certain they have been heard. In the words of Psalm 86:6-7: "Give ear, O LORD, to my prayer; listen to my cry of supplication. In the day of my trouble I call on you, for you will answer me." The Spirit intercedes for us with sighs beyond our words, sighs beyond our weaknesses, sighs beyond our foolish, bumbling attempts to pray.

Before We Pray, God Hears

Many years ago, Rabbi Levi Yitz-hak stopped for the night at an inn where quite a few merchants were also staying. In the morning, a number of young Jewish merchants took time to pray. But because there was only a single pair of phylacteries in the place, one after the other, the young men hurried through their prayers, so the others could use the phylacteries as well. When they were all finished, Rabbi Yitz-hak called them together saying he had something to tell them. Looking gravely into their faces, he said: "Ma-ma-ma; va-va-va. Ma-ma-ma; va-va-va. Ma-ma-ma; va-va-va."

Soon the young men cried out to him: "What is the matter with you! Why are you acting like this?"

He responded, "Why surely you know what I am saying. Isn't this the very language you have just used, rattling off your prayers to God?"

For a moment the young men were taken back and stood silent. Then one of them said, "Sir, haven't you seen a child in the cradle, making nothing but babbling sounds, 'Ma-ma-ma; va-va-va?' None of the wisemen or scholars in the world can understand that child, it is true. But the moment he cries out, his mother knows exactly what he needs." Now when Rabbi Yitz-hak heard these words, he was struck by their truth. He began to dance for joy. From that day on, he was a new man.[391]

In Luther's words: "It is no small comfort to me that God will hear our cry, our prayer, our sighs."[392]

We know from Scripture that God will hear the prayers or sighing of the righteous, as the Psalter says: "The LORD fulfills the desire of all who fear the LORD, and also hears their cry" (Psalm 145:19).[393]

The Traditional Form of the Lord's Prayer

> Our Father who art in heaven,
>   hallowed be thy name,
>   thy kingdom come, thy will be done,
>   on earth as it is in heaven.

> Give us this day our daily bread;
> and forgive us our trespasses,
> as we forgive those who trespass against us;
> And lead us not into temptation, but deliver us from evil.
> For thine is the kingdom, and the power and the glory,
> forever and ever. Amen (Cf. Matthew 6:9-13).

The Lord's Prayer in its traditional English form is based on the King James Version of the Bible, published in England in 1611 CE. A beautiful form of the Lord's Prayer, it is a liturgical variation of Matthew 6:9-13, a variation that substitutes the words, "trespasses/trespass," for the King James Version's "debts/debtors."

Today many congregations use a more up-to-date translation of the Lord's Prayer. They do so to update the seventeenth century "thys" and "thine" to the twenty-first century "you" and "your." They do so to update the rather archaic "trespasses/trespass' to the more understandable "sins/sin." They do so because recent studies of the Greek text of Matthew 6:13 and Luke 11:4 indicate that the traditional "lead us not into temptation" might be more aptly translated as "do not bring us to the time of trial."

According to Matthew, Jesus presented the Lord's Prayer as the very center of and key to the Sermon on the Mount (Matthew 5:1-7:29). This suggests that, like the Sermon on the Mount, the Lord's Prayer is *eschatological* in nature; that is, it is concerned about *living now with the end of all things in mind*. It is, then, a prayer for today, to be prayed with God's name, kingship, and will, as well as our relationship to others as central to our concerns.

The Lord's Prayer: A Pattern or a Liturgical Prayer?

Martin Luther once said: "The Lord's Prayer is the greatest of all martyrs, for everybody tortures and abuses it."[394] That is, we tend to misuse it. We simply "say it" instead of "pray it." We repeat it again and again, all too often without thought or meaning. How ironic!—ironic because, according to Matthew, immediately before Jesus taught his disciples what we call the Lord's Prayer, he said: "In praying, do not heap up empty phrases as the Gentiles do."

In fact, according to Matthew's Gospel, Jesus designed the Lord's Prayer, not so much as a prayer to be repeated over and over again, but as a guide or pattern for prayer. He said: "Pray *like this*: 'Our Father. . . .'"

Yet this prayer took on a specific form early in the church's history, becoming a common liturgical prayer, perhaps as early as 65 or 70 CE.

As Luke's Gospel presents it, Jesus seems to teach his followers to use these words as a particular prayer, just as many rabbis in those days taught their disciples specific, repeatable prayers. Jesus says: "*When* you pray, say, 'Father, hallowed be your name. . . .'"

Which, then, is the Lord's Prayer meant to be? A specific, repeatable form of prayer? A carefully designed pattern for prayer? Who can say? Perhaps both, with an emphasis on thoughtful, meaningful prayer. In either case, as Karl Jacobson writes: "The Lord's Prayer *is* instruction; it is a prayer, yes, but a prayer that teaches us to pray. [It is] a teaching exercise."[395]

The Traditional Nature of the Lord's Prayer

According to Luke's Gospel, "Jesus was praying in a certain place, and . . . one of disciples said, 'Lord, teach us to pray. . . .' And he said, 'When you pray, say: "Father, hallowed be your name. Your kingdom come. Give us today our bread for the coming day. Forgive us our sins as we forgive those indebted to us, And bring us not to the time of trial" (Luke 11:1-4).

Clearly Luke's version of the Lord's Prayer is shorter than the version recorded by Matthew—perhaps because Luke's version is closer to the original prayer Jesus taught, while Matthew's version is an expanded, liturgical form of the prayer. In any case, the two versions give us the same basic prayer. Matthew's "Our Father in heaven" expands Luke's simple "Father." "Your kingdom come, your will be done, on earth as it is in heaven" is an extended *parallel* version of Luke's "Your kingdom come." And so on.

The content of the prayer is the kind of solid, traditional prayer that could be prayed by any Jewish believer. Every petition has its counterpart in the Old Testament. God as Father, God's holiness, God's kingly power, the petitions for bread, forgiveness, guidance—it's all basic Jewish teaching. The LORD is understood to be a caring Father, holy and completely different from the arbitrary gods of the nations round about Israel; the God of faithfulness whose kingdom comes again and again; the God who rules, not by force, but by grace—extending kingly power through goodness and mercy, justice and right.

Praying the Lord's Prayer Forwards

Whatever wording we might use, whether we use the Lord's Prayer as a *form* of praying or as a *norm* (pattern) for praying, it is essential, as Luther said, that we pray the Lord's Prayer "forwards," not "backwards."[396] We pray the Lord's Prayer *backwards* when our concern is mainly for ourselves—bread for ourselves, forgiveness for ourselves, making the way easy for ourselves. We pray the Lord's Prayer *forwards* when we hallow God's name, pray for God's kingly power, and, most importantly, trust in God as our gracious Father.

Sometimes people speak about "a religion that is relevant" or "a faith that works." This often means benefits for *me*, things going *my* way, exempting *me* from the world's troubles. It too often means attempting to manipulate God rather than listening to what God has to say through the Word and trusting in God's action and timetable. We pray the Lord's Prayer "forwards" when we acknowledge that God is holy, that is, quite different than we imagine God to be. For example, some of us imagine that God is pleased with us *if only* we show up in church, pay our dues, and sing God's praises. That's not right, of course.

> "I desire faithfulness and not sacrifice," says the LORD. "To obey is better than sacrifice" (Hosea 6:6; 1 Samuel 15:22).

> "Is not this is the *fasting* that I choose?" says the LORD. . . . "That you share your bread with the hungry; that you bring the homeless poor into your home; that you clothe the naked; that you care for your relatives; that you show kindness to fellow human beings; that you help the suffering" (cf. Isaiah 58:6a, 7, 10).

To pray the Lord's Prayer forward, then, is a practical business. It is not so much a religious practice as it is a commitment to trust and obey God in the events of every day.

Luther's Explanation

In his Large Catechism, Luther writes:

> The *first* thing to know is this: it is our duty to pray because God has *commanded* it. . . . Let no one think that it makes no difference whether I pray or not. . . . To pray, as the Second Commandment teaches, is to call upon God in every need. God requires this of us and has not left it to our choice. . . . By invocation and prayer God's name is glorified and used to good purpose. This you should note above all, so you may silence and repel any thoughts that would prevent or deter you from praying.[397]

> In the *second* place, we should be all the more urged and encouraged to pray because God has *promised* that our prayer will surely be answered. As God says in Psalm 50:15, "Call upon me in the day of trouble, and I will deliver you," and as Christ says in Matthew 7:7-8, "Ask and it will be given you," etc. "For everyone who asks receives."

> Such promises certainly ought to awaken and kindle in our hearts a desire and love to pray. For God testifies in the Word that our prayer is heartily pleasing to God and will assuredly be heard and granted.[398]

> *Furthermore,* we should be encouraged and drawn to pray because, in addition to this commandment and promise, God takes the initiative and puts into our mouths the very words we are to use. Thus we see how sincerely God is concerned over our needs, and we need not doubt that our prayer pleases God and will assuredly be heard.[399]

"Our Father. . . ."

"Father" is the most common personal term for God in the New Testament, and, according to the Four Gospels, it is the term regularly used by Jesus in prayer. This shouldn't surprise us. Addressing God as Father was not an uncommon practice among the people of Judea 2,000 years ago.[400] And, as we've seen in the Old Testament, too, the LORD God is addressed as Father.

But why "Father"? Isn't this term the product of a patriarchal system? Isn't it a term created by males in a male-dominated society, a term that portrays God as a male figure? So it would seem, and yet . . .

True enough, biblical authors often describe God in human terms—speaking of God's mighty hand, God's outstretched arm, God's eyes, ears, heart, etc. Such pictorial language communicates. We would be at a loss without it.[401] At the same time these authors teach us that God is holy, unique. That is, God is completely *other* than human beings and completely *different* from the gods of the nations round about Israel.[402]

At no time is the God of Israel portrayed as a male figure, as were the gods of the nations; nor is the LORD said to have a female partner like those false gods. Neither does the God of Israel produce offspring like those gods. Instead, the LORD *adopts* Israel as "son" and later *adopts* the Davidic king as "son." Moreover, the God of Israel is called "the living God," that is, the source of life, the creator of all things, and *as such* is called "Father."

God as Father—Simply a Metaphor?

Is the biblical reference to God as Father primarily a metaphor? Is it simply another picture for describing God, such as God as Shepherd, as Vinedresser, as Warrior, as Redeemer, etc.?

Clearly the term is sometimes used as a metaphor. For example, Psalm 103 reads, "As a father pities his children, so the LORD pities those who fear the LORD." And Proverb 3:12 declares, "The LORD reproves those whom the LORD loves, as a father reproves the son in whom he delights." Yet, more often, the term is more than a metaphor. While God's holy name itself is the principal Old Testament term for describing who and what God is (cf. pages 30-31), the term "Father" has special significance.

First, "Father" has special significance in describing God as Creator. The term "Father" reveals that the LORD is more than simply the grand architect of the universe (cf. 1 Corinthians 3:10) or the cosmic manufacturer of all things (cf. Hebrews 11:10). God the Father/Creator cares for, sustains, and remains in constant touch with creation. As Deuteronomy 32:6 puts it, "Is not the LORD your Father, who created you, who made you and established you?"

Second, the term "Father" has special significance in portraying God's unique relationship—first to Israel and later to each descendant of David who was anointed to be king of Judah (and therefore, the mediator between the LORD and the Jewish people).

> The LORD declares, "I am a Father to Israel, and Ephraim is my first-born" (Jeremiah 31:9) [cf. Exodus 4:22; Hosea 11:1; Deuteronomy 32:8; etc.].

> The LORD declares to David, "I will raise up your offspring after you. I will establish the throne of his kingdom forever. I will be his Father, and he shall be my son" (2 Samuel 7:12-14) [cf. Psalms. 2:7; 89:26; etc.].

God as Father, A Metaphor and More

Note the way the term "father" is used in the apocryphal book of 4 Ezra:

> Thus says the LORD Almighty:
> "Have I not entreated you as a father entreats his sons
>   or a mother her daughters or a nurse her children,
> that you should be my people and I should be your God,
> and that you should be my children
>   and I should be your father?
> I gathered you as a hen gathers her chicks" (4 Ezra 1:28-30).

The term is used, first, as a metaphor to describe the LORD Almighty, along with the parallel terms "mother," "nurse," and "hen." It is used, second, in direct parallel to the term "God," to describe the LORD Almighty's unique relationship with the people of Israel, whom the LORD Almighty addresses here as "my children." Taken together, and in parallel with the endearing metaphors "mother," "nurse," and "hen," these two uses of the term "Father" picture God as one who cares deeply for the chosen people.

In fact, a number of Old Testament references to God as Father emphasize the loving concern of the LORD for the chosen people, and indeed, for all people. Psalm 68, for example, declares:

> God is the Father of the fatherless and protector of widows
>   within God's holy habitation.
> God gives the desolate a home to dwell in;
>   and leads out the prisoners into well-being.

And in Jeremiah God is portrayed, appealing to the people, saying:
> I thought you would call me "My Father,"
> and would not turn from following me (Jeremiah 3:19).

The term "Father," then, is not simply an alternate word for Procreator, Ruler, or Master. In its use, both as a metaphor and as a description of God's unique relationship to Israel, the term "Father" reveals the very nature of God's gracious, caring character.

God, the Primal Father

Metaphor or not, isn't addressing God as Father an inappropriate practice in the twenty-first century? Shouldn't we follow certain modern translations of the Bible in using neutral, inclusive terms such as "Dear Parent in heaven" or "Dear Father/Mother"?[403] What about persons who have never known their fathers? What about persons who have been abused by their fathers, and therefore have a negative reaction to the term?

These are good questions. In response we can only point out *why* the authors of the Bible call God "Father." It is a term that describes God in a way no other biblical word does—a term that conveys both the creative power and the caring nature of God's relationship to humanity, and especially to God's chosen people.

God's fatherhood should not be confused with human fatherhood. Human fatherhood receives its meaning from who and what God the Father is, not the other way around. It is especially those who have not known their human fathers, or who have been ill-treated by their earthly fathers, who need the heavenly Father and who are "redeemed" and "renewed" as they come to know their heavenly Father.

In describing the recurring theme that haunted him in everything that he wrote, Thomas Wolfe said:
> The deepest search in life, it seemed to me, the thing that in one way or another was central to all living, was the human search for a father; not merely the father of one's flesh, not merely the father of one's youth, but the image of a strength and wisdom external to our need and superior to our hunger, to which the belief and power of our own lives could be united.[404]

"Abba! Father!"

According to the four Gospels, Jesus regularly called God, "Father," in his teaching as well as in his prayers. It should be no surprise, then, that "Father" is the characteristic word for God throughout the New Testament, used by its authors some 250 times.

Some New Testament scholars believe that, in speaking his native Aramaic, Jesus used an even more intimate word for God—the young child's word *Abba*, similar to the English "Papa" or "Dada." Jesus called the Father "*Abba*" in the Garden of Gethsemane as he struggled with the horror of the impending cross (Mark 14:36).[405]

As Paul writes on two occasions, it is our privilege to do the same:

> When we cry, "Abba! Father!" it is God's own Spirit bearing witness with our spirit that we are children of God, and if children, then heirs, heirs of God and joint heirs with Christ, provided we suffer with him in order that we may also be glorified with him (Romans 8:15-17).

> When the time had fully come, God sent forth the Son, born of woman, born under the law, to redeem those who were under the law, so that we might receive adoption as God's children. And because you are God's children, God has sent the Spirit of the Son into our hearts, crying, "Abba! Father!" So through God you are no longer a slave but a child of God, and if a child of God then an heir (Galatians 4:4-7).

Notice that it is the Spirit who enables us to cry, "Abba! Father," just as it was Jesus who first taught his disciples to address God with such intimacy. This simple childlike word for God lays down, once and for all, our relationship to God in Christ. It is a relationship of love and trust in the One who created us, who loves us, and who redeems us from sin and evil, through the death and resurrection of Jesus, God's Son.

God as Our Father

Notice how Jesus refers to God as "Father," according to the Gospels: First, he most often refers to God as "*the* Father," with the emphasis on the uniqueness of God as Father; that is, God as the origin and prototype of what Fatherhood is and means. Second, he alone, in all of scripture, refers to God as "*my* Father," and "*your* Father." Here the emphasis is on the personal nature of God's relationship to Jesus and to us. Finally, in his personal prayers Jesus addresses God as "Father" or as "my Father." In any case, it is Jesus who draws his followers into a relationship of trust and love in God the Father.

Helmut Thielicke writes:

> Of ourselves we can never arrive at the idea of being able to say, "Our Father." Only on one condition—and that condition would be tantamount to a miracle—could we say "Our Father." And that would be if the Father had *first* spoken to us. . . .

> And this is the point . . . it is Jesus Christ himself who teaches us the Lord's Prayer. . . .
>
> For in him and in him alone did the miracle occur. In him and only in him was the one condition fulfilled—the miracle and the condition that the Father should have spoken to us first.[406]

"God Is Truly Our Father. . . ."

In the introduction to his Small Catechism explanation to the Lord's Prayer, Luther writes: "Here we are encouraged to believe that God is truly our Father and we are God's children. We therefore are to pray to God with complete confidence just as children speak to their loving father."[407]

Quite clearly, Luther's emphasis in this explanation is *faith*. As we would expect, he explains that such faith has its source in God the Father, who, through Christ, encourages us "to believe that God is truly our Father and we are God's children." As Luther states elsewhere:

> Because God the Father composed [the Lord's Prayer] through the Son and placed it into his mouth, there is no need for us to doubt that it pleases God immensely.
>
> And so we come, on the basis of God's command and God's promise, and in the name of Christ the Lord; and we present ourselves before God with all confidence.[408]

In an earlier writing, Luther explains the opening words of the Lord's Prayer by praying:

> It is your will not only that we call you Father, but that all of us together call you Father, and so offer our prayers with one accord for all. Therefore, grant us love and unity so we may know and think of each other as true brothers and sisters, and pray to you, our one common Father. . . .[409]

Here the emphasis is on *the familial relationship* we are meant to experience with one another because we are God's children through Christ. A right relationship to God, then, is not simply vertical in design, it is horizontal as well. More accurately, a right relationship to God is triangular in design—leading each of us to relate rightly to one another and to ourselves as well.

"Our Father in heaven. . . ."

According to Luke's Gospel, Jesus teaches his disciples to address God as Father. Matthew's Gospel adds the qualifying phrase, "in heaven." Why? What's the purpose of the phrase "in heaven?' Is it to remind us *where* God the Father is—in heaven? Is it to identify *which* "father" we address—the one in heaven?

In fact, the expression, "in heaven" or "who art in heaven," is a Jewish phrase that refers, not primarily to location (*where* God is), or to identity (*which* "father" this is). It refers, rather, to the *uniqueness* of God, to the complete *otherness* of God.

We, quite naturally, tend to think of heaven as a place. The authors of the Bible, too, often use the word heaven in terms of location or place. They use the word to refer to the atmosphere and to the realm of the celestial. But most often they use the word to speak of the LORD as "the God of heaven," who alone is "above and beyond," if not apart from, all creation.[410] In the words of 1 Timothy: "The Lord God alone has immortality and dwells in unapproachable light, whom no human being has ever seen or can see" (1 Timothy 6:16). It is in this last sense—in terms of God's uniqueness from all created things—that Matthew qualifies "Father" with the phrase "in heaven."

The scriptures speak of God, not as distant, but as distinct from us. They speak of God as holy and hidden from our sight, yet present and involved with us at all times.

In its supernatural sense, then, heaven is not somewhere far off in space, far above us, beyond the stars. Heaven is the infinite in contrast to the finite, the eternal in contrast to the temporal, the glorious in contrast to the mundane. Heaven is the domain of God. It is a completely different dimension than time and space. It is "the beyond in our midst." In the words of Hans Küng:

> The heaven of faith is none other than the hidden, invisible, incomprehensible sphere of God, who is not withdrawn from the earth but rather, perfecting all things for good, grants a share in the divine glory and kingdom.[411]

As used in Matthew's version of the Lord's Prayer, then, the phrase, "Our Father in heaven," reminds us that we are praying to the one and only Father of us all, the awesome creator of all the world—who is ever near, ever caring, ever ready to bless and renew us in grace. Perhaps the wonder of God's dwelling place and presence cannot be depicted more perfectly than this:

> Thus says the high and lofty One who inhabits eternity, whose name is Holy: "I dwell in the high and holy place, and also with those who are of a contrite and humble spirit, to revive the spirit of the humble, and to renew the heart of the contrite" (Isaiah 57:15).

"Hallowed be your name. . . ."

In Hebrew thinking, nothing exists without a name. Genesis 2 suggests that creation is incomplete until every creature is given a name. Further, in Hebrew thinking, a name not only identifies what exists; it conveys the nature of that thing or person. Consider the names *Adam* and LORD.

The Hebrew word Adam derives from the root-word Adamah, meaning "soil" or "humus." The name Adam describes who and what we are—humans made of humus. The name LORD declares who and what God is—great in might, exalted in steadfast love and faithfulness.

Holiness Is of the Lord

We read in Leviticus 22:32-33:

> You shall not profane my holy name,
> I shall be hallowed among the people of Israel;
> I am the LORD who sanctify you,
> who brought you out of the land of Egypt to be your God:
> I am the LORD.

This Leviticus passage uses three words with the same Hebrew root—the adjective translated as "holy;" the verb translated as "I shall be hallowed;" the verb translated as "sanctify." The adjective declares what the LORD (the LORD's name) is—*holy*. The first verb declares what the people of Israel are called to do—*hallow the LORD*. The second verb declares what the LORD does for the people of Israel—*makes them holy*.

So what does it mean to call the LORD *holy*? The Hebrew word *qadosh* means "to be separated" or "to be set apart." As James Limburg writes: "The sense of 'holy' is separate, apart, totally different from the ways and works of anyone on earth."[412]

The meaning is not that the LORD is separated from creation or isolated from the creatures of this world. On the contrary, the LORD is intimately involved in creation and is the dynamic source of life in all creation. The meaning is rather that the LORD is unique, completely different, *"wholly other"* than any creature or created thing. In the words of the LORD, according to the prophet Hosea: "I am God and not human, the Holy One in your midst" (Hosea 11:9).

More specifically, the LORD is holy or *wholly other* in constantly doing what is right, good, and beneficial for the world. In the words of the prophet Isaiah: "The LORD of hosts is exalted in justice, the holy God is revealed as holy in righteousness." (5:16). In the vision of the last book of the Bible, the redeemed sing out:

> Great and wonderful are your deeds,
> O LORD God the Almighty!
> Just and true are your ways, O King of the ages!
> Who shall not fear and glorify your name, O LORD?

> For you alone are holy.
> All nations shall come and worship you,
> For your judgments have been revealed (Revelation 15:3-4).

Just, true, great, and wonderful—such is the holiness of the LORD. Such are the ways of the LORD.

*A People Made Holy **by** the LORD*

Both the people of Israel and the people of Christ are chosen by the LORD and set apart or sanctified for the LORD.

> You are a people holy to the LORD your God who has chosen you to be a people for the LORD's own possession, out of all the peoples that are on the face of the earth" (Deuteronomy 7:6).

> To the church of God which is at Corinth, to those sanctified in Christ Jesus, called to be saints together with all those who in every place call on the name of our Lord Jesus Christ (1 Corinthians 1:2).

Notice, then, by what means the people of Israel and the people of Christ are chosen and sanctified. The people of Israel are chosen and sanctified by means of God's saving action in delivering them out of slavery in Egypt. As we read in Leviticus 22:32-33, the LORD declares: "I am the LORD who sanctify you, who brought you out of the land of Egypt to be your God."

The people of Christ are chosen and sanctified by means of God's saving action in delivering them out of sin and death, through the cross and resurrection of Jesus. In the words of the New Testament:

> We have been sanctified through the offering of the body of Jesus Christ once for all (Hebrews 10:10).

> You have been washed, you have been sanctified, you have been put right with God in the name of the Lord Jesus Christ and in the Spirit of our God (1 Corinthians 6:11).

It is no ordinary thing to be chosen and sanctified by the saving action of the LORD. To be delivered from human bondage reveals the depths of God's grace. To be delivered from bondage to sin and death reveals the riches of God's love. Such salvation makes it clear that only through the actions of the God who alone is holy, can human beings be called and set apart to live beyond ourselves.

*A People Made Holy **to** the LORD*

We are, then, a people made holy (set apart) by God's grace. This means to be chosen by the LORD to live in accord with the LORD's purposes. In terms of the root meaning of the Hebrew word *qadosh*, it means to be separated, not *from* the world, but separated *to* the LORD and *for* the LORD *within* the world. In other words, God's people are not meant to be withdrawn from society any more than God is separated from creation. But they are to be different. They are meant to live by a different standard and for a different purpose They are "set apart" not *from* society, but *for* God's purposes *within* society.

For God's people Israel, this meant they were to be, for the LORD

. . . a kingdom of priests and a holy nation (Exodus 19:6).

. . . a light to the nations, that the LORD's salvation might reach to the end of the earth (Isaiah 49:6).

. . . thus fulfilling the covenant God made with Abraham, that through him and his descendants "all families of the earth will be blessed" (Genesis 12:3; 22:18; 26:4; 28:14; cf. Galatians 3:8-9,14).

For God's people in Christ, this means we are to be, for the LORD:

. . . a royal priesthood, a holy nation, a redeemed people, that we may declare the wonderful deeds of the One who called us out of darkness into God's marvelous light (1 Peter 2:9).

As Jesus prayed to the Father, according to John 17:

I do not pray that you take them out of the world, but that you keep them from the evil one. Sanctify them in the truth, your Word is truth. I have sent them into the world . . . so that the world may believe that you have sent me.

"You Shall Be Holy, for I Am Holy"

In both the Old Testament and the New, we hear a call to holiness based on God's holiness:

I am the LORD who brought you up out of the land of Egypt, to be your God; therefore you shall be holy, for I am holy (Leviticus 11:45).

As God who called you is holy, be holy yourselves in all your conduct; for it is written, "You shall be holy, for I am holy" (1 Peter 1:15-16).

The problem is, *we* can't do it. As Helmut Thielicke points out, there is no petition in the Lord's Prayer that asks God to make us sanctified persons. We are taught to pray, not "let us be hallowed," but "hallowed be your name." Why is this? As Thielicke suggests, "Jesus turns our attention away from ourselves and concentrates it upon the Father."[413] It's as if he is saying that holiness depends, not on *our* efforts to be holy, but on hallowing God's name, on trusting in God, on letting God work in our lives.[414] As Paul puts it, "... beholding the glory of the Lord, we are changed into the likeness of the Lord from one degree of glory to another; for this comes from the Lord, who is the Spirit" (2 Corinthians 3:18).

Encountered by God's Word, through proclamation and sacrament, we are drawn out of ourselves. Enlivened by God's Spirit at work in and through the gospel, we are drawn into God's holiness and, to some degree at least, enabled to reflect God's love, righteousness, and justice in our relationships with one another and with those around us. It is, as Luther would say, a holiness "alien" to our natures; a holiness we can know and exhibit only through the work of Christ's Spirit in us. So it is that we pray, not "may we be hallowed," but "hallowed be your name."

What It Means to Hallow God's Name

In his Small Catechism, Luther says: "God's name certainly is holy in itself, but we ask in this prayer that we may keep it holy."[415] But what does it mean to hallow or to keep God's name holy?

First, in the parallel phrases of Numbers 20:12, "To sanctify the LORD" is to "*trust in* the LORD."

Second, in the parallel phrases of Isaiah 29:23: To "hallow God's name" is to "*stand in awe* of the God of Israel."

Third, as Luther writes, taking his cue from Scripture:

> God's name is hallowed whenever God's Word is taught in its truth and purity and we as children of God live in harmony with it. Help us to do this, heavenly Father! But anyone who teaches or lives contrary to the Word of God dishonors God's name among us. Keep us from doing this, heavenly Father![416]

Fourth, as Luther says elsewhere: "God's name is hallowed when one calls upon, prays, praises, and magnifies God."[417]

To hallow God's name then is to trust and revere the LORD; to worship the LORD in awesome reverence; to teach and preach God's Word in its truth and purity; to live our lives in harmony with the Word; and to call upon, pray, and praise the LORD.

The Humbling Aspect of Prayer

Genuine prayer is a humbling event. This is particularly so in praying the first petition of the Lord's Prayer—if we truly pray it and not simply say it. Luther writes: "Among the seven petitions there is none greater for us to pray than, 'Hallowed be thy name.' ... In this petition God becomes everything and human beings become nothing."[418]

As Luther goes on to say:

> When we pray that God's name may be hallowed in us, this implies that it is not yet holy in us; if it were, we would not have to pray for it.
>
> No one on earth hallows God's name satisfactorily. . . . That is why I call this first petition an unlimited one, the foremost one, encompassing all the others. Anyone who could hallow God's name perfectly would no longer need to pray the Lord's Prayer.[419]

And so, Luther concludes: "This prayer is not only a petition, but also a wholesome lesson and an indicator of our wretched and accursed life on earth, *humbling* us in our own esteem."[420]

James Nestingen sums up Luther's thinking in these striking words:

> Calling out to God, praying for God's name, kingdom, and will, we are effectively praying against the old sinner in each of us, who would rather die than ask and whose defining efforts take place on behalf of our own good names, to build our own kingdoms, and to enforce our own wills.[421]

The Uplifting Aspect of Prayer

And yet, in Luther's thinking, to pray in a genuine way (from the heart), not only humbles us, but lifts us up as well. He says:

> There are some who recognize and deplore that they do not fully hallow God's name, who earnestly pray that they may do so, and who take seriously their wretchedness. And God grants what they ask.
>
> So then, if you have earnestly repented, if you are really humbled by the recognition of your wretchedness, then there comes the comforting teaching that will *lift you up* again. That is to say, this petition also teaches you not to despair, but to ask for God's grace and help. For you must be certain and firmly believe that God taught you to pray like this because God intended to grant your prayer to you. Thus the result of the prayer is that God does not count your sin against you and does not deal harshly with you. God looks with favor only on those who sincerely confess that they dishonor God's name and ever desire that it may be hallowed.[422]

Elsewhere Luther says:

There never is a time when we do not need to pray that God's name be hallowed, that the Word of God bear fruit, and that Christ's kingdom be extended. This is the whole life of the Christian in the presence of God, as Paul also teaches throughout his letters.[423]

"Your kingdom come. . . ."

As used in the New Testament, what is the meaning of the term "kingdom of God" or "kingdom of heaven"?

Jesus' parable of judgment seems to refer to *a place* when the King says to those at his right hand: "Come, O blessed of my Father, inherit the kingdom prepared for you from the foundation of the world" (Matthew 25:34).

Jesus includes the idea of *a particular people* when he says, "Let the children come to me, and do not hinder them; for to such belongs the kingdom of God" (Mark 10:14).

Jesus refers to the dominion of God's *power* when he says, "Truly, I say to you, there are some standing here who will not taste death before they see that the kingdom of God has come with power" (Mark 9:1).

Most often the New Testament term "kingdom" is used to refer to *God's kingly reign* and power. Such is the meaning of the petition, "Your kingdom come." It simply means, "LORD, come and reign over us." Matthew's version of the Lord's Prayer makes this clear. "Your kingdom come" is used in parallel with the phrase, "Your will be done." Clearly where God's will is done, God reigns as Lord. As the Psalmist prays: "Let your work be manifest among us and your glorious power among our children" (Psalm 90:17).

The Kingly Reign of the LORD

As we saw earlier, "*the* LORD *reigns*" is a key affirmation in the theology of the Old Testament. And "the kingship of God" was a constant declaration of faith among the ancient people of Israel. We see this most clearly in the Psalms and in the writings of Isaiah and Jeremiah. From the beginning of Israel's existence as a people, the LORD God was proclaimed as Israel's king. As Exodus 15:18 declares: "The LORD *will reign* forever and ever."

Furthermore, the covenant at Mount Sinai was a *royal* covenant in which the assembled tribes acknowledged the LORD as their king. Exodus 19:5-6 describes the LORD saying to the people, "You shall be to me a *kingly domain of priests* and a holy nation." George E. Mendenhall has shown that the very form of the Sinai covenant was royal—a covenant patterned along the lines of royal treaties common in the Middle East three thousand years ago.[424]

But why such an obviously *political* arrangement as "king and subject" between the LORD and the tribes of Israel? Why not simply a religious arrangement of "God and worshiper?" Perhaps because the LORD is not merely a god in the religious sense. Perhaps because the political term "king" speaks of the LORD's leadership in *the total life* of the people.

God's Royal Covenant with Israel

As we have seen, according to Exodus 19:4-6, the LORD says to the people of Israel, "You have seen what I did to the Egyptians and how I bore you on eagle's wings and brought you to myself. Now therefore, if you will obey my voice and keep my covenant, you shall be my own possession among all peoples, for all the earth is mine, and you shall be to me a kingdom of priests and a holy nation." A number of things stand out in this important passage:

The first is the *personal* character of the passage. The LORD addresses the recently rescued people "*I to you*, me to you." The LORD does for the people of Israel what they could never do for themselves. The LORD sets them free from bondage and establishes a covenant with them; thereby making them a special people with a unique purpose among all people of the earth.

The second is the *meaning* of the possessives in this passage: ". . . *my* voice . . . *my* covenant . . . *my* own possession . . . you shall be *to me* a kingdom of priests and a holy nation." No longer are the people the enslaved property of the Egyptians. They are the personal possession of the LORD God. In *this* is their freedom and their purpose for being. In *this* is the fulness of their lives.

The third is *the nature* of the covenant that the LORD makes with the tribes of Israel. It is a *binding* covenant. The Hebrew word, *berith*, translated here as "covenant," actually means "a relationship that confines." In agreeing to this covenant, the LORD and Israel bind themselves to each other. This mutual binding is signaled and sealed by blood. The animals used for the ceremony clearly represent the life of the people before the LORD. The blood is divided into two parts. Half is *dashed* on the altar. Half is *dashed* on the people. It is, then, a reciprocal agreement, binding the two partners of the covenant to one another.

From this point on Israel is to have "no other gods" and Israel is to be the LORD's "own possession" among all peoples. Furthermore, Israel is to make no binding covenant with other nations or their gods (Exodus

23:32); and the people are assured that the LORD will be faithful to this agreement with them throughout their generations (Exodus 20:6; cf. 34:6-7; Deuteronomy 7:9). But what if the people of Israel violate the covenant, failing to be what God calls them to be? There will be serious consequences to be sure. Nevertheless, God remains faithful, bound by honor to the covenant. In the words of Isaiah 54:

> "In overflowing wrath I hid my face from you for a time,
>   but with everlasting love I will have compassion on you.
> The mountains may depart and the hills be removed,
>   but my steadfast love shall not depart from you,
> and my covenant of peace shall not be removed," says the LORD.

Hundreds of years later, writing to Christians in Rome, Paul also proclaims God's commitment to the covenant with Israel, declaring, "The gifts and the call of God are irrevocable" (Romans 11:29.)

The fourth feature of this passage is *the purpose* of the people of Israel in relationship to the LORD and to the rest of humanity. The LORD declares: "You shall be to me a kingdom of priests and a holy nation."

This seems to suggest a kingdom of persons dedicated to the priestly task of prayer and sacrifice in behalf of others. But as Martin Buber says, it would be a mistake to understand the Hebrew word *kohen* (translated here as "priest") in terms of religious activity. As he points out, in early Arabian literature the *kahin* is the vessel used by a god in order to speak. And in courtly circles the *kohen* was the title of an official who was particularly close to and represented the king.[425]

In 2 Samuel 8:18 David's sons are called "priests" (*kohanim*); while in the corresponding passage in 1 Chronicles 18:17 David's sons are called "the chief officers at the king's hand." They are, then, not priests in a religious sense, but spokesmen, representatives of the king.

As Buber would teach us, it is from this point of view that Hosea (4:6) proclaims to a covenant-breaking Israel that the LORD rejects their vocation as God's *kohanim*. And it is from this point of view that a later prophet (Isaiah 61:6) promises Israel: "You shall be called *kohanim* of the LORD; you shall be named ministers of our God."[426]

This could be the way the term "priesthood" should be understood in the paraphrase of Exodus 19:6 used in 1 Peter to address Christians: "But you are a chosen race, a royal priesthood, a holy nation, God's own people, that you may declare the wonderful deeds of the One who called you out of darkness into God's marvelous light" (1 Peter 2:9).

The Active Kingship of the LORD

The prophet Balaam, of the land of Amaz, was hired by Balak, the king of Moab, to curse the people of Israel, but he could not do so. Instead, the LORD used Balaam to bless Israel. As Balaam declares to Balak, "The LORD their God is with Israel, acclaimed as a king among them. God brings them out of Egypt, and is like the horns of the wild ox for them. . . . now it shall be said of Jacob and Israel, 'See what God has done!'" (Numbers 23:21b-23).

Three notable things are said in this passage about the LORD's relationship to Israel: The LORD is declared to be *with Israel*; the LORD is acclaimed as *king* in Israel; the LORD *brings out* Israel from Egypt. These three things belong together in describing what the kingship of the LORD is all about. The LORD, Israel's king, is *with* her, *leading* her. Here is the very essence of God's kingship—not a ruler who gives orders from afar, but a king who is *with* the people, *guiding* them. Over and over again God the king is pictured "going with" the people (Exodus 33:16; Deuteronomy 31:6); "going before" them (Exodus 13:21; Numbers 14:14); "leading" the people (Exodus 7:4; 13:14; Psalm 106:9); "guiding them" (Exodus 15:13; Psalm 78:52).

In truth, the LORD is not primarily a religious figure in Israel's history. The LORD is a political figure who is intimately involved and concerned with the people, guiding them in the whole of their lives, twenty-four hours a day. The LORD is the king of their economics, their culture, their society, their aspirations, and yes, their politics.

The Nature of God's Kingship

> Pilate entered the praetorium again, summoned Jesus, and said to him, "Are you the King of the Jews?" Jesus answered, "My kingship is not of this world. If my kingship were of this world, those who are with me would fight, to prevent me from being handed over to the Jews; but my kingship is not from the world" (John 18:33, 36).

The Jewish people, Jewish leaders, and Pontius Pilate had a view of authority that emphasized power and positive results. Some Jews looked for a king who would rebuild the armies of Israel, drive out the Roman forces, and restore the people of Israel to a place of power and prosperity in the world. Pilate and the authorities in Rome looked for the same, in order to squelch and squash it. Other Jewish people were looking for a divine Messiah who would lead armies of angels to root out sin, overcome evil, and usher in the kingdom of God then and there.

Then, along came Jesus, calling disciples, blessing children, helping widows, cleansing lepers, accepting sinners, and caring for people of every kind. No warrior-king was he, but a friend to sinners; no lordly ruler, but a counselor and teacher; no fiery judge, but a brother to all.

Such was his *royal* conduct two thousand years ago and such is his kingdom to this day. "My kingdom is not of this world," he said. That is, his authority was not and is not like that of earthly princes. It had and it has a different origin, nature, and purpose. But neither was it or is it outside this world, divorced from this world, and unconcerned with this world.

The Truth of God's Kingdom

> Pilate said to Jesus, "So you are a king?" He answered, "You say that I am a king. This is why I was born, and this is why I have come into the world, to witness to the truth. Every one who is of the truth hears my voice." Pilate said to him, "What is truth?" (John 18:37-38).

Like Pilate, we ask the question, "What is truth?" Like Pilate, we are Western in our outlook. We have been taught to think "like Greeks" by our upbringing, learning, and environment. For us, as for Pilate, truth is something we can think through, investigate, and discover. The Greek word for truth literally means "to uncover the hidden." For us, then, as for Pilate, truth is mainly a matter of the mind. It is something that adds up, makes sense, coincides with the facts, and can be verified. In this understanding of the term, to *know* the truth is to grasp it, master it, and make it your own.

Truth as Jesus expresses it is quite different. For Jesus and the authors of the Bible, truth is not simply a matter of the mind, but a matter of the whole of life. In Hebrew thinking, truth refers to the "sound and solid reality that enhances life." In this understanding of the term, truth is not primarily something you can investigate, discover, or uncover. It is something that happens. It is something genuine, active, and invigorating.

Again, this truth isn't something you can grasp, master, and make your own. It is something that grasps you, involves you, and brings vitality and validity to your life. This truth adds up all right. It is sensible and as reliably solid as can be. But it is more than a matter of facts, reasoning, and verification. To *know* this truth is to be encountered by it, to experience it, and to live it out. This is why the writings we identify with John speak of "knowing the truth," "doing the truth," and "walking in the truth."[427] This truth is like giving birth, marriage, and making music. A physician can master "the facts" of giving birth (Greek style), but only a mother can experience the reality of it (biblical style). A single person can "know" all about marriage (Greek style), but only a married couple "know" marriage first-hand (biblical style). All of us can study and understand the basics of making music, (Greek style), but only musicians can "know" it from the inside out as they compose, play, sing, and create it (biblical style).

Like marriage and making music, the truth is not something you learn or master once and for all. It is a reality that needs to be practiced, lived out, and renewed again and again. Like marriage, the truth is an involvement in reality, a participation in living. Like making music, the truth happens and affects, not only the one making music, but all of us who hear it, second hand or not. Jesus said: "If you continue in my word, you are truly my disciples and you will know the truth, and the truth will make you free" (John 8:31-32). This does not mean "the truth that makes you free" can be known and experienced in the *teachings* of Jesus, or in teaching *about* Jesus, or by following the *example* of Jesus. That is Greek thinking. "The truth that makes you free" is known in touch with him, in *hearing* and *being grasped by* his word. He himself is reality in its most authentic, life-enriching creativity. As he so boldly put it, "I am the way, the truth, and the life."

"Your kingdom come"

"What does this mean?" Luther asks and answers:

> God's kingdom comes indeed without our praying for it,
> but we ask in this prayer that it may also come to us.

"When does this happen?" He asks and answers:

> God's kingdom comes when our heavenly Father gives us the Holy Spirit, so that by grace we believe God's holy Word and live a godly life on earth now and in heaven forever.[428]

In his Large Catechism Luther gives an expanded explanation:

> God's kingdom comes to us in two ways: first, it comes here, in time, through the word and faith, and secondly, in eternity, it comes through the final revelation (Christ's return). Now, we pray for both of these, that it may come to those who are not yet in it, and that it may come by daily growth here and in eternal life hereafter to us who have attained it.
>
> All this is simply to say, "Dear Father, we ask you, give us your Word, so that the gospel may be sincerely preached throughout the world and that it may be received by faith and work and live in us. May your kingdom prevail among us through the Word and the power of the Holy Spirit . . . and that we may live forever in perfect righteousness and blessedness."[429]

Elsewhere Luther writes: "The Kingdom is *not being* prepared, but *has been* prepared, while the sons and daughters of the Kingdom are being prepared, not preparing the Kingdom."[430]

Prayer's Humbling and Uplifting Aspects

Once again, Luther reminds us that to truly pray rather then simply to say the Lord's Prayer is a humbling experience. He declares:

> The second petition, like the others, does two things: it humbles us and it raises us up. It humbles us because it compels us with our own lips to confess our great and pitiable misery. . . . [For] we are the ones who impair and obstruct God's kingdom.[431]

We impair God's kingdom whenever we look primarily to our own interests rather than to God's purposes and to our neighbors' welfare. We obstruct God's kingdom by the things we say and do and by our failure to speak and to act when we should.

But the second petition also raises us up. Luther says:

> The kind teacher, our Lord Jesus, instructs us to pray and petition for rescue from our misery and not to despair. Those who confess that they impede God's kingdom and pray sorrowfully that this kingdom might still come to them, will, by their penitence and prayer, be pardoned by God.[432]

How, then, does God's kingdom (God's reign in our lives) come to us? It comes to us through the personal action of God, who calls us to ask for what God is so willing to give. In Luther's words:

> We do not pray, "Dear Father, let us come into your kingdom," as though we might journey toward it. But we pray, "May thy kingdom come to us." If we are to receive it at all, God's grace and kingdom, together with all virtues, must come to us. We will never be able to come into this kingdom. Similarly, Christ came to us from heaven to earth; we did not ascend from earth into heaven to him.[433]

"Your will be done. . . ."

We tend to think of "Your will be done, on earth as it is in heaven" as a separate petition of the Lord's Prayer. It is, in fact, a parallel phrase of the petition, "Your kingdom come." It does not occur in Luke's version of the Lord's Prayer, but is included in Matthew's expanded version of the prayer in order to clarify the petition, "Your kingdom come." For surely, where God reigns as king, there God's will is done.

As we know, Luther treats the phrase as a separate petition. Yet his explanations of the two phrases reflect the parallel nature of the two: "God's kingdom comes indeed without our praying for it . . ."[434] and "God's good and gracious will is surely done without our prayer. . . ."[435]

Actually, the purpose of the parallel poetry of the Bible is not simply to clarify by repetition. The corresponding words and phrases of such poetry are intended to appeal to our ears, hearts, and spirits as well as to clarify. Such is the case with the parallel phrases of the Lord's Prayer.

Having asked, "When does God's will happen?" Luther explains:

> God's will is done when God hinders and defeats every evil scheme and purpose of the devil, the world and our sinful self that would prevent us from keeping God's name holy and would oppose the coming of God's kingdom. And God's will is done when God strengthens our faith and keeps us firm in the Word as long as we live. This is God's gracious and good will.[436]

As we have seen, according to the four Gospels, God's kingdom is not far off somewhere, unknown and beyond call. It is "at hand," "in the midst of us" in Jesus and in the proclamation of the gospel. So we pray, "Your kingdom come," meaning, "O God, reign in us and among us."

In parallel, neither is God's will mysterious and unknowable. In Jesus and his Word, God's will is made clear and God's guidance accessible. So we pray, "Your will be done on earth as it is in heaven," meaning, "By your Holy Spirit, redirect our ways to conform to your ways."

The Will of God

There are people who believe that everything that happens is God's will. Such persons are sometimes called "fatalists." It is an uninformed, unrealistic philosophy at best. For example, it is clearly God's will that "You shall not kill; you shall not steal; you shall not commit adultery." Yet murder, theft, and adultery take place every day, in direct opposition to God's will. We might ask, "How can this be? Why does God allow such things? Doesn't God care? Is God less than almighty?"

On the contrary, as Psalm 135 declares, "Whatever the LORD pleases, the LORD does." But it does *not* please the LORD to force us to be obedient. We are not robots or puppets. We are human beings, created by God to think and to act as free, responsible persons.

In his little book, *The Will of God*, Leslie Weatherhead distinguishes "the *intentional* will of God," from "the *circumstantial* will of God" and "the *ultimate* will of God."[437] As applied to God's command, "You shall not kill": God's *intentional* will is that no one kill any one else. But because God has created us to be free, responsible human beings, God's *circumstantial* will allows such killing to take place. *Ultimately* not only will killing be eradicated from heaven and earth, but killing itself will be reversed and overcome by God's gift of eternal life.

What God intends and what God allows are two different things. But, in the end, nothing that happens can finally defeat God's gracious will.

God's Will in Action

Why doesn't God straighten everything out once and for all. Why doesn't God eliminate sin, death, and evil and restore us to paradise? That would be our idea of what God should be and do. But that is not God's nature and way at all. God will not violate our humanity, turning us into robots or puppets. In Christ, God has acted to eliminate sin, death, and evil all right, but in a way that is true to God's nature and in harmony with God's ultimate purposes for us and for all creation.

In view of human suffering and nature's disruptions, many people have concluded, "There is no God." Others, who believe in a Creator God, agree with J. S. Mills' famous dictum: "Either God is good, but not all-powerful, or God is all-powerful, but not good."[438] That is, God allows suffering, either because God is not good and doesn't care or because God is not almighty and can't help it.

But such conclusions fail to take into consideration: 1) the nature of a creation in the making; 2) the unfulfilled human task of stewardship of the earth; 3) the corruptive power of human sin; and 4) the gracious nature of God. As we have said, God refuses to eliminate sin and evil by force. God will not violate our humanity with overwhelming power. God will not fill in the gaps left by our failures as earth's stewards. Neither will God forcibly reverse the disruptions of nature that are built into the very fabric of the universe, and which, at times, are magnified by our sin. God cares about us, our place in creation, and creation itself too much to use such methods.

In Leslie Weatherhead's concept: to resort to force is often a sign of *weakness*, while to refrain from force is *power*.[439] Certainly God's purpose for us and for all creation is defeated if we do not fulfil our calling as willing stewards of the earth and as willing subjects of God's kingly rule. God's will for us is achieved only as our lives are redeemed and brought into harmony with God's purposes. If God wins our allegiance freely, God wins everything. If God overpowers and forces us to do what we should do, God's purposes are defeated. Therefore, God acts in ways that are true to God's nature and in harmony with God's purposes for us and for creation. These are the ways of Jesus, God's Son.

God's Will and Human Suffering

Affliction, suffering, and grief; such was the experience of the people of Israel about 587 BCE. The kingdom of David was in ruins, Jerusalem destroyed, the nation conquered by Babylon. How could this be? If the LORD was God, why should Israel suffer so? The brief text, Lamentations 3:31-33, speaks to such questions: "The LORD will not reject for ever. Although the LORD causes grief, yet, out of an abundance of steadfast love, the LORD will have compassion; for the LORD does not willingly afflict or grieve anyone."

First and foremost, the LORD does not willingly afflict or grieve anyone. Affliction, grief, disease, misfortune, bad times—none of these things is God's intentional will and none of them pleases God. Where do such things comes from then? If the LORD is a God of power and love, as the Bible teaches, why should anything happen that is contrary to the LORD's will? The answer is, the LORD is not a dictator. The LORD refuses to make robots of us or to make a mechanical machine of the world of nature. We are created to be both responsible and free; and the world of nature is created to be both orderly and flexible.

If in our freedom we violate our responsibilities, and if in its flexibility the world of nature pushes beyond the bounds of good order, the results will be detrimental to life. But God refuses to set aside either our freedom or nature's flexibility, because God values the potential for life and growth that go along with that freedom and flexibility.

God *allows* suffering, to be sure. But can suffering ever be God's intentional will? We should recognize, straight away, that there are different kinds of suffering, none of them pleasant, but quite distinct from one another in kind, cause, effect, and degree.

Not all suffering is evil or caused by evil. Quite apart from sin and evil, suffering appears to be part and parcel of human life. We might say it is a natural consequence of life in an unfinished world. As such, it would seem to be an intended part of God's will. That is, in this incomplete world as it is, in which human beings *struggle*, *learn* by trial and error, *progress* through inquiry and experimentation, and *develop* through interaction with one another and through engagement with the world and all its creatures—there is bound to be suffering.

In fact the good things of life cause suffering. Love causes suffering. Children, family, and friends cause suffering. The responsibilities and challenges of daily living cause suffering. It's a part of life, and not without its value in human development.

Whatever the cause, suffering *in itself* is not always good. Any benefit that results from suffering depends on a person's attitude and openness to what God will bring about through suffering. Luther is certain that for Christians, suffering is a means by which "we may be conformed to Christ." And we may be sure "that Christ will not only help us to bear this suffering but also turn and transform it to our advantage."[440]

What It Means to Pray, "Your Will Be Done"

Once again Luther reminds us of both the humbling effect and the exalting effect of a genuine praying of the Lord's Prayer:

> This petition has the same twofold effect as the preceding one, that is, it humbles and it exalts; it makes sinners and it makes righteous people; for God's Word always works both judgment and righteousness. . . . Judgment consists of nothing else but that we recognize our condition and judge and condemn ourselves. That is true humility and self-abasement. Righteousness is nothing else but recognition of one's self, followed by a plea and petition for God's mercy and help by which a person is then exalted before God.[441]

Elsewhere Luther teaches:

> The Lord's Prayer alone is enough to show that all of us are still sinners, for all the saints must also pray, "Hallowed be thy name, thy will be done, thy kingdom come," etc. Here they actually confess that they do not now adequately hallow God's name; *and yet* they could not even offer this prayer if the Spirit had not already begun to hallow this name. They confess that they do not yet fulfil God's will; *and yet* they could not pray this petition had they not already begun to fulfil it. . . . For this reason, they ask that in the future God's name be honored, God's will be obeyed, and God's kingdom be attained.[442]

Luther sums up his teaching of the first three petitions as follows:

> We are shown in these three petitions our need with regard to God, but in such a way that it redounds to our benefit. God's name is not only hallowed in itself, but in me. Likewise, God's kingdom not only comes of itself and God's will is done not only of itself, but rather in order that God's kingdom may come in me, that God's will may be done in me, and God's name be hallowed in me.[443]

"Give us today our daily bread."

This petition seems to be simple and straight forward, but it is not. The problem is with the adjective translated as "daily."[444] This adjective is an obscure Greek word that occurs in the New Testament only in the

Lord's Prayer (Matthew 6:11; Luke 11:3). A number of scholars think "daily" is not a proper translation of the word, but they do not agree on how it is to be understood. The most common interpretations are:

- To understand the word as the substantive of a phrase meaning "for today" (the most common understanding);[445]
- To understand it as deriving from a word meaning "for tomorrow;"[446]
- To treat it as a phrase meaning "necessary for existence;"[447]
- To conjecture that it is based on a term meaning "bread for the future."[448]

These interpretations would translate the petition as follows:

- "Give us today our daily bread;"
- "Give us today our bread for the coming day;"
- "Give us today the bread we need to live;"
- "Give us today the bread we need for what lies ahead.

A case can be made for each of these interpretations. In any case, it is a prayer of faith that counts on God to provide whatever is needed to live.

Our Allotted Portion of Bread

The obscure Greek adjective that is most often translated as "daily" is used in an old secular Greek letter in the sense of "ration," as in a soldier's or worker's food ration.[449] Two biblical passages come to mind: Exodus 16:4, in which God promises "a day's portion" of manna every day to the people of Israel as they make their way in the wilderness, and Luke 12:42, in which Jesus speaks of "the faithful and wise steward, whom the master sets over his household, to give them their portion of food at the proper time."

If this sense of the word stands back of the bread petition in the Lord's prayer, Jesus is teaching his disciples to pray, "Give us today our allotted portion of bread." It is, then, a prayer of dependance on God.

Luther's Explanation

> God gives us daily bread, even without our prayer, to all people, though sinful, but we ask in this prayer that God will help us to realize this and to receive our daily bread with thanks.[450]
>
> What does this mean?
>
> Daily bread includes everything needed for this life, such as food and clothing, home and property, work and income, a devoted family, an orderly community, good government,

favorable weather, peace and health, a good name, and true friends and neighbors.[451]

Again, as Luther explains: "When you pray for 'daily bread' you pray for everything that is necessary in order to have and enjoy daily bread and, on the contrary, against everything that interferes with enjoying it."[452]

It is one of the wonders of our faith that God cares about the simple, everyday things of our lives—our daily bread, drink, clothing, work, and play. We are invited to bring anything and everything to God in prayer. No matter how insignificant, unreasonable, or foolish our prayer, God hears and responds accordingly. More than this, we are invited to ask and expect great things from God. As Luther declares:

> God desires of us nothing more ardently than that we pray for many and great things. And, on the contrary, God is not pleased unless we ask and count on God with confident.
>
> Imagine a very rich and mighty emperor who invited a poor beggar to ask for whatever he might desire and was prepared to give great and princely gifts, and the fool asked only for a dish of beggar's broth. He would rightly be considered a rogue and a scoundrel who had made a mockery of his imperial majesty's command and was unworthy to come into his presence. Just so, it is a great reproach and dishonor to God if we, to whom God offers and pledges so many inexpressible blessings, despise them or lack confidence that we shall receive them and scarcely venture to ask for a morsel of bread.[453]

God's Providence and Our Responsibility

Confidence in the providential goodness of God abounds throughout the Scriptures, even in times of drought and famine. People of faith are certain that God will provide. But, of course, as a vital part of God's providential goodness, God has given us the responsibilities of work, planning, and efforts in behalf of others.

Those of us who live in the twenty-first century know that the earth produces plenty of food and goods to provide even for today's vast human population. The problem is distribution of such goods and the reluctance of those with plenty to share with the needy. Luther comments on God's providence and our responsibility:

> God sustains human beings in the same way that all other living creatures are sustained . . . , with fulness and sufficiency. No animal achieves its own living, but each has its own task to perform, after which it seeks and finds it food.

The little birds fly about and warble, make nests, and hatch their young. That is their task. Oxen plow, horses carry their riders, sheep furnish wool, milk, cheese. That is their task. It is the earth which produces grass and nourishes them through God's blessing.

Similarly, we who are human must work and occupy ourselves at something. At the same time, we must know that it is something other than our labor that furnishes us sustenance. It is God's blessing. Because God gives us nothing unless we work, it may seem as if our labor sustains us. But it is with us as with the little birds. The birds neither sow nor reap, but they would certainly die of hunger if they did not fly about to seek their food. That food, however, is not the result of their labor, but of God's goodness. For who placed their food where they can find it? Beyond all doubt it is God alone.[454]

"Forgive us our sins. . . ."

Luther calls the forgiveness of sins "a great, eternal, and unspeakable treasure."[455] He calls Christ's promise of forgiveness "the main thing in the sacrament." And he explains this petition of the Lord's Prayer, saying:

> We ask in this prayer that our Father in heaven would not hold our sins against us and because of them refuse to hear our prayer. And we pray that God would give us everything by grace, for we sin every day. So we on our part will heartily forgive and gladly do good to those who sin against us.[456]

Einar Billing writes:

> Anyone wishing to study Luther would indeed be in no peril of going astray in following this rule: Never believe that you have a correct understanding of a thought of Luther before you have succeeded in reducing it to a simple corollary of the thought of the forgiveness of sins.[457]

In Luther's own words:

> The chief teaching of the New Testament is really the proclamation of grace and peace through the forgiveness of sins in Christ. . . .[458]

> To believe in the forgiveness of sins through Christ is the highest article of our faith. And it is true that whoever believes this article has the forgiveness of sins.[459]

> I am completely steeped in and saturated with the article of the forgiveness of sins. I am dealing with it constantly,

day and night; and all my thoughts are of Jesus Christ, my only Savior, who has atoned and paid for my sins. I grant the law—and all the devils—nothing. If only a person can believe the forgiveness of sins, he or she is blessed.[460]

It shouldn't surprise us that forgiveness of sins is so central in Luther's thinking. Forgiveness is emphasized throughout the Small Catechism. The texts of the third article of the Creed and of the Lord's Prayer, along with many of the scripture texts that Luther quotes, underscore the forgiveness of sins. And Luther's explanations abound in lifting up forgiveness. He writes:

> I believe that Jesus . . . has freed me from sin . . . (2nd Article).

> In this Christian church day after day [the Holy Spirit] fully forgives my sins and the sins of all believers . . . (3rd Article).

> We ask in this prayer that our Father in heaven would not hold our sins against us . . . (5th Petition).

> In baptism God forgives sin, delivers from death and the devil, and gives everlasting salvation to all who believe . . . (Baptism 2).

> This cup is the new covenant in my blood, shed for you and for all people for the forgiveness of sins [Matthew 26:26] (Communion 1).

> These words assure us that in the sacrament we receive forgiveness of sins, life and salvation" (Communion 2).

In his explanations of the remaining parts of the Holy Communion, as well as of The Office of the Keys and of Confession, Luther highlights the place of forgiveness in Christian life and faith. Further, he highlights forgiveness in his evening prayer.

Beyond this, Luther comments:

> The doctrine of the forgiveness of sins is the most important of all, both for us personally and for our relations with others. As Christ continually bears with us in his kingdom and forgives all sorts of faults, so we should bear and forgive one another in every situation and in every way.[461]

Forgiveness Through Redemption in Christ

It is important to stress the centrality of God's forgiveness, especially in this day and age. There are those today who understand the gospel to be a message of God's acceptance and approval of anything and everyone no matter what. Quite the contrary! The gospel as proclaimed in the New Testament is a call to trust in God who is at work in and through Christ Jesus:

- To forgive our sins;
- To save us from guilt and shame;
- To redeem us from God's wrath and the judgment of the law;
- To give us new life; and
- To empower us with the Holy Spirit in our struggle with the repressive agents of sin and death.

The gospel, then, is radically different from a belief that God accepts and approves of everyone no matter what. It is the message of God's action to *change* things. It is the Good News of God's action to *rescue* us from bondage to sin and evil through the cross and resurrection of Jesus, and to set us in a new direction. As Paul writes: "Whoever is in Christ is a new creation. The old has passed away. The new has come" (2 Corinthians 5:17).

As Philip Watson interprets Luther: "In thus freely loving sinners [through Christ's self-giving sacrifice on the cross] . . . Divine love never for a moment condones their sin, nor compromises with evil, but seeks actively to overcome it."[462]

In Luther's striking words: "The start of a new creature accompanies this faith and the battle against the sin of the flesh, which this same faith in Christ both pardons and conquers."[463]

The Faith to Accept God's Forgiveness

Someone might say, "I need God's forgiveness, but I don't know if my faith is strong enough." But faith is not a matter of degree, of how strong or how weak it is. Faith is not something we create from somewhere deep within ourselves. Faith is simply receiving what God so willing gives and generates within us through the gospel. As Luther reminds us: "A Christian is not someone who has no sin or feels no sin. . . ."[464]

> Even though my conscience is troubled, and sin frightens me and makes my heart quake, it is written nonetheless: "Take heart, my child; your sins are forgiven" (Matthew 9:2).[465]

> So when we mess up and our consciences bother us we need to confess our sins and to hear again the promise: "If we confess our sins, God who is faithful and just will forgive our sins and cleanse us from all unrighteousness" (1 John 1:9).

But, "What if a particular sin keeps nagging me? What if some awful thing I've done keeps dragging me down?" When J. A. Aasgaard was a pastor in northern Wisconsin, a certain parishioner came to him one day to confess some awful thing he had done. The man was obviously weighed down by his sin. After hearing his confession, Pastor Aasgaard assured the man of God's forgiveness and pronounced God's absolution of the sin. Then, as the fellow was about to leave, he turned to Aasgaard and said, "Thank you pastor. But I still feel rotten about all this. Do you really think God has forgiven me for this sin?" To which Aasgaard answered, "What sin?" What sin indeed!

"I, I am the One who blots out your transgressions," says the LORD, "And I will remember them no more!" (Isaiah 43:25).

". . . as we forgive those who sin against us."

Forgiveness is a gift of God, freely given to anyone who asks God for this gift. But it loses its power if it is not put into practice toward others. Like a baton in a relay race, it is meant to be passed on. This is why we pray, "Forgive us our sins as we forgive those who sin against us" (Matthew 6:12). This is why the first Epistle of John urges us, "Beloved, if God so loved us, we also ought to love one another" (1 John 4:11). And, indeed, this is why Jesus tells us: "If you forgive others their trespasses, your heavenly Father will also forgive you; but if you do not forgive others their trespasses, neither will your Father forgive your trespasses" (Matthew 6:14-15).

The practice of forgiveness is never easy. Neither is it the cheap way out. God does not pat the sinner on the cheek and say, "There, there, your sin doesn't really matter." God calls us to confess our sins and to repent of our wrong doing, so that we may be forgiven and cleansed.

On our part, we do not help a wrong-doer by shrugging our shoulders, by pretending these wrongs do not matter, or by keeping silent about our feelings of pain. Neither does it help or change a wrong-doer to reject or condemn him or her. Forgiveness is costly for the one who is hurt and for the wrong-doer, because it calls for a one-to-one encounter, confession, and acceptance. It is never easy or cheap. In the end, it is a matter of God's grace. When we experience God's forgiveness, we are enabled to forgive those who hurt us. As Luther writes:

> The forgiveness of sins takes place in two ways: *first* inwardly, through the gospel and the Word of God, which is received by faith in the heart toward God; *second* outwardly through works.

> The outward forgiveness I show in my deeds is a sure sign that I have the forgiveness of sins in God's sight. On the other hand, if I do not show this in my relations

with my neighbor, I have a sure sign that I do not have the forgiveness of sins in God's sight but am still stuck in unbelief. . . . But if I look and find myself gladly forgiving my neighbor, then I can draw this conclusion and say, "I am not doing this work naturally, but by the grace of God I feel differently from the way I used to."[466]

The Sacrament of Forgiving Others

Luther considers the practice of forgiving others to be one of God's sacraments in our lives—a means through which God encounters and blesses us. He writes:

God has provided us with various means, ways, and channels through which to take hold of grace and the forgiveness of sins: first, baptism and the sacrament; but also prayer and absolution; and our forgiveness of others. And so, we are abundantly taken care of, and we can find grace and mercy everywhere. Where would you look for it any nearer than with your neighbor, with whom you live every day and toward whom every day you have ample reason to practice this forgiveness? It is inevitable that you should be offended, deeply and often.

It is, therefore, not only in the church or in the presence of the pastor, but in the very midst of our personal lives that we have *a daily sacrament or baptism*—one believer with another, including those in our own home. For if you take hold of the promise through this act [of forgiving others], you have the very thing that you receive in baptism. How could God have endowed us more richly with grace than by hanging such *a common baptism* around our necks and attaching it to the Lord's Prayer—*a baptism* that we discover within ourselves when we pray and forgive our neighbors?[467]

Luther goes on to declare that the ways and means God has given us "are all linked together and whoever has one should have them all or keep none of them." He writes:

Whoever is baptized should also receive the sacrament; whoever receives the sacrament must also pray; and whoever prays must also forgive. If you do not forgive, you have a terrible sentence here: your sins will not be forgiven either, even though you are in a Christian company and are enjoying the sacrament and other benefits. In fact your sins will damage and damn you all the more on account of this.[468]

Repentance and Forgiveness

> If your brother sins, rebuke him. If he repents, forgive him. Even if he sins against you seven times in a day, and turns to you seven times, and says, "I repent," you must forgive him (Luke 17:3-4).

Repentance and forgiveness go together, as do repentance and faith. To repent, in Hebrew understanding, is "to turn around;" "to go the other direction." To repent, in Greek understanding, is "to change one's mind' or "to be transformed in mind." Repentance, then, is *a turning* from sin to God. It is *a transformation* from wrong doing or wrong thinking to what is right.

As the New Testament describes it, repentance takes place through the working of God's Spirit who—through the proclamation of law and gospel—convicts us of sin, assures us of God's love and forgiveness through Christ, and calls us to faith in God (cf. John 16:7-11; Acts 5:30-32; Romans 2:4; 2 Corinthians 7:8-10).

Clearly, then, repentance is an essential element in faith. And, at the same time, repentance is an essential factor in receiving forgiveness. As we read in the treatise *Instructions for the Visitors of Parish Pastors in Electoral Saxony* (written by Philip Melanchthon and approved and enhanced by Luther):

> Christ says we are to preach repentance and forgiveness of sins in his name [Luke 24:47].
>
> Many now talk only about the forgiveness of sins and say little or nothing about repentance. There neither is forgiveness of sins without repentance nor can forgiveness of sins be understood without repentance. It follows that if we preach the forgiveness of sins without repentance that the people imagine that they have already obtained the forgiveness of sins, becoming thereby secure and without compunction of conscience. This would be a greater error and sin than all the errors hitherto prevailing. Surely we need to be concerned lest, as Christ says in Matthew 12 [:45], the last state becomes worse than the first.
>
> Therefore we have instructed and admonished pastors that it is their duty to preach the whole gospel and not one portion without the other.[469]

"Lead us not into temptation"
"Save us from the time of trial"

These are two versions of the sixth petition of the Lord's Prayer. The question is, which of the two is the more accurate translation? A literal translation of the Greek New Testament presents three possibilities:

1) "Do not bring us into temptation . . ."
2) "Do not bring us into testing . . ."
3) "Do not bring us into trial . . ."

The first possibility, the traditional translation, doesn't *seem* to make a lot of sense. As we read in the Epistle of James, "God tempts no one" (1:13; cf. Sirach 15:11-12).

The second possibility is unacceptable for the opposite reason. The authors of the Bible clearly teach us that God often *tests* believers, *tries* us, or *puts us through difficult times*, if you will.[470] God does this so that we might see ourselves as we really are; so that we might see our need for God's presence in our lives; so that we might be enriched in character, as we learn to cope with such difficulties with fortitude, resolve, and trust in God.

This suggests that the third possibility *may* be what Jesus had in mind. However, the translation, "Save us from the time of trial," is problematic. Not only does it paraphrase "do not bring us into" as "save us from"; but more importantly it adds the words, "the time of," to the Greek word translated as "trial." However, there is no definite article here in the Greek phrase. Perhaps we could translate the phrase literally, "Do not bring us into trial." Or, if we are going to paraphrase or add words, we might more judiciously translate the phrase, "Do not bring us into *times of* trial."[471]

"God Tempts No One to Sin"

It could be said that Luther's explanation of sixth petition of the Lord's Prayer disclaims that prayer's traditional translation. Luther writes:

> God tempts no one to sin, but we ask in this prayer that God would watch over us and keep us so that the devil, the world, and our sinful self may not deceive us and draw us into false belief, despair, and other great and shameful sins.
>
> And we pray that even though we are so tempted we may still win the final victory.[472]

What then is the meaning of all this for us today? We might say: If it is true that God tests us and tries our faith; and since, in fact, we live in a world of temptation, trials, and troubles, we should not only pray the

Lord's Prayer, but the kind of prayer that Jesus and his apostles teach us again and again: "Lord, keep us steadfast and close to you through all the troubles, the trials, and the temptations that we face day by day."

". . . and deliver us from evil."

As we would expect, this phrase does not appear in Luke's version of the Lord's Prayer, but is part of the liturgical version presented by Matthew. It is, then, not an additional petition, but a parallel phrase that compliments and augments the prayer, "Do not bring us into times of trial."

The phrase could be translated, "but deliver us from the evil one," referring to the devil. But because it stands in parallel to the more general phrase, "times of trial," it might better be translated as the more general, "but deliver us from evil.' This is a common kind of prayer among God's people. For example, the Psalmist prays: "Rescue me, O my God, from the hand of the wicked, from the grasp of those who are unjust and cruel" (Psalm 71:4).

Again, as we read in 2 Timothy 4:18: "The Lord will rescue me from every evil and save me for his heavenly kingdom. To him be the glory for ever . . . ." Luther's explains this phrase:

> We ask in this inclusive prayer that our heavenly Father would save us from every evil to body and soul, and at our last hour would mercifully take us from the troubles of this world into heaven.[473]

"For the kingdom, the power, and the glory are yours. . . ."

The phrase, "For the kingdom, the power, and the glory are yours, now and forever," is not an original part of either Matthew's version or Luke's version of the Lord's Prayer. The early church added it as a doxology to its liturgical use of the prayer.

The Didache, a second century CE manual of church order, includes Matthew's version of the Lord's Prayer with the addition of a short doxology, "For yours is the power and glory forever." We are not certain when the longer, more traditional doxology began to be used.[474]

Doxologies have long been common in Jewish worship and are used in praise of God in both the Old and New Testaments. The Greek word *doxology* literally means "word of glory." The purpose of a doxology is to praise God with words of adoration. To attach this doxology to the Lord's Prayer is an appropriate finale of praise to God. In fact, the doxology recalls and reinforces the opening petitions of the prayer.[475]

- God's glory is exalted in the hallowing of God's name.
- God's kingdom is embraced in the prayer for its coming.

- God's power is acknowledged in the call that God's will be done.

The petitions for bread, forgiveness, and deliverance are prayers for the gifts of God's kingdom. They are gifts that are granted through God's power and that express God's glory. As the psalmist prayed:

> All your works shall praise you, O LORD,
>   and all your saints shall bless you!
> They shall speak of the glory of your kingdom,
>   and tell of your power,
>   to make known to all people your mighty deeds,
>   and the glorious splendor of your kingdom
>   (Psalm 145:10-12).

"Amen."

Amen is a word we use often in the church. It comes from a Hebrew root-word meaning, "to be firm," "to be true," "to be certain." It is an exclamation that means, "Yes!" "I agree!" "Let it be so!"

Luther concludes his explanation of the Lord's Prayer by writing:

> Amen means yes, it shall be so. We say Amen because we are certain that such petitions are pleasing to and heard by our Father in heaven. For God the Father has personally commanded us to pray in this way and has promised to hear us.[476]

Elsewhere Luther writes:

> It is good to remember that this word expresses the faith that we should have in praying every petition. Christ says, "Whatever you ask in prayer, you will receive, if you have faith" (Matthew 21:22).
>
> If we conclude our prayer with the word "Amen," spoken with confidence and strong faith, it is surely sealed and heard. But without this conclusion neither the beginning nor the middle of the prayer serves any purpose.
>
> So, the little word "Amen" means the same as truly, verily, certainly. It is a word uttered by the firm faith of the heart. It is as though you were to say, "O my God and Father, I have no doubt that you will grant the things for which I petitioned, not because of my prayer, but because of your command to me to request them and because of your promise to hear me. I am convinced, O God, that you are truthful, that you cannot lie. It is not the worthiness of my

prayer, but the certainty of your truthfulness, that leads me to believe this firmly. I have no doubt that my petition will become and be an Amen.[477]

The word "Amen" is used in the Bible in three quite specific ways. It is used, first of all, as *a word of affirmation*. This is the most common use of the word in the Bible and this is the way the word is meant to be used in Christian worship. It is our way of saying *"Yes"* to a prayer or a greeting or a benediction. This is why the person who prays or preaches or gives the benediction need not say Amen. The word is designed to be a word of affirmation by the people.

Second, "Amen" is used in the Bible as *a pledge of certainty*. It is Jesus who uses the word in this way. Some seventy-five times he is quoted as beginning his comments by saying, "Amen," or "Amen, Amen, I say to you. . . ." He does so, not only to get attention or to emphasize what he is saying, but to certify the truth of what he is about to say with his very self.

The third use of "Amen" in the Bible is as *a title for Christ* (Revelation 3:14). The message is, Jesus not only speaks the truth and lives the truth, he is the very embodiment of the truth. He brings reality into the lives of all those who trust in him. In the words of Paul:

> As surely as God is faithful, our word to you has not been Yes and No. For God's Son, Jesus Christ, whom we (Silvanus, Timothy and I) preached among you was not Yes and No; but in him it is always Yes. For all the promises of God find their Yes in him. That is why we utter the Amen through him, to the glory of God (2 Corinthians 1:18-22).

Luther comments:

> The Holy Spirit is the sort of teacher who is sure and makes people sure, and does not let them toss and dangle, for "in Christ it is not yes and no, but yes and amen" (2 Corinthians 1:19). St. Paul teaches and confidently asserts a *confident reality* in Christ, a full, certain, sure understanding upon which a person can die and risk everything.[478]

THE SACRAMENTS

Among the promises Jesus has given his followers are what many of us call "sacraments." Sacrament, from the Latin *sacramentum*, means "a sacred act or oath that binds," and was used, ages ago, to identify the oath by which a soldier bound himself to military service.

The Latin Vulgate version of the New Testament uses *sacramentum* several times to translate the Greek word *mysterion*.[479] Such is the case with 1 Timothy 3:16, which, in English, reads: "Great indeed is the *mystery* of our religion: Christ was manifested in the flesh, vindicated in the Spirit, seen by angels, preached among the nations, believed on in the world, taken up in glory."

The Greek word *mysterion* in this passage refers to a revelation so astounding it can only be grasped by faith. To translate *mysterion* as *sacramentum* may intend to suggest that the mystery that is "Christ manifested in the flesh" is, at the same time, God's binding pledge to us of forgiveness and salvation. In any case, to call certain promises of Jesus "sacraments" is to emphasize the binding nature of those promises to those who receive them in faith and who, thereby, participate in the mystery that is Christ Jesus.

Lutherans and some other Protestants recognize two sacraments: Holy Baptism and Holy Communion. Roman Catholic and Eastern Orthodox Christians acknowledge seven sacraments: Holy Baptism, Holy Communion, Confirmation, Penance (Confession), Holy Orders, Marriage, and Anointing of the Sick.

Strictly speaking, God's Word is the one sacred means by which we are drawn to Jesus and his life-giving salvation. As Paul writes: "The gospel is the power of God for salvation to everyone who has faith" (Romans 1:16). In Luther's words: "The Word, I say, and only the Word, is the vehicle of God's grace."[480] And Jesus has ordained that the Word be conveyed to us both *audibly* (by word of mouth) and *visibly* and *physically* (through the sacraments).

Only Holy Baptism and Holy Communion are characterized by what Luther considers the three essential components which identify a sacrament:

1. Jesus' *command* establishing it;
2. Jesus' *word of promise* conveyed in and through it; and
3. *An earthly element* in and through which the promise is conveyed [Christ manifested in the flesh, as it were].

Jesus' Command Instituting the Sacraments

The first essential component of a sacrament is Jesus' command establishing it. Jesus said to his disciples, "Go. . . make disciples. . . baptizing them. . . teaching them to observe all that I have commanded you . . ." (Matthew 28:19-20). Jesus took bread . . . and said to them, "Take, eat, this is my body." And he took a cup . . . saying, "Drink of it, all of you, for this is my blood of the covenant . . ." (Matthew 26:26-28).

Of course Jesus has given his disciples other important commands that are vital for Christian life and faith, but none of these commandments is "a sacrament." None of them conveys his word of promise in and through an earthly element.

Luther says regarding baptism: "You must esteem baptism as something high, glorious, and excellent; for here there is a divine word and command, which institutes and confirms baptism."[481]

The Earthly Elements in the Sacraments

The second essential component of a sacrament is an earthly element, chosen by Jesus, by which his word of promise is conveyed to us. In baptism that element is water; in Holy Communion, bread and wine.

Why does Jesus consider it appropriate to convey God's word of promise to us in such a way? He does so in order that we may more easily sense and grasp his word of promise. As Luther writes:

> Faith must have something to believe—something to which it may cling and upon which it may stand. . . . it must be external so that it can be perceived and grasped by the senses and thus brought into the heart, just as the gospel is an external, oral expression. In short, whatever God effects in us is done through such external ordinances.[482]

Jesus often used such down-to-earth ways to convey his word and his ways to others—using mud for the blind man's eyes (John 9:6-7); touching the lips and ears of the deaf mute and looking up to heaven (Mark 7:32-35); kneeling and writing in the dust in front of the woman caught in adultery (John 8:6); and so on.

Christ's Word of Promise in the Sacraments

The central and most essential component of a sacrament is *Jesus'* word of promise which is conveyed in and through the earthly element of his choosing. As Luther put it: "To constitute a sacrament there must be, above all things else, a word of promise, by which faith may be exercised."[483]

In Holy Baptism, Jesus' word of promise is: "Whoever believes and is baptized will be saved" (Mark 16:16). In Holy Communion, his promise is: "Take, eat; this is my body. Drink of it, all of you; for this is my blood of the covenant, poured out for many for the forgiveness of sins" (Matthew 26:26, 28).

But is "Whoever believes and is baptized. . . ." etc. an authentic saying of Jesus? It was surely not part of the original manuscript of Mark's Gospel (cf. page 112 above). However, it does express the faith and practice of the early church and of the teaching of the New Testament. That is, it is in relationship with Jesus, in faith, that we are saved and set free to live a more abundant life. And in the New Testament baptism always accompanies faith and is the sign and seal of that faith-union with him. As Paul wrote to the Galatians: "In Christ Jesus you are all children of God through *faith*. For as many of you as were *baptized* into Christ have put on Christ" (3:26-27).

The Letter to the Colossians also expresses the essential bond of faith and baptism in Christ: "You were buried with Christ in *baptism*, and you were also raised with him through *faith* in the power of God, who raised him from the dead" (Colossians 2:12).

The Transforming Power of God's Promises

As with all of God's promises, these promises are life-changing because God's Spirit is at work in and through them (1 Thessalonians 1:5; cf. Acts 10:44; Ephesians 1:13) to energize and empower those who hear and receive them (1 Thessalonians 2:13; cf. Romans 1:16). As the authors of the New Testament describe it, the power of God's Word:

- Awakens faith (Romans 10:17; cf. John 8:30; 17:20).
- Generates new birth (1 Peter 1:23; cf. James 1:18).
- Saves (Romans 1:16; 1 Corinthians 1:18; cf. James 1:21).
- Sets free (John 8:31-32).
- Enlivens (John 6:63; Philippians 2:16; I John 1:1).
- Cleanses (John 15:3; 17:17; cf. Ephesians 5:26).
- Builds up (Acts 20:32).
- Produces fruit (Colossians 1:5-6; cf. Acts 10:36; Hebrews 5:13; 6:5).

Luther comments:

> The Scriptures assign many different names to the Word of God because of its many virtues and effects. It is indeed all things and all powerful [Hebrews 1:3; 4:12].[484]

Through the oral preaching of the Word, which enters the ears and touches the heart by faith, and through the holy Sacraments our Lord God accomplishes all these things in Christendom, namely, that people are brought to faith, are strengthened in faith, are kept in pure doctrine, and in the end are enabled to withstand all the assaults of the devil and the world.[485]

Beyond all the might and power of the world and of all creatures, Christ proves his ability to draw the hearts of people to himself through the Word alone and to bring them to his obedience without any compulsion or external force at all. . . . Viewed superficially, this looks like a trifling thing, without any power, like any ordinary human speech and word. But when such preaching is heard, his invisible, divine power is at work in human hearts through the Holy Spirit.[486]

The Cross and Resurrection in the Sacraments

Death and resurrection are highlighted in the sacraments, in and through the components of the sacraments.

- In Baptism a person is "immersed" in the waters of baptism *to depict* and *to initiate* that person's union with Jesus in his death and burial; and the person is "raised up" out of those waters *to depict* and *to initiate* that person's union with the risen Lord Jesus (Romans 6:3-11; Colossians 2:12).

- In Communion Jesus' *words* from the Last Supper are repeated to declare that his self-sacrifice of himself for his followers is renewed through the gifts of his glorified body and blood, given in and with bread and wine. Thereby, in Paul's words, "As often as you eat this bread and drink the cup, you proclaim the Lord's death until he comes" (1 Corinthians 11:26).

What is begun and depicted in Holy Baptism—a life-long relationship with Jesus who calls us to die daily to sin and, by faith, to rise up to new life in him—is sustained by Jesus himself through the preaching of the gospel and through the gifts of his body and blood in Holy Communion.

The Action of Christ in the Sacraments

The sacraments, then, are not primarily something *we* do. They are "means" through which the Lord is active among us here and now. That is, Jesus did not establish the sacraments as memorial rites that we reenact to commemorate his life, death, and resurrection. They are "vehicles" of God's redeeming action, by which we are incorporated into Jesus' saving death and resurrection. Jesus himself is present and active in the sacraments. He himself is the baptizer at every baptism—at work through the agency of water and the person doing the baptism. As Luther writes:

> To be baptized in God's name is to be baptized, not by human beings, but personally by God. Although it is performed by human hands, it is truly God's own act.[487]

Jesus himself is the host whenever his Supper is celebrated—bestowing his benefits via bread and wine through the agency of those who distribute these elements. As Luther says:

> It is not our activity or speech but the edict and decree of Christ that make the bread the body and the wine the blood. We hear these words, "This is my body" . . . as coming from Christ's own mouth who is present and says to us, "Take, eat, . . ." We hear Christ himself, through the pastor's mouth, speaking to us. . . .[488]

As Luther concludes:

> It is true that when you are baptized and when you partake of the Holy Supper you hear a human being. But the Word that you hear is not that of a human being; it is the Word of the living God. It is God who baptizes you; it is God who absolves you from sins; and it is God who commands you to hope in God's mercy.[489]

The Sacraments as Safeguards

As Philip Watson points out, the sacraments guard against three errors. Because the sacraments have been instituted by Jesus to convey God's word of promise through earthly elements: They restrain our attempts to "devise our own ways to God;" they challenge any claim to a direct "spiritual" knowledge of God; they prevent us from thinking that the gospel is simply "the teaching of Jesus" or a set of religious doctrines.[490]

Luther had much to say about this over the years. For example:

> God's intrinsic nature is altogether unknowable. . . . For this reason God condescends to meet us on our level of understanding and comes to us in images, in coverings as it were, in a simplicity adapted to a child, so we might be enabled to know God in some measure.

> God approaches us in these visible forms, deals with us, and puts these forms before us to keep us from degenerating

into erratic and vagabond spirits who indeed carry on discussions about God, but are profoundly ignorant of the One whose unveiled majesty cannot be comprehended. God sees that this way of knowing God is impossible for us, for as Scripture says, 'God dwells in unapproachable light' (I Timothy 6:16). Those who adhere to the ways and means in which God has chosen to meet us truly understand God. But those who boast of visions, revelations, and enlightenments and follow them are either overwhelmed by God's majesty or remain in utter ignorance of God.

Let no one therefore contemplate the unveiled Divinity. Rather let us flee from such contemplations as from hell and the veritable temptations of Satan. Let it be the concern of each of us to abide by the signs by which God is personally revealed to us, namely, God's Son, born of the Virgin Mary and lying in his manger among the cattle; the Word, Baptism, the Lord's Supper; and absolution. In these images we see and meet a God whom we can bear, One who comforts us, lifts us up into hope, and saves us.[491]

PART FOUR

THE SACRAMENT OF HOLY BAPTISM

Origins of the Sacrament of Holy Baptism

Baptism, the complete immersion of a person in water, is mentioned in the Old Testament only in the instance of Naaman, commander of the army of Syria. As we read in 2 Kings 5:14: "Naaman went down and *immersed* himself seven times in the Jordan River. . . ."

In the Septuagint, the Greek translation of the Old Testament, the word used here is *baptizein*. In the Hebrew language of the Old Testament the word used here is *tabal*. Both these words mean to immerse. In the case of Naaman it is self-immersion, seven times, on one occasion, at the direction of the prophet Elisha. So, it is not baptism as an established ritual practice.

It is true that the Jewish people often used water as a means of ritual cleansing from various impurities (cf. Numbers 15:1ff.). And the Old Testament occasionally speaks in a symbolic way of the washing away of impurity or sin (Psalm 51:7; Ezekiel 36:17; Zechariah 13:1). But baptism as a ritual or as a sacrament is unknown in the Old Testament.

Proselyte Baptism

As Joachim Jeremias indicates, baptism as a ritual practice first came into being among the Jews during the century before Jesus was born. This baptism was designed for proselytes, that is, for non-Jews who desired to become members of the Jewish community of faith.[492]

At that point in history, orthodox Jews considered Gentiles to be impure and did not associate with them. According to the practice developed by rabbis of that century, Gentile converts were *made fit* to be received into the Jewish community by a process of purification that concluded with the ritual cleansing of baptism. More specifically, a Gentile man who converted to Israel's God was carefully taught, catechized, circumcised, and seven days after circumcision, baptized, that is, fully immersed in water; a Gentile woman who converted to Israel's God was carefully taught, catechized, and then baptized (immersed); a child of a Gentile convert was circumcised (if a male) and baptized (immersed).

In those days, then, proselyte baptism was the final, crucial step in the purification necessary for a Gentile to be accepted into the Jewish community of faith. And because this baptism was a complete immersion of the convert, *perhaps* it symbolized, not just the washing away of impurity, but also death to that person's old self and the raising to life of a new self. In fact, Jewish writings from those days describe such a proselyte as "renewed," "recreated," "a new-born child;" as one who had passed "from death to life." And, the "new-born" person was usually given a new name.[493]

John's Baptism

In the third decade of what we now call the CE:

> John the baptizer appeared in the wilderness, preaching a baptism of repentance for the forgiveness of sins. And people from all the country of Judea and all of Jerusalem went out to him and were baptized by him in the Jordan River, confessing their sins (Mark 1:4-5).

The Jewish people must have been shocked by the words and actions of John the Baptist. They were well aware that Gentile proselytes were required to be purified by baptism before being accepted into the fellowship of God's people. What a surprise, then, that John declared to them, God's chosen people, "Repent, for God's kingdom is at hand!" (Matthew 3:2) and called on them, God's people, to be baptized!

It is a stunning word from the prophet, calling the Jewish people to repent and to be purified, as if they were Gentiles. Moreover, he calls them to be baptized to prepare for the coming of the Messiah-King. He declares: "I baptize you with water for repentance, but he who comes after me . . . will baptize you with the Holy Spirit and with fire" (Matthew 3:11; Mark 1:8; Luke 3:16)). And surprisingly, great numbers of the Jewish people came to be baptized, confessing their sins. As Luther declares:

> John comes as "the voice of one crying" . . . and preaches to all people a baptism of repentance, and by this preaching he claims unceasingly that all people are sinful.
>
> . . . it is not only written concerning John that he preached a baptism of repentance, but "into" or "for the forgiveness of sins" is added. That is to say that through it people are prepared for grace, which effects the remission of sins. Sins are remitted only to those who are dissatisfied with themselves, and this is what it means to repent.[494]

Jesus Baptized by John

Then came another surprise. As we read in Matthew 3:13-15:

> Jesus came from Galilee to the Jordan River to be baptized by John. John would have prevented him, and said, "Do you come to me? I need to be baptized by you." But Jesus said to him, "Let it be so now, for it is fitting for us to fulfil all righteousness in this way."

As Matthew presents it, John considered Jesus to be the Messiah; and so, he was surprised that Jesus came to be baptized. As John himself declared, the Messiah, as God's royal agent, would baptize with holy wind and fire—separating the wheat from the chaff, the good from the bad (Matthew 3:11-12). Why, then, should the Messiah be baptized, an act of repentance meant for sinners? Because, in the Messiah's own words, "It is fitting for us to fulfil all righteousness in this way." And this means, what? Notice what happened according to Matthew 3:16-17:

> When Jesus was baptized, just as he came up from the water, the heavens opened, and he saw the Spirit of God coming down like a dove and alighting on him. And a voice came from heaven saying: "This is my Son, the beloved, with whom I am well pleased."

- First of all, then, "Jesus was baptized." He deliberately took his place *with* sinners.
- Second, ". . . he came up from the water. . . ." This is the initial sign of *how* he would minister to sinners such as we. He went down into and came up out of the water—symbolic, not simply of cleansing, but of drowning, of death and burial, and of resurrection to new life.
- Third, ". . . the heavens opened, and he saw the Spirit coming down on him like a dove; and a voice came from heaven, saying, '*This is my son, the beloved, with whom I am well pleased.*'"

It is a graphic message: the heavens opened—his mission originating with God; the Spirit descending on him—his mission empowered by God; a voice coming from heaven—his mission verified by God.

Notice that the voice from heaven is quite specific: "*This Is my Son,*" God's words to David's son, the Messiah king (Psalm 2); "*the beloved,*" Abraham's son Isaac whom he must sacrifice (Genesis 22); "*with whom I am well pleased,*" God's words for Israel, God's servant to all the world (Isaiah 42).

In his baptism, then, Jesus is designated as *God's son,* the true Messiah, the deliverer of justice. He is designated as *the beloved one,* the sacrificial lamb of God who must die. He is designated as *the well pleasing servant of God*, true Israel, called to be God's light to the nations. It all adds up to the way of the Cross, the way of self-sacrifice and death.

In receiving John's baptism for sinners, Jesus took his place, not just *with* us sinners, as one of us; he took his place *for* us, *in our behalf*. In the language of the New Testament, *he exchanged places* with us, the righteous for the unrighteous—taking our sins, giving us his righteousness; assuming our guilt, giving us his innocence; dying and rising in our behalf, setting us free from the curse of God's law, free from God's wrath, free from death and evil.[495]

This is what Jesus means when he says, "It is fitting for us to fulfil all righteousness in this way." Because of who he is and what he has done, we who are unrighteous are made righteous by God's grace.

Jesus' Baptism and his Cross

There is a case to be made that Jesus himself expresses the meaning and purpose of baptism as it came to be known and practiced by the first Christians. Referring to his coming death, Jesus says to his disciples: "I have a baptism with which to be baptized; and how constrained I am until it is accomplished!" (Luke 12:49-50; cf. Mark 10:38).

It would seem that these words of Jesus stand back of what Paul writes to the assembly of believers in Rome:

> Do you not know that all of us who have been baptized into Christ Jesus were baptized into his death? Therefore we have been buried with him by baptism into death, so that, just as Christ was raised from the dead by the glory of the Father, so we too might walk in newness of life. For if we have been united with him in a death like his, we will certainly be united with him in a resurrection like his (Romans 6:3-5).

This much seems clear:

- By being baptized by John, Jesus identifies himself with those who come to be baptized in repentance for their sins.
- By calling his coming death "a baptism he must accomplish," Jesus is saying his death has a purpose; a purpose in behalf of sinners no doubt.
- Following his resurrection, Jesus distinguishes baptism in the Spirit from John's baptism, saying, "John baptized with water, but before many days you will be baptized with the Holy Spirit" (Acts 1:5).

- And Jesus commissions his followers to make disciples of all nations, by baptizing and teaching them in the name of the Father, the Son, and the Holy Spirit (Matthew 28:18-20; cf. Mark 16:15-16; Luke 24:47; Acts 1:8).

"What Is Holy Baptism?"

Luther asks in his Small Catechism. He answers: "Baptism is not water only, but it is water used together with God's Word and by God's command."[496]

Here are the three components that Luther considers necessary in a sacrament—the earthly element, *water*; Jesus' command, "Go, make disciples, *baptizing* them; and Jesus' word of promise, "Whoever *believes* and *is baptized* will be saved." As Luther describes it elsewhere:

> When water and the Word of God come together, then it is baptism. But you say, can water benefit me? No. What then? Baptism. But isn't it water? No. It is water connected with God's Word; and so it must be something more than water. That's why we declare that the water amounts to nothing, but baptism does. Baptism, then, is water *with* the Word of God, and this is the essence and whole substance of baptism.[497]

The Sign, the Significance and the Faith

In his 1519 treatise on baptism,[498] Luther writes: "In this holy sacrament we must pay attention to three things: the sign, the significance of it, and the faith."[499]

As Luther indicates in this treatise and elsewhere:[500]

> *The sign* of baptism is a person's complete immersion in water;

> *The significance* and effect of baptism is a person's union with Christ Jesus in his death, burial, and resurrection; a union that calls that person to die *daily* to sin, and so, to be raised up *daily* to "walk in newness of life."

> *The faith* is a person's commitment to Christ who, in baptism, unites us with himself and calls us to "fight against sin and slay it, even to our dying breath" in the power of the Holy Spirit given to us in baptism.[501]

The three components of baptism, "water used together with God's Word and by God's command." indicate what baptism *is*. The three things in baptism, "the sign, the significance and the faith," indicate the *meaning and purpose* of baptism.

The Sacrament of Holy Baptism | 197

The Importance of the Sign of Baptism

For Luther, then, to be baptized is to be fully immersed in water. It is to be plunged beneath the water and to be drawn up again out of the water. And so, it is *a sign,* as well as *a means*, of unity with Jesus in his death, burial, and resurrection (Romans 6:4).

To be true to the *sign* of baptism, every candidate for baptism should be immersed, adult and infant alike. Today most Christian churches baptize by sprinkling or pouring water on a person's head, as was the custom in Luther's day. But if Luther had his way, we would immerse. He writes:

> Baptism is *baptismos* in Greek and *mersio* in Latin, and means to plunge something completely into the water, so that the water covers it. . . . This usage is demanded by the significance of baptism itself.[502]

> I would have those who are to be baptized completely immersed in the water, as the word (*baptismos*) says and as the mystery indicates. It's not that I deem this necessary, but it would be well to give a thing so perfect and complete a sign that is also complete and perfect. And this is doubtless the way in which it was instituted by Christ."[503]

"What benefits does God give in Baptism?"[504] Luther asks, then he explains: "In baptism God forgives sin, delivers from death and the devil, and gives everlasting salvation to all who believe what God has promised."

"What Is God's promise?" Luther asks. Our Lord Jesus Christ says: "Whoever believes and is baptized will be saved" (Mark 16:16).

"How can water do such great things?" Luther then asks. And he explains:

> It is not water that does these things, but God's Word with the water and our trust in this Word. Water by itself is only water, but with the Word of God it is a life-giving water which by grace gives the new birth through the Holy Spirit.[505]

St. Paul writes in Titus 3:

> God saved us . . . in virtue of God's own mercy, by the washing of regeneration and renewal in the Holy Spirit, which God poured out on us richly through Jesus Christ our Savior, so that we might be justified by grace and become heirs in hope of eternal life.

Again we see, that in Luther's judgment, God's Word is the one sacred means through which God gives us the salvation that Jesus accomplished once for all two thousand years ago. God brings us the Word through *speech* (preaching, witnessing one to one, and the mutual conversation of believers); and through *sacrament* (baptism and holy communion). And again we see the all importance for Luther of faith in God's Word.

"What does Baptism mean for daily living?"[506] Luther immediately goes on to ask. Then he explains:

> It means that our sinful self, with all its evil deeds and desires, should be drowned through daily repentance; and that day after day a new self should arise to live with God in righteousness and purity forever.

St. Paul writes in Romans 6:

> We have been buried with him by baptism into death, so that, just as Christ was raised from the dead by the Father's glory, we too might walk in newness of life.

But who wants to drown and die? Certainly not our sinful selves. We may be "new persons" in union with Christ in faith, but as long as we live *the old me* in us struggles for life and lordship in our lives. We are, in Luther's words, *simul justus et peccator*, at one and the same time justified and sinners (made right before God in Christ; sinners in fact).[507] And so, day after day, *the old me* struggles with God's Spirit for the upper hand in our lives.

How, then, is *my sinful self* to be drowned through daily repentance, so that *a new self*, created in Christ, can come forth? To repent means "to turn away from sin." But this is possible only by that faith in Jesus that the Holy Spirit creates in us through the gospel. As Luther says: "Faith justifies and fulfils that which baptism signifies. Faith is the submersion of the old me and the emerging of the new."[508]

Faith, then, which leads to repentance, is the means of drowning the old me. Caught up as we are in a daily struggle between *the old me* and *"the new life of the Spirit"* (Romans 7:6), we continually need to hear the gospel through which God's Spirit works. Then we will be strengthened in faith and enabled to attend to the drowning of *the old me* through daily repentance.[509]

"The Washing of Water with the Word"

Baptist Christians believe and teach that baptism is simply "water used according to God's command." They do not believe God's Word is at work in baptism. They teach that adults who become Christians are baptized:

- As an act of obedience to Jesus' command;
- As a sign of unity with Jesus—immersed in water, symbolic of death and burial to one's old self; emerging from the

water, symbolic of being raised to a new life in Christ Jesus;
- As a witness to others of a believer's identity with Christ Jesus.

Lutherans believe and teach that baptism is water used together with God's Word.

- We believe and teach that baptism is "a means of grace" through which God acts in the lives of the baptized (adults and children).

  > Turn and be baptized every one of you in the name of Jesus Christ for the forgiveness of sins and you will receive the gift of the Holy Spirit. For the promise is to you and to your children and to all who are far away, every one whom the Lord God calls (Acts 2:38-39).

- We, too, believe that baptism is a sign of unity with Christ Jesus and a witness of our identity with him,[510] but more than that, we believe it is a sign that gives what it represents.

  > It *represents* cleansing and it *gives* cleansing: ". . . be baptized and wash away your sins . . ." (Acts 22:17). "Christ loved the church and gave himself up for her, that he might sanctify her, having cleansed her by the washing of water with the Word. . . ." (Ephesians 5:25-27).

  > It *represents* our unity with the Lord in his death, burial, and resurrection; and *gives* that very unity: "We have been buried with him by baptism into death, so that, just as Christ was raised from the dead by the Father's glory, we too might walk in newness of life" (Romans 6:4).

"Whoever Believes and Is Baptized Will Be Saved"

The Roman Catholic consecration of baptismal water tends to leave the impression that, by God's power, baptism is effective in a person's life *ex opere operato* (automatically). This chant of consecration is:

> May the Holy Spirit descend upon this water, which has been prepared that man may be born again, and make it fruitful by mingling with it his mysterious power; so that a new heavenly race, conceived by sanctification, may be reborn as a new creation, and arise from the immaculate bosom of this divine source.[511]

Lutherans believe and teach that God's gifts of forgiveness and the Holy Spirit are received by those who are baptized in a response of faith in the Lord. Indeed, it is quite clear from the New Testament that faith in Jesus and baptism go hand in hand *and* that baptism apart from faith in Jesus makes no sense. Again, as Luther writes in the Small Catechism:

> In baptism God forgives sin, delivers from death and the devil, and gives everlasting salvation to all who *believe* what God has promised.[512]

> It is not water that does these things, but God's Word with the water and *our trust* in this Word.[513]

Elsewhere Luther writes:

> In the last chapter of Mark [16:16] Christ says, 'Whoever believes and is baptized will be saved.' He puts faith before baptism for where there is no faith, baptism does no good.[514]

> Unless faith is present or is conferred in baptism, baptism will profit us nothing; indeed, it will become a hindrance to us, not only at the moment it is received, but throughout our lives.[515]

> We know that wherever there is *a divine promise*, there *faith* is required, and that these two are so necessary to each other that neither can be effective apart from the other. For it is not possible to believe unless there is a promise, and the promise is not established unless it is believed. But where these two meet, they give a real and most certain efficacy to the sacraments. Hence to seek the efficacy of the sacrament apart from the promise and apart from the faith is to labor in vain. . . .[516]

The Covenant of Baptism

Martin Luther identifies baptism as the means by which God makes a life-long covenant with us. He writes:

> Through my baptism God, who cannot lie, is personally bound in a covenant with me.[517]

> This blessed sacrament of baptism helps you, because in it God is allied with you and becomes one with you in a gracious covenant of comfort.[518]

Elsewhere Luther writes that God has made "a pact of freedom" with us in baptism.[519]

As Luther sees it, this covenant is valid as long as we live. We are never through with its promise and significance. We may drift apart from it, lose faith in it, even reject it; but it continues to be valid. In Luther's words: "Baptism is such a great thing, that if you turn again from sins and appeal to the covenant of baptism, your sins are forgiven."[520]

Valid though it always is, the covenant of baptism is efficacious in our lives *only* as we respond to Jesus' word of promise in faith. His word of promise alone calls (and recalls) us to faith and generates (and can regenerate) new life within us. In Luther's words: "If we hear and firmly believe that in the covenant of baptism God receives us sinners, spares us, and makes us pure from day to day, then our heart must be joyful, and love and praise God."[521]

The meaning of this covenant is clear. We are called to take up the cross everyday. We are called to die daily to *the old me* within us, so that, in Christ, we might walk in newness of life. Luther writes: "It establishes a covenant between us and God to the effect that we will fight against sin and slay it, even to our dying breath. . . ."[522]

The Validity of Holy Baptism

As we have just seen, baptism is valid and valuable in itself, without regard to our response, efforts, or behavior; simply because Jesus has promised, "Whoever believes and is baptized will be saved." Nevertheless, baptism does not operate magically or automatically.

On the one hand, once we have been baptized—"washed in water with the Word" (Ephesians 5:26)—God's claim is on us. Nothing can change that. We are marked with the cross of Christ Jesus forever.

On the other hand, baptism is not some sort of heavenly voodoo that does its wonders apart from our faith or response. After all, Jesus says, "Whoever *believes* and is baptized will be saved."

As Luther writes his Large Catechism:

> When the Word accompanies the water, baptism is valid even though faith be lacking. My faith does not constitute baptism, but receives it. Baptism does not become invalid even if it is wrongly received or used, for it is bound, not to our faith, but to the Word.[523]

But as he also writes in the Large Catechism:

> Faith alone makes the person worthy to receive the salutary, divine water profitably. Since these blessings are offered and promised in the words which accompany the water, they cannot be received unless we believe them wholeheartedly. Without faith baptism is of no use, although in itself it is an infinite, divine treasure.[524]

And he concludes:

> So you see plainly that baptism is not a work which we do but is a treasure which God gives us and faith grasps, just as the Lord Christ upon the cross is not a work but a treasure

comprehended and offered to us in the Word and received by faith.[525]

The Life-giving Waters of Baptism

If baptism was "**water** only," it would be no more than a religious ceremony, similar to the water purification rites of orthodox Jews.

If baptism was merely "*water used in response to Christ's **command***," it would simply be an act of human obedience to Christ, a symbol of unity with him, and a witness to a person's identity with Christ—which is what Baptist Christians believe it to be.

But because baptism is "*water used together with **God's Word** and by Christ's command*," it is an act of God in which the Holy Spirit *unites* us with Christ Jesus in his death and resurrection; *gives* us forgiveness of sins; *grafts* us into the Body of Christ, the community of those who belong to him; and thereafter, *renews* us in Christ day after day as we trust in him.

The Continuing Reality of Holy Baptism

As we have seen, in his Small Catechism Luther emphasizes the importance of baptism for *daily* living, *daily* repentance, and *daily* renewal in Christ. As he writes elsewhere: "Let us all regard our baptism as a daily garment that is to be worn all the time. Every day we should be found in faith and amid its fruits; every day we should be suppressing our old self and growing up in the new."[526]

In Luther's thinking, then, baptism is not a solitary event, but a continuing reality. It is not restricted to the day we were baptized. It is designed to exercise an on-going vitality to be lived out in the give and take of everyday. And so, we shouldn't say, "I *was* baptized," but "I *am* baptized."

Baptism is an on-going reality:

- First, because Jesus' word, "Whoever believes and is baptized will be saved," is an *enduring* promise (Mark 16:16);
- Second, because our new-birth into Christ Jesus, initiated in baptism, is a *living* reality (Titus 3:5-7);
- Third, because the forgiveness of sins and the gift of God's Spirit, given in baptism, are *continually* needed, *never failing* gifts to us (Acts 2:38);
- Fourth, because our faith in Jesus, called forth by his baptismal promise, is meant to be exercised in *daily* repentance and trust (Mark 16:16);

The Sacrament of Holy Baptism | 203

- Fifth, because, as baptism signifies, our union with Jesus in his death, burial and resurrection calls us to die *daily* to sin so we might *daily* be raised up to "walk in newness of life" (Romans 6:4). In Luther's words: "One thing only has been enjoined on us to do all the days of our lives—to be baptized, that is, to be put to death and to live again through faith in Christ."[527]

"Baptism is in Force All Through Life"

As Christians, then, we are never done with the waters of baptism, its washings, its drownings, its death, and its resurrection to life again. The initial event of our baptism is essential, of course. But it is the meaning of baptism for daily living that Luther sees as vital. And so he writes:

> . . . baptism is in force all through life, even until death. . . .[528]

> The sacrament of baptism, even with respect to its *sign*, is not a matter of the moment, but something permanent. Although the ceremony itself is soon over, the thing it signifies continues until we die, yes, even until we rise on the last day. For as long as we live we are continually doing that which baptism *signifies*, that is, we die and rise again.

> You have been once baptized in the sacrament, but you need continually to be baptized in faith, continually to die, continually to live. Baptism swallowed up your whole body and gave it forth again. In the same way, that which baptism signifies [death and resurrection] should swallow up your whole life, body and soul, and give it forth again at the last day, clad in the robe of glory and immortality. We are therefore never without the sign of baptism nor without the thing it signifies.[529]

Implications of the Continuing Reality of Baptism

The first implication of the continuing reality of baptism is that the initial event of baptism is *unrepeatable*. It is unrepeatable simply because it is "in force all through life," "permanent," "perpetual."

The Anabaptists of Luther's day taught that a person should be baptized *only after* coming to faith in Christ. After all, they argued, Jesus said, "Whoever believes and is baptized will be saved." That's the right order of things. First, a person must believe, then be baptized. Therefore, a person who becomes a believer as an adult, even though baptized as an infant, must be re-baptized.

If baptism were no more than a sign of unity with Christ Jesus and a witness to one's faith in him, the Anabaptists might have a point. But if, as Luther taught, baptism is a means of grace in which God is at work, then the practice of re-baptizing, now, as well as back then, is highly suspect.

As Luther argues, the sure *foundation* of baptism is not faith, but Jesus' Word of command and promise. Who can say for certain that any particular person has genuine faith? But Jesus' Word of command and promise is certain beyond doubt. Luther writes:

> The unchanging Word of God, once spoken in the first baptism, ever remains standing, so that afterwards [those baptized] can come to faith in it, if they will. . . . Its power does not derive from the fact that it is repeated many times or is spoken anew, but from the fact that it was commanded once to be spoken.
>
> Granted, baptism is not of benefit to anyone who is without faith . . . but the baptism is not thereby incorrect, uncertain, or of no meaning.[530]

A second implication of the continuing reality of baptism is the *life-long struggle* between "the old me" and "the new life of the Spirit" initiated by God in baptism.[531] Luther writes:

> A Christian life is nothing else than a daily baptism, once begun and ever continued. We must keep at it incessantly, always purging out whatever pertains to the old Adam, so what belongs to the new self may come forth.
>
> In baptism we are given the grace, Spirit, and power to suppress the old me so that the new may come forth and grow strong.[532]

A third implication of the continuing reality of baptism is the *enduring validity* of our baptism, to which we may return even after we have abandoned it in unbelief. As Luther writes:

> Baptism remains forever. Even though we fall from it and sin, nevertheless we always have access to it so that we may again subdue the old me. But we need not again have the water poured over us. Even if we were immersed in water a hundred times, it would nevertheless be only one baptism, and the effect and significance of baptism would continue and remain. Repentance, then, is nothing else than a return and approach to baptism, to resume and practice what was earlier begun but abandoned.[533]
>
> When we rise from our sins or repent, we are merely returning to the power and the faith of baptism from which

we fell, and finding our way back to the promise then made to us, which we deserted when we sinned. For the truth of the promise once made remains steadfast, always ready to receive us back with open arms when we return."[534]

Baptized and Justified

Paul writes:

> Don't you realize that those who are unrighteous will not inherit the kingdom of God? . . . And such were some of you. But you were washed, you were sanctified, you were justified in the name of the Lord Jesus Christ and in the Spirit of our God (1 Corinthians 6:9, 11).

Paul is referring here to those who have been baptized. The Greek root word, translated here as "washed," is used three other times in the New Testament to refer to baptism (Acts 22:16; Ephesians 5:26; Titus 3:5). The word is normally used to refer to bathing one's whole body.

But notice the three key words used here in tandem—"washed," "sanctified," "justified." Is Paul saying that a person who is baptized into Christ is "sanctified" and "justified?" He is.

Not that a person is "made just and holy" *ex opere operato* (automatically, magically), simply by being baptized. After all, the heart of Paul's teaching is that we are justified by God's grace alone through faith alone (Romans 3:24; etc.). And yet, it is through baptism that God initiates most of us into the family of faith. It is through baptism that we receive the gifts of forgiveness and the Holy Spirit (Acts 2:38). It is through baptism that we are incorporated into the death and resurrection of Christ (Romans 6:3-4).

Paul is speaking of being justified by faith (Galatians 3:24) when he writes in Galatians 3:26-27: "For in Christ Jesus you are all children of God through faith. For as many of you as were baptized into Christ have put on Christ."

It is "in Christ" (baptized into Christ, belonging to Christ, believing in Christ) that we are made holy and just in God's sight. Again, as Paul writes: "God has made Christ Jesus our wisdom, our righteousness and sanctification and redemption" (1 Corinthians 1:30).

The Inclusive / Exclusive Nature of Baptism

Baptism is *inclusive* in this sense: every one who is baptized into Christ is "baptized into one body," the assembly of believers (I Corinthians 12:13). Every one who is baptized is assured of God's grace, through the promise proclaimed in baptism. Every one who is baptized is called to daily die to sin and to be raised up to "walk in newness of life." The *inclusive* nature of baptism, endures because it is based on God's Word of promise; a Word we can count on and return to as long as we live.

At the same time, baptism is *exclusive* in nature. Baptism marks us with the cross of Christ forever, so to speak; and sets us apart to be disciples of Christ Jesus our Lord. In Luther's words:

> Baptism is an external sign or token that so separates us from all those who are not baptized that we are thereby known as a people of Christ, our Leader, under whose banner of the holy cross we continually fight against sin.[535]

But, of course, continually valid though it is, baptism is of no value unless we live out Christ's call in faith. As Luther writes: "Where faith is present with its fruits, there baptism is no empty symbol, and the effect accompanies it; but where faith is lacking, it remains a mere unfruitful sign."[536]

As we saw earlier (page 130), the community of believers—within which baptism and the other signs of God's grace are present and employed—is visible enough. The marks of the church remove all doubt as to *where* the people of God may be found. However, *who* the true believers are is known only to God and remains hidden within the wider community.

The Right Use and Abuse of Baptism

Luther speaks of *a right use* as well as *a misuse* of baptism. What he says about this may seem contradictory; but his comments are consistent with his understanding of the Christian faith.

On the one hand, Luther encourages us to count on the fact that we are baptized, especially in the face of sin and doubt. He writes:

> We must boldly and without fear hold fast to our baptism, and set it high against all our sins and terrors of conscience. We must humbly admit, "I know full well that I cannot do a single thing that is pure. But *I am baptized*, and through my baptism God, who cannot lie, is personally bound in a covenant with me. God will not count my sin against me, but will slay it and blot it out."[537]

On the other hand, Luther writes:

> All of us who were baptized and reborn through baptism are indeed called Christians, but we do not all remain true to baptism. . . . It is idle to say . . . *"I am baptized* and numbered among the Christians."
>
> Christ wants no one to boast of being . . . a Christian, saying, *"I am baptized.* . . ." This is not enough. It must be your

concern to believe, to conduct yourself as a Christian should, to be upright in your heart and outwardly in your life, and to be able to take pride in the Lord Christ and your faith.[538]

Indeed, Luther warns us not to think we are saved just because we were baptized once upon a time. He writes:

> There are people who think that they are Christians because they have been baptized. They relax the reins. They are not concerned about conquering sins, but follow their desires."[539]

> This verse, "Whoever believes" . . . makes it a matter of everyone's conscience to realize that to be saved a person must believe and not pretend that it is sufficient for a Christian to be baptized.[540]

How do we account for these apparently contrary statements? It's a matter of our response. To trust in *the fact* that we were once baptized does nothing for us. What matters is *a living faith in Christ* who calls us in and through baptism.

Like the Lord's Supper, baptism is *a means* of God's redeeming action in our lives, not *an end* in itself. Neither baptism nor the Lord's Supper is meant to be the object of our devotion. It is our Lord himself, and his ever-valid Word of promise extended in baptism, that we are called to trust. This is *a right use* of baptism.

Luther addresses both the right use and misuse of baptism in his Large Catechism. He writes:

> To appreciate and use baptism aright, we must draw strength and comfort from it when our consciences oppress us, and we must retort, "But *I am baptized*! And if I am baptized, I have the promise that I shall be saved and have eternal life, both in soul and body."[541]

However, he also writes in his Large Catechism:

> Just by allowing the water to be poured over you, you do not receive baptism in such a manner that it does you any good. But it becomes beneficial to you if you accept it as God's command and ordinance, so that, baptized in God's name, you receive in the water the promised salvation. This the hand cannot do, nor the body, but the heart must believe it.[542]

Clearly then, it is as *a means* of God's redeeming action, as well as *a sign*, that baptism exercises its value and purpose. By the activity of

God's Spirit, it is baptism's continuing double-mission—*one*, to proclaim Jesus' sure Word of salvation to those who are burdened by their sins; and *two*, to call to repentance (death to self) and to faith (resurrection to new life) those who are self-satisfied and secure in their sins.

The Faith of the Baptized

In Matthew 18:1-6 Jesus is reported to say:

> Whoever welcomes one such child in my name welcomes me; but whoever causes one of the little ones who believe in me to sin, it would be better for that person to have a great millstone hung around the neck and to be drowned in the depth of the sea.

Who are "the little ones who believe" in Jesus? Are they children? Are they the newborn in the faith, whatever their actual age? In the context in which Matthew quotes Jesus, "the little ones who believe" are quite certainly children. In the context in which Mark and Luke use this quotation, it is not as certain.

But surely children cannot believe in Jesus, can they? Surely little ones, who do not know what Jesus has done for them, cannot believe in him. So said the Anabaptists in Luther's day. So say many people today. But the issue is not as clear cut as it may seem. Let's not forget what faith is and how it works:

- Faith is the trusting response of one person to another person.
- The exercise of such faith is a vital part of us the day we are born. It is as natural as breathing, eating, exercise, and sleeping. It is as necessary as nurture, care, and love.
- Faith does not depend on intellectual knowledge or reasoning. It depends on the interaction of one person with another person. The action and conduct of the one generates trust in the other.
- As far as faith in Jesus is concerned, God's grace always precedes and generates a person's response of faith. How? It is in and through the community of faith that God the Spirit is at work, generating faith in Jesus through the witness (by word, deed, and demeanor) of that community to the gospel. Wherever the community of faith bears witness to the gospel, there the Holy Spirit is at work. And surely the Spirit's work includes the children of believers within the community.

Infant Baptism

Does any New Testament text assert that children should be baptized? No. Does any New Testament text assert that children should not be baptized? No. Does any New Testament text support the practice of baptizing children? Yes. There are several such texts.

Before we look at those supporting texts, we might ask, "If baptizing children was a regular practice among first century believers, why didn't the authors of the New Testament tell us so clearly?" Because, as the British scholar Alan Richardson writes: "In the missionary situation of the apostolic church, as on the mission field today, baptism would be for the most part adult."[543]

It is "in the missionary situation" in which the New Testament authors did their writing. So what they record "for the most part" is the baptism of adult converts to the faith; but as we shall see, not to the exclusion of children. And so, we turn now to their writing that supports the baptism of children.

First of all, according to the Book of Acts, those who are moved by Peter's proclamation of the gospel on the day of Pentecost, ask, "What shall we do?" And Peter responds:

> Repent and be baptized every one of you in the name of Jesus Christ for the forgiveness of your sins; and you shall receive the gift of the Holy Spirit. For the promise is to you and to your children and to all that are far off, every one whom the Lord our God calls (Acts 2:38-39).

Peter says, "The promise is to you and to your children." What promise? The promise of the forgiveness of sins and the gift of the Holy Spirit to be received in baptism. Of course this text does not prove that the children were to be baptized then and there, but it is surely indicates that God's promise was extended to them.

Second, the author of the Book of Acts tells us that on at least two occasions, the apostle Paul baptized entire households—those of Lydia of the city of Thyatira (Acts 16:14-15) and those of the jailer from the city of Philippi (Acts 16:30-33).

Were there children in these households? Who knows? Nevertheless, when the head of the household, Lydia or the jailer, responded to the gospel in faith, *everyone* in the household was baptized. Why? Because in the culture of those times the household was understood to be the source and center of life, with a cohesiveness that endowed every member of the household with a common character and spirit. We read, for example:

- Joshua declared, "Choose this day whom you will serve. As for me and my house, we will serve the LORD" (Joshua 24:15).
- King David said, "Does not my house stand firm with God? For God has made with me an everlasting covenant" (2 Samuel 23:5).

As Johannes Pedersen writes, concerning biblical times:

> The man forms a complete unity with the whole of his family, his 'house,' and his property. Psychic community means, above all, a common will and so a common responsibility. The man is the centre of this common will. He does not act for himself alone, but for the whole of his house. Whatever he has done, the house, the family has likewise done, for together they form an organism so closely knit that no single part thereof can be separated as something independent.[544]

As Alan Richardson has written:

> . . . objections to the practice of baptizing the infant children of Christian parents arise from the rationalistic and individualistic attitudes of renaissance humanism rather than from a right understanding of NT teaching about faith and justification.
>
> But the solidarity of the family, or more accurately the household, would mean, in baptism as in other matters, that when the head of the household took a decisive step, he committed every member of his 'house,' and what happened to him happened to all.[545]

For the early church, then, baptizing the entire household of a believing head of the house (children and all) would be as natural as can be.

Third, we read in the Letter to the Colossians:

> In Christ you were circumcised, not with a circumcision that cuts away the flesh, but with the circumcision of Christ, that sets you free from bondage to your sinful self. For in baptism you were buried with Christ and also raised with him, through faith in the active power of God, who raised him from death (Colossians 2:11-12).

This passage calls baptism "the circumcision of Christ." Circumcision, of course, was the Old Testament *sign* of God's covenant with Abraham and his descendants. God said to Abraham:

> This is my covenant that you shall keep, between me and you and your descendants after you. Every male among

you shall be circumcised. You shall be circumcised in the flesh of your foreskin, and it shall be a sign of the covenant between me and you. He that is *eight days old* among you shall be circumcised; every male throughout your generations. . . . So shall my covenant be in your flesh an everlasting covenant (Genesis 17:10-13).

As Luther writes:

> This is a weighty passage, as people say. Therefore we must note it, for it is clear evidence that God received the children of the Jews into the fellowship of the people of God and of eternal grace.[546]

> If this was brought about with the Jews in the Old Testament through the medium of circumcision, why would God not do the same thing with the Gentiles through the medium of the new covenant of baptism?[547]

Indeed, since the descendants of Abraham were circumcised as infants, and since the Colossian letter calls baptism "the circumcision of Christ," one would think that *if* infant baptism was *not* the normal practice of the early church, this passage would say so. But no. Since baptism is likened to circumcision here, it is quite likely that baptizing the children of believers was the normal practice of the early church.

Furthermore, as we saw earlier,[548] in the century before Jesus was born, when Jewish rabbis adopted the practice of baptizing Gentile converts to Israel's God, the children of those converts were always baptized as well. Since this practice would have been well known among the early Christians, most of whom were Jewish, surely the baptism of children would have been expressly rejected if it was not a legitimate practice of the early church.[549]

Fourth, from the Gospel of Mark:

> People were bringing little children to Jesus, that he might touch them; and the disciples rebuked them. But when Jesus saw it he was indignant, and said to the disciples, 'Let the little children come to me; do not prevent them; for to such belongs the kingdom of God. Truly, I tell you, whoever does not receive the kingdom of God like a little child will never enter it.' And he took them up in his arms, laid his hands upon them, and blessed them (Mark 10:13-16).

Martin Luther writes: "The text about children ought not to be passed over lightly. . . .[550] In fact Luther calls this text: ". . . a promise and command for the baptism of children. . . ."[551]

A number of modern biblical scholars agree with Luther.[552] To be sure, Mark, Matthew, and Luke, say nothing about baptism in this text. But, as these scholars say, there is more to this text than meets the eye. They are convinced that *the very form* in which the story is told indicates that it was used in the first century church in connection with child baptism.

- They show that the comment used by Jesus in this text:[553] "Let the little children come to me; do not *prevent* them" corresponds to a formula commonly used in first century baptism, "What is to *prevent* me from being baptized?" (Acts 8:36; cf. Acts 11:17; Matthew 3:13-14). "Can any one *prevent* water, that these should not be baptized?" (Acts 10:47).
- They remind us that the early church practiced "the laying on of hands" at baptism as the evangelists report Jesus doing to the children here (cf. Acts 8:15-17; 19:5-6).
- They point out the similarity of language and theology in this incident with that of John 3, especially the parallel declarations: "Whoever does not receive the kingdom of God like a little child will never enter it," and "Unless one is born of water and the Spirit, one cannot enter the kingdom of God" (3:5).

Of course, the reasoning presented here does not *prove* that Mark 10:13-16 was used in the first century in connection with child baptism, but it is *evidence* of a sort that should not be lightly dismissed.

Fifth, Paul writes: "The unbelieving husband has been sanctified through his wife, and the unbelieving wife has been sanctified through her husband. Otherwise your children would be unclean, but as it is, they are holy" (1 Corinthians 7:14). Why are the children of parents, only one of whom is a believer, considered "holy"? *Perhaps* because these children have been baptized.

Sixth, one might argue that the overall outlook of the New Testament favors the practice of child baptism. An expression of that outlook is the following incident from Mark 9:34-37:

> When the twelve discussed among themselves which of them was the greatest, Jesus called them and said to them,"Whoever wants to be first must be last of all and servant of all." Then he took a little child and put it among them; and taking it in his arms, he said to them, "Whoever welcomes one such child in my name welcomes me, and whoever welcomes me welcomes not me but the one who sent me.'"

This passage is one of many that reveals the unexpected, topsy-turvy nature of God's Kingdom, as taught by Jesus. He says, 'Whoever wants to be first must be last of all and servant of all.' He says, "Whoever is least among you is the greatest" (Luke 9:48) and "Let the greatest among you become as the youngest, and the leader as one who serves" (Luke 22:26).

How contrary to how we think and act! We tend to think, "Unless we become like adults, we will never enter the kingdom." But no. To qualify for God's kingdom is to become like a child; that is, *to turn* to become like a child and *to welcome* such children. God's kingdom, and Christ's church as well, is precisely the community that has to do with children. Every new Christian, whatever that person's actual age, is a newborn babe who must be nourished, encouraged, and taught the basics of life and faith. Like a child, that person must learn by trying, failing, trying again, falling short, asking for forgiveness, being forgiven, being renewed, slowly growing, slowly maturing.

It may seem contradictory, but to grow in Christ is to become more and more like a little child; not child*ish*, but child*like;* that is, *open* to God and others, *dependent* on God and others, without deceit or status or claims, quick to respond and to trust, quick to forgive and forget.

The very nature of the Christian life is to begin as a child, to need parents, brothers, and sisters in the faith to nourish and guide us; and again and again, *to turn* to become like little children. No wonder many of us believe that child baptism has been the norm in the church from the very beginning.

There is no doubt in Luther's mind that the children of believers are to be baptized. Some of Luther's additional reasons include the following:

> St. Augustine writes, child baptism has come from the apostles."[554]

> For over a thousand years there were hardly any other but child baptisms. If this baptism is wrong then, for that long period, Christendom would have been without baptism, and . . . it would not be Christendom.[555]

> That the baptism of infants is pleasing to Christ is sufficiently proved from God's own work. God has sanctified many who have been thus baptized and has given them the Holy Spirit. Even today there are not a few whose doctrine and life attest that they have the Holy Spirit."[556]

> If we are going to change or do away with traditional customs, it is necessary to prove convincingly that these are contrary to God's Word.[557]

Christ's commission to make disciples of *all* nations, baptizing them in the name of the Father, the Son and the Spirit excludes no one.[558]

Is Baptism a Necessity?

According to the New Testament, *faith in God's Son* is the key to eternal life. As Martin Luther declares over and over again, it is only as we respond to the crucified, resurrected Jesus in faith that we are saved. And it is only as we respond to him in faith that the Word and the sacraments become meaningful and efficacious for us. Luther writes:

> The sacraments do what they do, not by their own power, but by the power of faith, without which they do nothing at all. . . .[559]

> Many receive the sacraments and obtain from them neither life nor godliness, but whoever believes is godly and will live.[560]

> Without faith, no sacrament is of any use, indeed, it is altogether deadly and pernicious.[561]

Is baptism, then, necessary for a person to become a child of God? Luther would probably respond, "Certainly it is necessary, though it is not absolutely necessary." In fact, he writes:

> Christ says, "Whoever believes and is baptized will be saved, but whoever does not believe will be condemned" [Mark 16:16]. He shows us in this word that faith is such a necessary part of the sacrament that it can save even without the sacrament, and for this reason he did not add, "Whoever does not believe and is not baptized."[562]

Again, as Luther says a number of times in a number of ways: "God is able to save without baptism. . . ."[563] But he hastens to add:

> But in the church we must judge and teach, in accord with God's ordered power, that without that outward baptism no one is saved.

> Attention must be paid to the Word, and baptism must be sought. The Eucharist must be received, and absolution must be required. All these are indeed externals, but they are included in the Word. Hence the Holy Spirit works nothing without them.[564]

A Summary of the Meaning and Practice of Baptism

- Baptism is founded on faith in Jesus; a faith engendered by God's Spirit at work through the proclamation of God's Word.

- Baptism is "the washing of water with the Word," that is, God's Word of promise, "Whoever believes and is baptized will be saved."
- Baptism is meant for every believer and for the children of every believer.
- Baptism is *a means of grace,* through which forgiveness of sin and the gift of the Holy Spirit is given to every believer.
- *The sign* of Baptism is immersion in water; the *significance* of baptism is a union with Jesus in his death, burial and resurrection, that calls us to die daily to sin, and so, be raised up daily to "walk in newness of life."
- Baptism, then, is meant to be an continuing reality in our lives.

THE OFFICE OF THE KEYS

According to the New Testament, Jesus speaks about four keys: the key of knowledge, the key of interpretation, the key that binds, and the key that sets free.[565] He is using pictorial language of course, with each key representing something important for faith and life. Knowledge and interpretation are basic to life and faith, that's certain. So are the keys that bind and set free.

According to Matthew's Gospel Peter was the first to be promised the keys that bind and free. To Peter Jesus said: "I will give you the keys of the kingdom of heaven. Whatever you bind on earth will be bound in heaven, and whatever you loose on earth will be loosed in heaven" (Matthew 16:19).

Peter, the rock—the first apostle to acknowledge Jesus as Messiah; the first to be encountered by the risen Jesus; the first to publicly proclaim Jesus as Lord; the first leader of the young church. But the other apostles were encountered by the risen Jesus as well. They proclaimed him as Lord. They became leaders of the young church and they, too, were promised and given the keys of the kingdom. In fact, Jesus promised and gave these keys to *all* of his disciples, as well as to future believing men and women. See Matthew 18:18 and John 20:22-23.

The office of the keys, then, has been given to all God's people. We, like the first Christians, are stewards of the kingdom, keepers of the keys that bind and set free. What, then, is the office of the keys? As we read in the Small Catechism, "It is that authority which Christ gave to his church to forgive the sins of those who repent and to declare to those who do not repent that their sins are not forgiven."[566]

One is the key of censure and indictment. The other is the key of forgiveness and reconciliation. The first is *the Law* that calls us into question and condemns us when we have gone wrong. The second is *the gospel* which encourages and assures us when things have gone wrong, and which announces God's forgiveness when we confess our sins and seek God's mercy. Indeed, the two are meant to work together, the first preparing for the second, so that recognizing when we go wrong, we might be led to repent and to be restored.

How are the keys that bind and set free put to work in the faith and life of our people today?

First, they are put to work in the preaching of the Law that exposes and judges our sin, and in the preaching of the gospel that calls us to repent of our sins to receive God's forgiveness through Christ Jesus.

Second, the keys are put to work in the actions of the congregation. In the words of Matthew 18:15-17,

> If a fellow believer sins against you, go to that person by yourself and point out the fault. If he or she listens, you will be reconciled to each other. If he or she does not listen, take one or two others with you, so that every word may be confirmed by two or three witnesses. If he or she refuses to listen to them, tell the whole congregation. If that fails, let that person be to you as a Gentile or a tax collector.

Third, the keys are put to work in the General Confession of the Church, in worship, where the power of sin and its consequences are announced, where confession is honestly made, and where absolution is proclaimed in Jesus' name.

Fourth, the keys are put to work in *the conversation* of two believers—either in counseling or in private confession in which one person listens and applies the keys to the other; or in a time of "mutual consolation" in which two persons who trust one another openly confess their failings and assure and encourage one another in the name of Christ.

Luther sums up the purpose of the keys beautifully:

> The intention of the key that binds is that we heed its threatening and so come to fear God. . . . The intention of the key that looses is to make us believe its consolation and promise, and so learn to love God and receive a joyful, confident, and peaceful heart.[567]

CONFESSION

In this part of his Catechism Luther asks and answers six questions:[568] What is private confession? What sins should we confess? What are such sins? How might we confess our sins privately? What if we are not troubled by any special sins? How may we be assured of forgiveness?

In his answer to the question, "What sins should we confess?" Luther makes a distinction between one's confession of sin before God and before a pastor. While we confess *to the Lord* our basic sinfulness as well as particular sins, "*before the pastor* we should confess only those sins that trouble us in heart and mind."

Elsewhere Luther explains the value of private confession as follows:

> I have a high regard for private confession, for here God's word and absolution are spoken privately and individually to each believer for the forgiveness of sins, and as often as desired the believer may have recourse to it for this forgiveness, and also for comfort, counsel, and guidance. So it is a precious, useful thing for souls, as long as no one is driven to it with laws and commandments but sinners are left free to make use of it, according to each one's need. . . .[569]

> There is much that is beneficial and precious in private confession. First of all, the absolution, in which your neighbor absolves you in God's stead, is just as if God were speaking. That should indeed be comforting to us. . . . Such absolution God has put into the mouth of a human being, hence it is most comforting, especially to burdened consciences, to receive it there.[570]

Luther also speaks of the value of private confession for himself:

> I will allow no one to take private confession away from me, and I would not give it up for all the treasures in the world, since I know what comfort and strength it has given me. No one knows what it can do except someone who has struggled often and long with the devil. Yea, the devil would have slain me long ago, if the confession had not sustained me.[571]

Few things are worse than unresolved anguish, bitterness, or guilt. Such things can never be dismissed from one's being. They may be repressed, buried away; but they remain active, at work, eating away at body and soul. We need the keys of the kingdom to set us free. This "cure without equal,"[572] as Luther calls it, is to admit these things to a listening, *trustworthy* person who knows how to open our lives to Christ.

It isn't easy to confess our sins to another person. We are ashamed and we fear that we will be humiliated or rejected, but it's worth the risk. As Luther puts it:

> There are many doubtful matters that a person cannot resolve or find the answer to alone, and so shares a troubling problem with another believer. What harm is there if a person is humbled a little before a neighbor, puts himself or herself to shame, looks for a word of comfort from that neighbor, and believes it, as if hearing it personally from God.[573]

Again he says:

> When we have laid bare our conscience to another believer and privately made known the evil that lurked within us, we receive from that person's lips the word of comfort spoken by God personally. And, if we accept this in faith, we find peace in the mercy of God speaking to us through that person.[574]

Must One's Sins Always be Made Known?

Normally we should confess our sins to persons whom we have wronged. But there are times when we should not. In one of her novels Florence Barclay illustrates one of those times. Lucy Mallory, a rather self-righteous lady, had lied to Diana Rivers. It bothered Lucy, and so she later confessed her lies to Diana. In doing so however, Lucy hurt Diana deeply. Diana wrote to her husband, expressing her pain, wondering what he thought of Mrs Mallory's action. He replied:

> If confession is merely the method adopted by a stricken and convicted conscience for shifting the burden of its own wrong-doing by importing to another the knowledge of that wrong, especially if that knowledge will cause pain, disappointment, or perplexity to the innocent heart—then I hold it to be both morbid and useless.[575]

In today's language, if, to sooth my conscience, I confess a previously unknown sin to someone, thereby causing that person pain, I simply add injury to insult. The burden should rather be mine to bear, to confess to the Lord, and, perhaps, to confess to a third person whom I trust.

PART FIVE

THE SACRAMENT OF HOLY COMMUNION

Origins of the Sacrament of Holy Communion

What is often called the Sacrament of Holy Communion was founded by Jesus during his Last Supper with his twelve apostles. This sacrament is identified in the New Testament as the Lord's Supper (I Corinthians 11:20), the Lord's Table (I Corinthians 10:21), and the Breaking of Bread (Acts 2:42). Over the centuries this sacred act has been identified by other terms as well, including the Sacrament of Holy Communion, the Sacrament of the Altar, Mass, and Eucharist. Luther uses all these terms in his writing.

Descriptions of the Last Supper are given in four New Testament texts, written by four different authors—Matthew 26:20-30; Mark 14:17-26; Luke 22:14-38; I Corinthians 11:23-25.

What Was the Occasion or Setting for the Last Supper?

The authors of the Synoptic Gospels (Matthew, Mark, and Luke) tell us that all of the events of Jesus' passion, including the Last Supper, took place *on* the day of the Passover (Matthew 26:20; Mark 14:17; Luke 22:14-15).

The author of John's Gospel tells us that the events of Jesus' passion, including the Last Supper, took place "*before* the festival of the Passover" (13:1), on "the day of preparation for the Passover" (19:14, 31, 42)—the day that the Passover lambs were sacrificed.

Note: In first century Judea, each day was calculated to begin at sunset and to end the following sunset. So the day we call Good Friday began at sunset on what we call Maundy Thursday. So, as the Synoptic Gospels describe it, the events of Jesus' passion—the Last Supper, Gethsemane, his arrest, trial, crucifixion, and burial—all took place on Good Friday.

If the Synoptic Gospels are right, the Supper had its setting in the solemn ritual of a Passover meal. If John's Gospel is right, the Supper had its setting in a more ordinary meal, on the day before Passover. Whatever the case, what Jesus does and says is anything but ordinary.

"What is Holy Communion?"[576]

Luther asks in his Small Catechism. Then he answers:
"Holy Communion is the body and blood of our Lord Jesus Christ given with bread and wine, instituted by Christ himself, for us to eat and drink."

"Where do the Scriptures say this?" he then asks. And he answers: "Matthew, Mark, Luke, and Paul say . . ." then gives a harmonized description of the founding of the Lord's Supper based on those four sources. In this study, however, we will look at what each source or author has to teach us.

What Jesus Is Doing and Saying During the Last Supper?

Mark 14:22-24 tells us:

> As they were eating, he took a loaf of bread, and after blessing it, he broke and gave it to them, and said, "*Take, this is my body.*" And he took a cup, and after giving thanks he gave it to them, and they all drank from it. And he said to them, "*This is my blood of the covenant which is poured out for many.*"

Notice, first, what Jesus is *not* doing here. He is *not* breaking the bread as a symbol of his crucifixion. The Greek root-word *klao*, translated here as *broke*, occurs twenty-six times in the New Testament, *always* in reference to breaking bread and in every case means to break bread in order to distribute it.[577] Furthermore, Jesus' body was not broken on the cross. It was beaten, bruised, punctured, and stabbed, but not broken. As Luther writes:

> The wine and bread here cannot be *the likeness* of the body and blood of Christ as the text of the Supper speaks of them. I pass over the fact that John utterly repudiates the application of the word "breaking" to the suffering of Christ, when he writes that not a bone of Christ was broken, "that the Scripture might be fulfilled, 'Not a bone of his shall be broken.'" Scripture therefore does not allow us to refer 'breaking' to Christ's suffering or death.[578]

What, then, is Jesus doing at the Last Supper? He is doing what any host would do at a Passover meal or at any meal, festive or ordinary. He blesses and shares, first the bread, then the cup, with every one at the table. The disciples understand exactly what this means. In the culture of that day, to be given a portion of the bread that was blessed and to share a drink from the cup that was blessed was to be fully accepted as *one who belongs* in the company of those gathered there.

But, of course, Jesus not only carries out these acts of acceptance, he speaks. In blessing and sharing the bread, he says, "Take, this is my body;" and by this act and word, indicates that he is *giving himself* to his followers. In blessing and passing the cup, he says, "This is my blood of the covenant, which is poured out for many;" and by this act and word, indicates that he is *giving up his life* for them, and "for many" — and thereby, establishes a covenant with them. It is a covenant in which Jesus binds himself to them and to those who come after them, in a fellowship based on his self-giving sacrifice. It is a covenant designed to be renewed and shared by them whenever they gather together to eat this bread and drink this wine, and, by so doing, participate with one another in Jesus' life-giving benefits.

The Communion of All Believers in Christ

In his 1519 treatise on Holy Communion, Luther writes that the sacrament has three parts: the sign, the significance, and the faith.[579]

> *The sign* is "the bread and wine that must be used in eating and drinking" in communion with other believers.
>
> *The significance* or effect of this sacrament is . . . the complete union and the undivided fellowship of the saints with Christ and with one another. . . .
>
> The third part of the sacrament . . . is *the faith* on which everything depends.[580]
>
> To receive this sacrament in bread and wine, then, is nothing else than to receive a sure sign of this fellowship and incorporation with Christ and all saints.[581]

Over the years Luther continues to teach that the significance of the Lord's Supper is the unity and fellowship of believers with their Lord. He teaches this *at the same time* as he emphasizes that Christ's body and blood are given to us in the bread and the wine of the Supper. Indeed, in Luther's mind the two teachings go together, the fellowship with Christ and others depends on Christ's pledge and gift of himself in the sacrament.

In 1525 he writes: "*This fellowship* is really a participation, so that in communion with each other they receive the common body of Christ, as Paul himself said, 'We who are many are one body, for we all partake of the same loaf.'"[582]

In 1528 Luther writes: "The sacrament of the Supper must indeed prefigure and signify something, viz. *the unity of Christians* in one spiritual body of Christ through one spirit, faith, love, and the cross, etc."[583]

In 1544 he writes: "The sacrament, according to Christ's intention, is ordained and instituted for this purpose, that one should administer or give it to other Christians as *a communion* and common meal to strengthen and comfort them in faith."[584]

As for "the *faith* on which everything depends"—for Luther, that faith is simply a person's heart-felt trust in Christ Jesus and the promise that he gives to us in the sacrament.

Luke's Quite Different Account

> And he took a loaf of bread, and having given thanks, he broke and gave it to them, saying, *"This is my body which is given for you. Do this in remembrance of me."* And he did the same with the cup after supper, saying, *"This cup that is poured out for you is the new covenant in my blood"* (Luke 22:19-20).

Here is a definite command, *"Do this. . . ;"* and here is a definite promise, "This is my body . . . *given for you.* This cup . . . is *poured out for you. . . ."*

By the way, Jesus' command, "Do this. . . ." was not restricted to the event of the Last Supper or for the apostles only. All first century believers regularly participated in the Lord's Supper. As Paul puts it, "The cup of blessing that *we* bless. . . . The bread that *we* break. . . ." (1 Corinthians 10:16). The Lord's Supper is meant for every follower of Jesus.

What, then, according to Luke, does Jesus ask us to do? As Luther says: Jesus commands that we do "the whole ordinance of the Supper."[585] That is, Christ asks us to take bread, to give thanks, to break and give it to one another, to declare again what Jesus says is happening here, "This is my body given for you," and to eat it. Christ asks us to take the cup, to give thanks, to share it with one another, to declare again what Jesus says it happening here, "This cup, poured out for you, is the new covenant in my blood," and to drink it.

But why does Jesus ask us to do this? According to both Luke and Paul, he says. "Do this *in remembrance of me."* The word "remembrance" is crucial here. In English the word means "to bring to mind" or "to recall the past." But the Greek word *anamnesis* that we translate as remembrance, and the Hebrew word *zakar* that stands behind it and informs it, means something more than simply "to bring to mind" or "to recall the past." It is a word that calls for *an active response* to *an enduring, significant command* or *person* or *reality.* We read for example:

The people of Israel were commanded to "Remember the Sabbath day to keep it holy" (Exodus 20:8). They did so by setting aside the seventh day of every week to *honor* the LORD and to *allow* their servants and their work animals to rest, as well as themselves. We are told that, "The LORD remembered Hannah" (1 Samuel 1:19) by *answering* her prayer. Leaders among the believers in Jerusalem asked Paul and Barnabas to "remember the poor" (Galatians 2:10), that is, to *help* them.

Even the English word "remembrance" or "remember" can mean *an active response* to *an enduring, significant reality* or *person*. We remember our friends' birthdays by congratulating them personally or by sending them cards. We remember the 4th of July by celebrating that day as the founding of our nation. The Jewish people remember the Passover by preparing it, eating it, and dramatizing it. And we remember Jesus by participating in the Lord's Supper in which we believe he is present and active "for us."

We come to the Lord's table, then, not to re-enact the first Lord's Supper as a reminder of something that happened long ago. The Lord's Supper is not a memorial meal. It is an "eating" and "drinking" in which we, along with other believers, are *actively responding* to our crucified, risen Lord, who is present and active in our lives here and now. In Luther's words:

> You should mark well the words 'in remembrance of me,' for with it Christ wants to induce and encourage you, out of love and gratitude to him and in praise and honor of his suffering, *to participate* in the sacrament gladly.[586]

Participating in the Body and Blood of Christ

Paul writes: "The cup of blessing that we bless, is it not a participation in the blood of Christ? The bread that we break, is it not a participation in the body of Christ?" (1 Corinthians 10:16).

Luther writes:

> This verse has been the life-giving medicine of my heart in my trials concerning this sacrament.[587]

> This text I have extolled, and I do still, as my heart's joy and crown.[588]

Luther extols these texts so highly, first, as we have seen, because in writing "The cup that *we* bless, the bread that *we* break," Paul shows that the Lord's Supper was not a once only event between Jesus and his apostles, but a Supper intended for all believers down through the ages.

He does so, second, because as Paul indicates, to eat the bread and to drink from the cup of the Lord's Supper is *the means* by which we participate in Jesus' body and blood.

He does so, third, because the word *participation* clearly shows that the bread and cup of the Lord's Supper are not mere symbols of Jesus' body and blood, but the means for *receiving and sharing* his body and blood.

The Greek word translated as "participation" is *koinonia*. No single English word can adequately translate the full meaning and intent of *koinonia*. It takes several English words to begin to grasp its meaning; words such as "participation," "communion," "fellowship," and "sharing."[589]

This means that to eat the bread and to drink the wine of this Supper, and, thereby, to participate in the body and blood of our Lord, is to be caught up into union with him and his people. Automatically? Magically? No. This eating and drinking is always an exercise of faith. As Luther writes: "Whoever goes to the sacrament must firmly believe that what Christ says is in fact true, that his body is given 'for you,' and his blood shed 'for you.'"[590]

The Earliest Account of the Lord's Supper

The earliest New Testament account of the Lord's Supper is Paul's declaration in 1 Corinthians 11:23-25:

> I received from the Lord what I also passed on to you, that on the night he was betrayed, the Lord Jesus took bread, and when he had given thanks, he broke it, and said, *"This is my body which is for you. Do this in remembrance of me."* In the same way also he took the cup after supper, saying, *"This cup is the new covenant in my blood. Do this, as often as you drink it, in remembrance of me."*

This account gives no indication that Jesus founded it during the Passover meal. In fact, Paul's words seem to suggest that the setting of the Lord's Supper was an ordinary evening meal. Specifically, Paul uses the Greek word for leavened bread (*artos*), rather than the word for unleavened bread (*azumos*), which would be appropriate for a Passover meal.

This does not prove that the Last Supper did not originate within the setting of the Passover meal. But it does suggest that the Lord's Supper, as practiced in the early church, was quite distinct from the Passover meal. It was *the Lord's Supper*, exalting *his* name, proclaiming *his* death. It was *a new covenant* in his blood, succeeding the old covenant, conveying *new* benefits. And in contrast to the Passover meal, the Lord's Supper was a *weekly* or *occasional* celebration, not a once a year event.

If the Lord's Supper did originate within the Passover meal, one might have expected Jesus to identify himself with the Passover Lamb as the ideal symbol of his sacrificial death. But no. He took bread and wine and identified himself with those elements.

The Lord's Supper, then, is different. Whatever its connection with the Passover meal, it moves beyond that meal in a new and distinct way. This is why Luther writes: "We are properly to distinguish [the celebration of the Passover] from the sacrament of Christ's body and blood."[591]

Luther goes further. He writes:

> If Christ had intended to institute a Supper in which, *not* his body and blood, *but a likeness* of his body and blood were present, he would properly have left us the old Mosaic supper with the paschal lamb. For, beyond all measure, conclusively . . . in every respect, and quite beautifully this [lamb] *represents, prefigures* and *typifies* his body given for us and his blood shed for us. . . . Why then should he so foolishly abolish this fine Old Testament supper and substitute a supper that in meaning and in essence is altogether *insignificant in comparison* with it?

> For in the Old, at least, there is a lamb, a *living* body, offered for the people, that *represents* the body of Christ much more lucidly and clearly than simple bread, which is an obscure simile in comparison with a lamb. And . . . there is the blood of the lamb which *represents* the blood of Christ much more lucidly and clearly than the wine. In a word, this Supper is in no way comparable to the old one in *significance* and *similarity*.

> No doubt Christ spoke these words ["This is my body. This is my blood."] *in contrast* with the old paschal lamb, which he *abrogates* here, as if to say, "Up to now you have eaten a lamb, the body of an animal. But here in its stead is *my body—mine, mine,* I say in perfect clarity." . . . This he does to express the *presence* of Christ's body in the Supper with all possible clarity.[592]

"What benefits do we receive from this sacrament?"[593] Luther asks in his Small Catechism. Then he answers:

> The benefits of this sacrament are pointed out by the words, given and shed for you for the remission of sins. These words assure us that in the sacrament we receive forgiveness of sins, life, and salvation. For where there is forgiveness of sins, there is also life and salvation.

Luther bases this teaching on what Jesus says according to Matthew's account of the Last Supper, for only Matthew quotes Jesus as saying: "Drink from it, all of you, for this is my blood of the covenant, which is poured out for many *for the forgiveness of sins*" (Matthew 26:28).

How do we reconcile Matthew's reference to the forgiveness of sins with what Jesus says according to the other three accounts of the Lord's Supper? This much is certain: In all four accounts Jesus invites his disciples to receive what he gives them, the bread of which he says, "This is my body." In all four accounts Jesus invites his disciples to receive the cup he passes to them, calling it "my blood of the covenant."

Most of us understand these words and actions of Jesus to be a pledge of self-giving which would shortly be carried out on the cross. And as the New Testament authors unite in declaring, in his self-giving sacrifice on the cross, Jesus has acted to deliver us from sin, death, and evil. In any case Luther is certain that Jesus gives us "forgiveness of sins, life, and salvation" in the sacrament. As he writes on another occasion:

> We treat of the forgiveness of sins in two ways. First, how it is achieved and won. Second, how it is distributed and given to us. Christ has achieved it on the cross, it is true; but he has not distributed or given it on the cross. He has not won it in the supper or sacrament; there he has distributed and given it through **the word**, as also in the gospel, where it is preached. He has won it once for all on the cross. But the distribution takes place continuously, before and after, from the beginning to the end of the world.

> If now I seek the forgiveness of sins, I do not run to the cross, for I will not find it there. Nor must I hold to the suffering of Christ in knowledge or remembrance, for I will not find it there. But I will find in the sacrament or gospel **the word** which distributes, presents, offers, and gives to me the forgiveness which was won on the cross. Therefore, whoever has a bad conscience from sins should go to the sacrament and obtain comfort, *not* because of the bread and wine, *not* because of the body and blood of Christ, *but* because of **the word** which in the sacrament offers, presents, and gives the body and blood, given and shed for me. Is that not clear enough?[594]

"**How can eating and drinking do all this**?"[595] is the third question Luther asks with regard to this sacrament. And he answers:

> It is not eating and drinking that does this, but the words, *given and shed for you for the remission of sins*. These words, along with eating and drinking, are the main thing in the sacrament. And whoever believes these words has exactly what they say, forgiveness of sins.

As Luther writes elsewhere:

If we wish to observe and understand the mass properly we must give up everything that the eyes see and the senses suggest—be it vestments, bells, songs, ornaments, prayers, processions, elevations, prostrations, or whatever happens in it—until we first grasp and fully ponder **the words of Christ**, by which he performed and instituted the mass and commanded us to perform it. For therein lies the whole mass, its nature, work, profit, and benefit. Without the words nothing is derived from the mass.

So if you would receive this sacrament and testament worthily, see to it that you give emphasis to these living words of Christ, rely on them with a strong faith, and desire what Christ has promised you in them; then it will be yours, then you will be worthy and well prepared.[596]

The Validity of Holy Communion

As Luther teaches:

The Lord's Supper was not invented or devised by any human being. It was instituted by Christ without human counsel or deliberation. Therefore, just as the Ten Commandments, the Lord's Prayer, and the Creed retain their nature and value even if we never keep, pray, or believe them, so also this blessed sacrament remains unimpaired and inviolate even if we use and handle it unworthily.[597]

As Luther says elsewhere:

Our unbelief does not alter God's Word. . . . Christ does not found his sacrament upon our use of it. What he says or ordains remains, no matter whether one uses it rightly or wrongly.[598]

Nevertheless, as he emphasizes often in any number of ways: "Whoever receives these words and *believes* that they are true *has* what the words declare. But whoever does not believe has nothing, but lets this gracious blessing be offered in vain."[599]

The Word and the Sign

Luther writes:

Let us learn that in every promise of God there are two things which one must consider: the word and the sign. In baptism—the words of the baptizer and the immersing in water; in the mass—the words and the bread and wine. The words are the divine vow, promise, and testament. The signs are the sacraments, that is, sacred signs. Now as the testament is much more important than the sacrament, so the words are much more important than the signs. For the signs might well be lacking, if only one has the words; thus without sacrament, yet not without testament, one might be saved. For I can enjoy the sacrament in the mass every day if only I keep before my eyes the testament, that is, the words and promise of Christ, and feed and strengthen my faith on them.

We see, then, the best and greatest part of all sacraments and of the mass is the words and promise of God, without which the sacraments are dead and are nothing at all, like a body without a soul, a cask without wine, a purse without money, a type without fulfillment, a letter without the spirit, a sheath without a knife, and the like.[600]

Everything depends on these words. Every Christian should and must know them and hold them fast. We must never let anyone take them away by any other kind of teaching, even though it were an angel from heaven. They are words of life and of salvation, so that whoever believes in them has all sins forgiven through that faith, is a child of life and has overcome death and hell. Language cannot express how great and mighty these words are, for they are the sum and substance of the whole gospel. This is why these words are far more important than the sacrament itself, and a Christian should make it a practice to give far more attention to these words than to the sacrament.[601]

A Sign and Seal of the Word

Having considered Luther's comments cited in the last few pages, we are not surprised to hear that, time and again, Luther declares:

> The chief and foremost thing in the sacrament is the word of Christ, when he says: "Take and eat, this is my body . . ." [etc.].[602]

> God's Word plays the chief part in the sacraments.[603]

> All sacraments must become such through the word, which is the most essential part in all sacraments.[604]

What might surprise us is Luther's oft-repeated conviction:

> The chief reason for holding mass outwardly is the word of God which no one can do without.[605]

> Had there been no preaching, Christ would never have instituted the mass. He is more concerned about the word than the sign.[606]

In Luther's judgment, then, the sacrament is a servant of the Word, created by Jesus as a sign and seal of his promises. As Luther explains:

> The mass is nothing else than the divine promise or testament of Christ, *sealed* with the sacrament of his body and blood.[607]

> Christ has affixed to the words of his testament a powerful and most precious seal and sign: his own true flesh and blood under the bread and wine. For we poor human beings, living as we do in our five senses, must always have along with the words at least one outward sign to which we may cling and around which we may gather—*in such a way, however*, that this sign may be a sacrament, that is, that it may be external *and yet* contain and signify something spiritual, in order that through the external we may be drawn into the spiritual.[608]

For Luther, then, Jesus' Word is "the chief and foremost thing," with the sacrament as a seal or guarantee of his word. And, as Luther would put it, this sign is no wax or paper seal.[609] It is a living sign and seal. It is Jesus' body and blood given in and with bread and wine.

What is Central in Faith, Life, and Worship

There are those today who assert "the centrality of the Eucharist in the life of the congregation" and claim that "Holy Communion has been the principal act of Christian worship since New Testament times."[610]

There is no question about the vital role of the Lord's Supper in our lives. But to claim it is "central in the life of the congregation" and to call it "the principal act of Christian worship" is to overstate its purpose.

Luther, for one, always affirmed the vital importance of the Supper. He called it "a great treasure"[611] and "a gift which God has given to us and which we should take and receive with thanks."[612] But Luther never considered this sacrament "central" or "the principal act of Christian worship." His emphasis is quite different. Again and again he declares:

> The preaching and teaching of God's Word is the most important part of divine worship.[613]

> The worship of God lies especially in preaching the Word, because by teaching the gospel one worships God.[614]

> The Word of God is the greatest, most necessary, and most sublime part of Christendom, for the sacraments cannot

exist without the word, but indeed the word can exist without the sacraments. . . .[615]

You know that the greatest divine service is the preaching of the Word of God, and not only the greatest divine service, but also the best we can have in every situation.[616]

In truth, there is no greater mercy on earth than when God's Word is preached, and again, no greater woe than when God's Word is not preached.[617]

"Proclaiming the Lord's Death until He Comes"

As most commentators suggest, the very act of celebrating the Lord's Supper is a proclamation of the Lord's death until he comes. This conviction is based on Paul's words: "As often as you eat this bread and drink the cup, you proclaim the Lord's death until he comes" (1 Corinthians 11:26). Luther agrees with this, for he writes: "We eat and drink and *in so doing* remember him and proclaim his death."[618]

Again he seems to affirm this conviction when he writes:

When I say, "This is the body, which is given *for you*, this is the blood, which is poured out *for you* for the forgiveness of sins," I am there commemorating him; I proclaim him and announce his death. Only it is not done publicly in the congregation but is directed at you alone.[619]

But beyond this, Luther is certain that Jesus instituted his Supper to underscore the proclaiming of his Word, by serving as a sign and seal of the Word and as a means of conveying the Word. As he says: "When celebrating the Sacrament we should preach a sermon and not forget Christ; for the Lord's Supper was instituted for the sake of the proclamation."[620]

Unfortunately, the mediaeval Roman Church neglected preaching the gospel and turned the Lord's Supper into something it was not meant to be. In contrast to the centrality of the Word in the Supper, the mediaeval church taught that the Supper was a "re-offering to God of Christ's sacrifice of himself on Calvary." As a result, instead of *serving* as a seal of Jesus' Word and a means of God's grace, the sacrament became all-important in itself.

Even in our own day the Supper, at times, seems to be elevated into an event celebrated quite apart from the proclamation of the Word. Such a practice in his day led Luther to declare:

It is a bad situation that in our time so much stress is laid on saying and having masses said, while unfortunately

> neglecting the most important part, the one for which the masses were instituted, namely, the proclamation.[621]

> . . . we hold that the sacrament is less important than preaching.[622]

This, in turn, is the reason he says: "It is highly important to lead the people back from the sacrament to the words, and to accustom them to pay much more attention to the words than to the sacrament."[623]

Of course, this can happen only through preaching and teaching.

Preaching the Word

It is no surprise to hear Luther saying: "A Christian congregation should never gather together without the preaching of God's Word and prayer, no matter how briefly."[624] After all, he believed, as Paul taught, that "the gospel is the power of God for salvation to every one who has faith" (Romans 1:16) and that "faith comes from what is heard and what is heard comes by the preaching of Christ" (Romans 10:17).

And, after the preceding quotes from Luther, it is no surprise to hear Luther say:

> There should be preaching at the mass at all times.[625]

> Christ's intention is that we should preach about him and his death in the sacrament and publicly confess him, as he says: "Do this in remembrance of me." That is, as Paul says, "Proclaim my death until I come."[626]

What may surprise us is Luther's oft-repeated conviction:

> It is better to omit the sacrament than not to proclaim the gospel.[627]

> Christ has so strictly commanded that the gospel and this testament be preached that he does not even wish the mass to be celebrated unless the gospel be preached. As he says, "As often as you do this, remember me." And as Paul says, "You shall preach his death."[628]

> The Word, the Word, I say, merits more regard than the whole sacrament with all that it is and can do, for the Word is the chief thing. Where it is a question of making decisions and choices, one should rather let the whole sacrament go than forsake a single letter or tittle of the Word.[629]

It all goes back to Luther's heart-felt conviction: "The words and deeds of Christ are not dead histories, but living things held forth by God's Son so that we might live through them."[630]

Discerning Christ's Body

The Lord's Supper was celebrated in the assembly at Corinth as part of a full meal (an early church practice called "a feast of love"). But it was being practiced in a thoughtless manner. In Paul's words: "Each of you goes ahead with your own meal so that one is left hungry while another gets drunk. What? Do you despise the assembly of God? Do you humiliate those who have nothing?" (1 Corinthians 11:17-22).

It is because of such behavior that Paul declares, "It is not the Lord's supper that you eat" (11:20). Several commentators suggest it is also this behavior Paul has in mind when he goes on to write:

> Whoever eats the bread or drinks the Lord's cup in an unworthy manner will be guilty of profaning the body and blood of the Lord. Let us examine ourselves, and so eat of the bread and drink of the cup. For those who eat and drink without discerning the body eat and drink judgment upon themselves 1 Corinthians 11:27-29).

To treat other believers in such a way disrupts the fellowship the Supper is meant to nourish. Such behavior fails to "discern the *body* of Christ"—his *body* given in the Supper as well as his *body*, the assembly of believers. It is, at the same time, a failure to take seriously the awesome nature of Christ's gift of himself to us in the Supper.

Luther understands the text on "discerning the body" to refer to Christ's body given in the Lord's Supper. He nevertheless knows and teaches that the very purpose of the Supper underscores the value and status of all believers and their practice of love toward one another. As we read in *Instructions for the Visitors of Parish Pastors in Electoral Saxony*:

> The people are to be taught that this sign has been instituted not only to awaken faith but also to instruct us in love, as Paul says in I Cor. 10: 'It is one loaf and it is one body, for we all partake of the same loaf.' We are not to harbor envy and hatred, but each is to care for the other, to help the other with alms and every kind of service that God has commanded us.[631]

Eating Flesh and Drinking Blood

According to the Fourth Gospel, Jesus declared: "Truly, truly, I say to you, unless you eat the flesh of the Son of man and drink his blood, you have no life in you. Whoever eats my flesh and drinks my blood has eternal life" (John 6:53-55).

Luther writes:

> The sixth chapter of John does not refer to the sacrament in a single syllable. Not only because the sacrament was not yet instituted, but even more because the passage itself and the sentences following plainly show that Christ is speaking of faith in the incarnate Word. He says: 'My words are spirit and life' [John 6:63], which shows that he was speaking of a spiritual eating, by which whoever eats has life.[632]

We think Luther is right. John, chapter six, is not about the Lord's Supper. We refer to John 6 here to address a misunderstanding of what is happening when we eat and drink the Lord's Supper. Opponents of the first Christians called them cannibals, because they claimed they were receiving the Lord's body and blood in the Supper. Today, those who believe that the Lord's Supper is merely symbolic say similar things about those of us who believe we receive Jesus' body and blood in the Supper. They speak as if we were literally chewing Jesus' earthly flesh and swallowing his human blood. But our understanding is not so crude. Here is Luther's explanation:

> We poor sinners are not so foolish as to believe that Christ's body is in the bread in a crude visible manner. . . .[633]

> We do not say Christ's body is present in the Supper in the same *form* in which he was given for us—who would say that?—but that it is the same body that was given for us, not in the same form or mode but in the same *essence* and nature.

> Did not Jesus eat with the disciples after his resurrection? Certainly he was no longer with them in the manner in which he had once been with them, in mortal form and limited to this life in the present world.[634]

It is his immortal, glorified body and blood our Lord gives us in his Supper.

"When Is a person rightly prepared to receive this sacrament?"[635] Luther asks with regard to this sacrament in the Small Catechism. His answer is:

> Fasting and outward preparations serve a good purpose. However, that person is well prepared and worthy who believes these words, *given and shed for you for the remission of sins*. But anyone who does not believe these words, or doubts them, is neither prepared nor worthy, for the words *for you* require simply a believing heart.

In his Large Catechism Luther writes:

> Whoever hears these words and believes that they are true *has* what the words declare. But whoever does not believe

The Sacrament of Holy Communion | 235

has nothing, but lets this gracious blessing to be offered in vain and refuses to enjoy it. The treasure is opened and placed at everyone's door, yes, on everyone's table, but it is your responsibility to take it and confidently believe that it is just as the words tell you.

Since this treasure is fully offered in the words, it can be grasped and appropriated only by the heart. Such a gift and eternal treasure cannot be seized by the hand. Fasting and prayer and the like may have their place as an outward preparation and children's exercise so that one's body may behave properly and reverently toward the body and blood of Christ. But what is given in and with the sacrament cannot be grasped and appropriated by the body. This is done by the faith of the heart which discerns and desires this treasure.

But suppose you say, "What if I feel that I am unfit?"

People with such misgivings must learn that it is the highest wisdom to realize that this sacrament does not depend upon our worthiness. We are not baptized because we are worthy and holy, nor do we come to confession pure and without sin; on the contrary, we come as poor, miserable people, precisely because we are unworthy.[636]

Certainly Luther is in agreement with what Philip Melanchthon wrote in *Instructions for the Visitors of Parish Pastors in Electoral Saxony*: "It shall be taught that they alone are worthy to receive the sacrament who show true repentance and sorrow for their sins. . . ."[637]

And yet, Luther urges us not to trust in our repentance, but to trust solely in Jesus' promise of forgiveness; for how can we ever be sure that our repentance is true or sincere. In Luther's words:

God's promise in the sacrament is sure; our contrition is never sure. For this reason God would have us build not on our uncertain contrition, but on God's sure promise, so we may be able to persist in every time of trouble.[638]

Through no attitude on your part will you become worthy, through no works will you be prepared for the sacrament, but through faith alone, for only faith in the word of Christ justifies, makes a person alive, worthy, and well prepared. Without faith all other things are acts of presumption and desperation. A just person lives not by his or her attitude but by faith. For this reason you should not harbor any doubt because of your unworthiness. You go to the sacrament because you are unworthy and so that you may be made worthy and be justified by him who seeks to save sinners and not the righteous. When, however, you believe Christ's word, you honor it and thereby are righteous.[639]

Should the Lord's Supper be Withheld from Anyone?

In Luther's thinking, the sacrament should be withheld from someone *only* because of unbelief *or* refusal to repent of sin *or* ignorance regarding the sacrament. Of this last reason, he writes:

> We do not intend to admit to the sacrament and administer it to those who do not know what they seek or why they come.[640]

> People run by custom to the sacrament and do not know why they should use the sacrament. Thus, whoever does not know why the sacrament should be received is not to be admitted to it.[641]

> No one shall be admitted to the sacrament who has not previously been to the pastor, who shall inquire if that person rightly understands the sacrament, or is in need of further counsel, etc.[642]

Should Children Receive the Lord's Supper?

As we have just seen, Luther is convinced: "One ought to give the sacrament to no one who is unable to explain what is being received and why he or she goes to the sacrament."[643]

Does this mean Luther would exclude children from the Lord's Table? No. At least not if the parents, in league with their pastor, properly prepare their children. As Luther writes:

> Let every head of a household remember it is a personal duty, by God's injunction and command, to teach or have taught to his or her children the things they ought to know. Since they are baptized and received into the Christian church, they should also enjoy this fellowship of the sacrament so that they may serve us and be useful, for they must all help us to believe, to love, to pray, and to fight the devil.[644]

What about infants? Some pastors and people advocate giving the sacrament to infants (an accepted practice in Orthodox churches for a thousand years.) It is doubtful Luther would approve. After all, can infants "know what they seek and why they come"?[645] Are infants "able to explain what they are receiving or why"?[646]

Some advocates of infant communion argue that, in contrast to many adults, infants are open and unopposed to what God does in their lives; therefore, we should not withhold the benefits of the Supper from them. Consider these comments by Luther:

> It is heresy to hold that the sacraments give grace to those who place no obstacle in the way.
>
> I continue to hold and insist that this doctrine is un-Christian, misleading, and heretical. . . . The reception of the sacrament requires not only genuine repentance for sin, but the worthy reception of the sacraments also requires that there be a firm faith within the heart.[647]

Differences in Understanding the Lord's Supper

It is ironic that the Lord's Supper, which is designed by Jesus to unite us with him and with one another, has become a divisive issue among Christians. We simply do not agree on what the Supper is or what Jesus intends it to be.

Roman Catholics believe and teach that:

> . . . the bread and wine are *changed* into the body and blood of Christ. By the power of Christ working through the priest the bread and wine, though appearing to be bread and wine, become Christ.[648]

Baptists believe and teach that the Lord's Supper is simply "bread and wine" which *symbolize* the broken body and shed blood of Jesus for us on the cross. Therefore believers eat this bread and drink this wine in order to remember and to give thanks for Jesus' sacrifice in our behalf.

Lutherans believe and teach that "Holy Communion is the body and blood of our Lord Jesus Christ *given with* bread and wine. . . ."

We agree with Roman Catholics and Baptists that Jesus' death on the cross is at the heart of Holy Communion. That is, we believe that what Christ offered once for all on the cross—his body and his blood—he gives to us again in the bread and wine of his Supper. In Luther's words:

> God's divinity is not given to us unconcealed; for God said, 'Human beings shall not see me and live.' God must be disguised in flesh and blood, in the Word, in the outward ministry, in baptism, and in the Lord's Supper where we receive Christ's body and blood in bread and wine to eat and to drink. God must be concealed in forms to which the Word is added, so that we may hear of God's presence. Then the Word is not an empty sound; the bread is not

plain bread; the wine not plain wine; and baptism not simple, common water. To be sure, it remains water, bread, and wine, but not only that; it is now called God's bread, God's Word, God's water, God's flesh, and God's blood.[649]

Sacrament or Symbol?

Baptists and other Christians today readily believe that Jesus fed the five thousand with five small loaves of bread and two relish-size fish. But they do not believe that the exalted risen Christ gives us his glorified body and blood in and through the bread and wine of the Lord's Supper.

They understand the Supper to be a memorial meal that is symbolic of what Jesus accomplished on the cross—giving his body and shedding his blood to redeem us from sin, death, and evil. They understand Jesus' words, "This *is* my body" and "This *is* my blood of the covenant" to mean "This *symbolizes* my body" and "This *symbolizes* my blood."

Luther takes Jesus' words to mean what they say, "This *is* my body; this *is* my blood." He rejects a symbolic view of the Supper and declares:

> They say it is not fitting that Christ's body and blood should be in the bread and wine. . . .
>
> I might say equally well that it is not reasonable that God should come from heaven and enter into the womb; that he who nourishes, sustains, and encompasses all the world should tolerate being nourished and encompassed by the Virgin. Likewise, that Christ, a king of glory, at whose feet all angels must fall and before whom all creatures must tremble, should thus humble himself below all people and allow himself to be suspended upon the cross as a most notorious evil-doer and that by the most wicked and desperate of men. And I might conclude from this that God did not become a human being, or that the crucified Christ was not God.[650]
>
> The glory of our God is precisely that for our sakes God comes down to the very depths, into human flesh, into the bread, into our mouth, our heart, our bosom; moreover, for our sakes God consents to be treated ingloriously on the cross, and on the altar, as St. Paul says in I Corinthians 11, that some eat the bread in an unworthy manner.[651]

Gift or Sacrifice?

A fundamental disagreement between Lutherans and Roman Catholics concerns what happens in the celebration of the Lord's Supper. Roman Catholics believe and teach:

Christ offered himself to his Father once upon the cross. He continues to offer himself, day after day, minute after minute in that re-offering of his sacrifice of Calvary in which we now have a part, the eucharistic sacrifice of the Mass.[652]

We agree that Christ offered himself "*once* upon the cross," but we do not agree that "he continues to offer himself, day after day" in what we know as the Lord's Supper. Neither do we agree that he "offered himself to his Father." Quite the opposite. As Luther writes:

> Where is it written, that the mass is a sacrifice, or where has Christ taught that one should offer consecrated bread and wine to God? Do you not hear? Christ has sacrificed himself *once*; henceforth he will not be sacrificed by anyone else. He wishes us to remember his sacrifice. Why are you then so bold as to make a sacrifice out of this remembrance? Is it possible that you are so foolish as to act upon your own devices, without any scriptural authority?[653]

Indeed, "scriptural authority" is quite clear: "Christ has appeared *once for all* at the end of the age to remove sin by the sacrifice of himself" (Hebrews 9:26). Cf. Hebrews 7:27; 9:12, 28; 10:10; Romans 6:10; 1 Peter 3:18. And, "For by *a single offering* he has perfected for all time those who are sanctified" (Hebrews 10:14; cf. Hebrews 10:12).

Notice, in particular, that Roman Catholic doctrine maintains that *the very sacrifice* that took place on the cross is "renewed" on the altar in what is called "the sacrifice of the mass," and is offered to God the Father, again and again, at each and every mass. As this doctrine asserts:

> That one comprehensive and final, unique and sacrificial death of Jesus Christ takes place at the Mass; not a new sacrificial death, but the same sacrificial death renewed. That which happens on the altar during the Consecration is in truth the same as the sacrifice of the cross, and so it remains the very core and center of our religion.
>
> The priest takes the paten with the host saying: "Receive, O holy Father, almighty and eternal God, this spotless host"; and after that, takes the chalice with the wine saying: "*We offer* unto thee, O Lord, the chalice of salvation, beseeching thee thy clemency that it may ascend as a sweet odor before thy divine majesty, for our own salvation, and for that of the world. Amen."[654]

In contrast to this doctrine, Jesus says of the cup, "This is my blood of the covenant poured out *for many*," (Mark 14:24; Matthew 26:28; cf.

Hebrews 9:28). And we read in I Peter 3:18 "Christ died for sins once *for all*, the righteous *for the unrighteous*". As Luther believes and teaches:

> We must clearly distinguish here between what *we offer* and what we do *not* offer in the mass.
>
> We should, therefore, give careful heed to this word 'sacrifice,' so that we do not presume to give God something in the sacrament, when it is *God* who in it gives us all things.
>
> What sacrifices, then, are we to offer? Ourselves and all that we have, with constant prayer that 'Thy will be done, on earth as it is in heaven'. With this we are to yield ourselves to God's will to make of us what suits and pleases God. In addition we are to offer whole hearted praise and thanksgiving for the unspeakable, sweet grace and mercy that God has promised and given us in this sacrament.[655]

What Creates the Lord's Supper?

Is it the God-given power of the priest to change bread and wine into Christ's body and blood as Roman Catholics claim?[656] Is it the consecrating authority of a priest who has been properly ordained within the historic episcopate as Episcopalians declare?[657] Is it the eucharistic prayer, "Pour out your Holy Spirit . . . on these gifts of bread and wine"? or ". . . we ask you . . . with your Word and Holy Spirit to bless us . . . and these your own gifts of bread and wine"?[658] Could it be "the laying on of hands" by the pastor upon the elements of the Supper, as we sometimes see?

It is none of these things. No New Testament teaching or early church practice supports such suppositions. *What,* then, makes the Lord's Supper what it is meant to be? It is the word of the Lord himself, who is present with those who gather in his name to do as he directed, "Do this in remembrance of me." As Martin Luther puts it again and again:

> *The Word* must make the element a sacrament; otherwise it remains a mere element. No saint on earth or angel in heaven can transform bread and wine into Christ's body and blood.[659]
>
> It is not by *our* doing, speaking or work that bread and wine become Christ's body and blood, much less is it by the chrism or consecration. It is rather *Christ's command and institution*. For Christ commanded that when we meet together and speak his words with reference to bread and wine, then it is to be his body and blood. Here, too, we do

nothing more than administer and bestow bread and wine along with his words. So it is not our work or speaking but the command and ordinance of Christ that make the bread the body and the wine the blood.[660]

As we read in *Instructions for the Visitors of Parish Pastors:* "It is to be remembered that so great a miracle happens through no merit of the priest but because Christ has ordained that when we commune his body is present."[661]

Who Should Officiate at the Lord's Supper?

As indicated earlier Luther gave no credence to the doctrine that a God-ordained order of priests has been given the unique power (denied to others) to transform bread and wine into Christ's body and blood. Luther goes so far as to say, "I will not tolerate the '*superpriest*' in this common and universal sacrament."[662] That is, he will not tolerate the idea that by virtue of ordination a priest has a unique role to play in the Lord's Supper.

Notice Luther's words, "this common and universal sacrament." He holds that the Lord's Supper is Christ's gift to the entire assembly of believers and that every believer is qualified "to consecrate or to administer the sacred bread and wine."[663] He writes accordingly:

> We hold that this function, too, like the priesthood, belongs to all, and this we assert, not on our own authority, but that of Christ who at the Last Supper said, 'Do this in remembrance of me.' . . . Christ spoke this word to *all* those present and to those who in the future would be at the table, to eat this bread and to drink this cup. So it follows that what is given here is given to all.
>
> A further witness is the word of Paul in 1 Cor. 11, "For I received from the Lord what I also delivered to you," etc. Here Paul addresses all the Corinthians, making each of them, as he himself was, a consecrator.[664]

Luther is on solid ground here. Nowhere do the authors of the New Testament suggest that only certain individuals are authorized to administer the Lord's Supper. Further, as William Barclay writes: "There is no evidence from the earliest time that the celebration of the Eucharist was a priestly function or an episcopal function."[665]

Nevertheless, by the middle of the second century C.E., celebrating the Lord's Supper, along with other duties, became the responsibility of a single pastoral leader in most congregations—probably as a measure to guard against false teachings within the congregation and against opposition from without. But as Barclay writes: "It is at least possible to argue that the Church took the wrong way when it took from the layman the right to celebrate the sacraments and confined it to either an ecclesiastical or a priestly class."[666]

But if *any Christian* may celebrate the Lord's Supper (and as Luther also declares, if any Christian may preach, baptize, and absolve others from sin), why do we normally commit this responsibility to an ordained pastor? We do so for the sake of *good order* (1 Corinthians 14:40). As Luther writes:

> Because we are all priests of equal standing, no one must push forward and take [the pastoral office], without our consent and election, to do that for which we all have equal authority. For no one dare take for one's self what is common to all without the authority and consent of the community.[667]

> It is true that all Christians are priests, but not all are pastors. For to be a pastor one must be not only a Christian and a priest but must have been charged with an office and a field of work. This call and command make pastors and preachers.

> For God's will is that nothing be done as a result of one's own choice or decision, but everything as a consequence of a command or a call.[668]

In Luther's view, then, the difference between a pastor and others in a particular community of faith is simply that the pastor has been *called* to carry out certain duties *in behalf of* that community.

Luther's view is in sharp contrast to the teaching of other denominations. Anglicans, for example, teach that "there has always been a clear distinction between clergy and the laity;" a distinction, not of function, but of "status," "order," and "character."[669] Indeed, Anglicans teach that ordained ministry "is not an extension of the common Christian priesthood but belongs to another realm of the gifts of the Spirit."[670]

Luther finds no warrant for such teaching in the New Testament and says so in several of his writings.[671] As Heinrich Bornkamm writes:

> By restoring its New Testament meaning to the priesthood (I Peter 1:5; Revelation 1:6; 5:10) Luther abolished the notion that a special class is required in order to perform certain functions. He thereby cleansed Christendom of *an element quite alien* to the message of Jesus.[672]

The Sacrament of Holy Communion

Celebrating the Lord's Supper

Luther writes:

> In order that we might safely and happily attain to a true and free knowledge of this sacrament, we must be particularly careful to put aside whatever has been added to its original simple institution by human zeal and devotion: such things as vestments, ornaments, chants, prayers, organs, candles, and the whole pageantry of outward things. We must turn our eyes and hearts simply to the institution of Christ and this alone, and set nothing before us but the very word of Christ by which he instituted the sacrament, made it perfect, and committed it to us. For in that word, and in that word alone, reside the power, the nature, and the whole substance of the mass.[673]

It is ironic that in celebrating the Lord's Supper some clergy seem quite caught up in "the whole pageantry of outward things;" outward things such as burses, veils, corporals, palls, patens, purificators, proper vestments, gestures, and positions.[674] As Luther would be the first to say, such things and practices are not "wrong." Care, respect, and good order are always important in public worship. The question is, do such practices contribute to or detract from what is central in the celebration of the Lord's Supper?

In Luther's mind we should do what we can to emphasize what is central in the sacraments, "the very word of Christ," in which "reside the power, the nature and the whole substance" of both sacraments. As he writes:

> We should do nothing with greater zeal than to set before our eyes, meditate upon, and ponder the words of Christ in order to exercise, nourish, increase, and strength our faith in them.[675]

Differing Communion Practices

Lutheran congregations differ quite a bit in their communion practices—practices that go beyond what is called "high church" ritual with burses, palls, incense, etc. or "low church" ritual with unadorned bread and wine.

To begin with, congregations differ in how the elements of Holy Communion are presented. Certain congregations practice bringing bread and wine to the table or altar as part of the offering. As advocates of this practice put it: "The offering of the bread and wine is a sign of what human labor has done to the gifts of God—making wheat into bread and grapes into wine. Thus we offer our whole selves and our whole lives to him."[676] A further interpretation of this practice might be: The Lord takes what we have and offer, blesses it, and in and through it offers us his very self.

Other congregations begin the hour of worship with the bread and wine already on the table, as an indication that the Lord's Supper comes from God to us.

Another practice in many congregations is the custom of calling the Lord's Supper, "the Eucharist." Eucharist is an ancient title and for that reason is revered by many. But what does this title mean and where did it come from? *Eucharist* is the Greek word for thanksgiving, a word used in the New Testament when Jesus gave thanks before breaking the bread for distribution at the Last Supper. As Luther points out:

> ... the ancients called this office *eucharistia* or *sacramentum eucharistie*, that is, a thanksgiving. For in this sacrament we should thank God according to Christ's command, and we should use and receive the sacrament with thanks. In the course of time, however, through misunderstanding, this word came to be applied only to the sacrament.[677]

Luther is quite right. Many people today use the word only as a name for the sacrament, without further thought as to the meaning of the word. This is why it would be well for pastors to occasionally preach on the meaning and purpose of the sacrament.

Paul, of course, uses the titles "the Lord's Supper" and "the table of the Lord" (1 Corinthians 11:20; 10:21) which clearly emphasize who is the host, the giver, and the gift in the sacrament. In Luther's words:

> We know that the Supper is the Lord's in name and in reality, not the supper of Christians. For the Lord not only instituted it, but also prepares and gives it himself, and is himself cook, butler, food, and drink. . . ."[678]

Many congregations celebrate the Lord's Supper by placing Jesus' words of institution within what is called a eucharistic prayer. Advocates of eucharistic prayer appeal to "the wider practice of the Christian church" (Roman Catholic, Eastern Orthodox, and Anglican). They think "the barrenness" of setting the words of institution apart as declaration has "obscured the richness of prayer, praise, and thanksgiving."[679]

Originally, of course, Jesus' words of institution were not a prayer, but a pledge and invitation from Jesus to his disciples. Indeed, it might be said that to place Jesus' words of institution within a prayer tends to obscure the purpose of his words as pledge and promise, because it intermingles what he says within what we are saying. In Luther's penetrating words:

> We must separate the mass clearly and distinctly from ceremonies and prayers that have been added to it by the holy fathers. We must keep these two as far apart as heaven and earth, so that the mass may remain nothing else than the testament and sacrament comprehended in Christ's words.[680]

Is the Lord's Supper a Necessity?

In Luther's mind the Lord's Supper is Christ's priceless gift to us. Is it absolutely necessary? No. Is it needful? Yes. Could one do without it? Yes. Should one do without it? No.

On the one hand, as Luther writes:

> The Eucharist is not so necessary that salvation depends on it. The gospel and baptism are sufficient, since faith alone justifies and love alone lives rightly.[681]

> It is certainly true that you can have life, righteousness, and salvation without the sacrament, but you cannot have life, righteousness, and salvation without the Word, even though you were to receive the sacrament not only three times a day, but even three times an hour.[682]

> Paul says, 'One believes with the heart and so it justified.' He doesn't say that it is necessary to receive the sacraments, for one can become righteous by faith without the sacraments (so long as one does not despise them). But without faith, no sacrament is of any use, indeed, it is altogether deadly and pernicious.[683]

On the other hand he writes:

> We go to the sacrament because we receive there a great treasure, through and in which we obtain the forgiveness of sins. Why? Because the words are there through which this is imparted! Christ bids me eat and drink in order that the sacrament may be mine and may be a source of blessing to me as a sure pledge and sign—indeed, as the very gift he has provided for me against my sins, death, and all evils.[684]

> Those who claim to be Christians should prepare themselves to receive this blessed sacrament frequently.[685]

> It was no idle jest or plan when God established and instituted this sacrament for us human beings. Therefore

God does not want to have it despised, neglected, or unused; much less does God want us to regard it as unnecessary and insignificant. Rather, God wants us to exercise ourselves in its use faithfully.[686]

A Summary of the Meaning and Practice of the Lord's Supper
- The Lord's Supper is *an eating and drinking* established by Jesus for his followers.
- The Lord's Supper is *a pledge* of Jesus' self-giving sacrifice for us and *a means* of participating in his body and blood.
- The Lord's Supper is *a covenant* in which Jesus binds himself to us, and we are bound to him and to one another in a community of faith, a covenant sealed by the blood of Jesus for the forgiveness of sins.
- *The sign* of the Lord's Supper is eating and drinking the bread and wine of the Supper; its *significance* is the fellowship Jesus creates, as together, we receive his body and blood in and with the bread and wine.
- When we eat *this* bread and drink *this* wine, we "remember him," that is, we *actively respond* to him in faith; and, in doing so, we proclaim his death until he comes.

ENDNOTES

LSC The Small Catechism, Martin Luther, *The Book of Concord*, T.G. Tappert, trans. & ed. (Philadelphia: Muhlenberg Press, 1959), 338-356.

LC The Large Catechism, Martin Luther, *The Book of Concord*, T.G. Tappert, trans. & ed. (Philadelphia: Muhlenberg Press, 1959), 357-461.

WA *Weimar Ausgabe*, D. Martin Luthers Werke, (Weimar: Kritische Gesamtausgabe), 1883ff.

LW *Luther's Works:* American Edition, Jaroslav Pelikan & Helmut T. Lehman, general eds. (St. Louis: Concordia Publishing House / Philadelphia: Fortress Press), 1955ff.

HK Haus- & Kirchen-Postille: *The Complete Sermons of Martin Luther*, J. Lenker & E. Klug, eds, Vols. 1-7 (Grand Rapids: Baker Books, 2000).

HK Haus- & Kirchen- Postille: *The Complete Sermons of Martin Luther*, J. Lenker & E. Klug, eds. (Grand Rapids: Baker Books, 2000), vols. 1-7.

[1] Gordon Rupp, *The Righteous of God* (London: Hodder and Stoughton, 1953), 84.

[2] WA 5:176.

[3] WA 1:361 [LW 31:51]; WA 13:657 [LW 20:136]; WA 7:52 [LW 31:348].

[4] WA 13:113 [LW 18:111]; cf. WA 45:229-230, 240 [LW 12:118; 135]; WA 36:569 [LW 28:124].

[5] WA 8:685 [LW 45:70].

[6] WA 10-2:40 [LW 36:265, 266].

[7] WA 19:76 [LW 53:64].

[8] The letters CE abbreviate the words Common Era (the era common to Christians and Jews). Previously scholars spoke of the years before Jesus' birth as BC (before Christ) and the years after his birth as AD (*Anno Domini*, Latin for year of the Lord). In deference to the Jewish people, scholars today use BCE (before the common era) and CE (common era) to identify the years before and after Jesus' birth.

[9] WA 30-1:128 [LC:361].

[10] *The Book of Concord*, T. G. Tappert, trans. & ed. (Philadelphia: Muhlenberg Press, 1959), 339.

[11] WA 30-1:126, 126-127 [LC:359].

[12] WA 39-2:199 [LW 34:316-317].

[13] WA 14:631-632 [LW 9:94].

[14] WA 6:356 [LW 35:83].

[15] WA 42:503 [LW 2:337].

[16] WA 50:316-317 [LW 47:71].

[17] WA 45:701 [LW 24:263].

[18] WA 44:703 [LW 8:170]; cf. WA 30-1:178 [LC:407]; WA 26:204 [LW 40:277]; WA 39-1:542; WA 39-2:274; etc.

[19] WA 10-1-1:675 [LW 52:245].

[20] WA 5:171.

[21] WA 14:640 [LW 9:112]

[22] WA 7:801 [LW 44:241].

[23] WA 30-1:133 [LC:365];cf. WA 19:384 [LW 19:186-187].

[24] WA 30-1:243 [LSC:342].

[25] WA 20:65 [LW 15:55].

[26] WA 45:596 [LW 24:148].

[27] WA 41:148 [LW 13:289, 290].

[28] WA 6:209 [LW 44:30].

[29] WA 30-1:135 [LC:367].

[30] WA 11:446 [LW 36:293]; cf. WA 1011:715 [LW 52:277]; WA 45:651 [LW 24:209]; WA 4:243 [LW 11:377].

[31] *Theology Today*, Vol. 57, No. 3:378.

[32] WA 30-1:134, 135f, 136 [LC:366, 367, 368].

[33] WA 6:209 [LW 44:30].

[34] WA 14:611, 642 [LW 9:70, 117].

35 WA 6:233-234 [LW 44:60].
36 WA 30-1:139 [LC:371].
37 WA 31-2:570 [LW 17:397].
38 WA 43:442-443 [LW 5:21].
39 WA 42:631 [LW 3:117].
40 WA 40-2:329 [LW 12:312].
41 WA 40-2:329 [LW 12:312]; cf. WA 14:577 [LW 9:41]; WA 45:523 [LW 24:68].
42 Exodus 3:14; 33:19.
43 WA 42:48 [LW 1:65].
44 Dietrich Bonhoeffer, *Christ the Center* (New York: Harper and Row, 1960/66), 107.
45 Ibid., 59.
46 Ibid., 22.
47 See Claude Tresmontant, *A Study of Hebrew Thought* (New York: Decslee Company, 1960), 46-47.
48 Cf. Johannes Pedersen, *Israel: Its Life and Culture*, Vol. I (Copenhagen: Branner Og Korch, 1926), 245-249.
49 "The *Shield* of Abraham" (Genesis 15:1); "the *Fear* of Isaac" (Genesis 31:42, 53); "the *Rock* of Israel" (Genesis 49:24); "the *Shield*" (Deuteronomy 33:29), "the *Fear*" (cf. Isaiah 2:10, 19, 21; Job 25:2) and "the *Rock*" (2 Samuel 23:3; Isaiah 30:29; cf. Deuteronomy 32:4; etc.) of the whole people of Israel.
50 WA 30-1:140 [LC:371].
51 WA 30-1:243f [LSC:342].
52 WA 30-1:243F [LW:51:142].
53 WA 40-2:296 [LW 12:81].
54 Martin Buber, *Moses* (Oxford: East & West Library, 1946), 132.
55 Ibid., 132.
56 Martin Buber, *The Prophetic Faith* (New York: Macmillan, 1949), 53, 54.
57 WA 30-1:151 [LC:383].
58 WA 30-1:67 [LW 51:147]; cf. WA 30-1:148 [LC:380]; WA 26:86-87 [LW 28:336-337].
59 WA 6:39 [LW 45:278].
60 WA 8:624 [LW 44:327].
61 WA 8:623 [LW 44:326].
62 WA 30-1:244 [LSC:342].
63 WA 30-1:144 [LC:376].
64 WA 30-1:145 [LC:377]; cf. WA 16:375 [LW 35:166].
65 WA 30-1:244 [LSC:343].
66 WA 30-1:111 [LW 51:183f]; cf. WA 301:214 [LC:439].
67 WA 30-1:156 [LC:388]; cf. WA 42:635 [LW 3:122]; WA 44:648 [LW 8:94].
68 Patrick Miller, *The Ten Commandments* (Louisville: Westminster John Knox Press, 2009), 223ff.
69 WA 11:251 [LW 45:91].
70 WA 11:248 [LW 45:87].
71 WA 30-1:244 [LSC:343].
72 WA 56:473 [LW 25:464].
73 WA 30-1:244 [LSC:343].
74 WA 30-1:159 [LC:390-391].
75 WA 30-1:160 [LC:391].
76 WA 6:207 [LW 44:26-27].
77 *The Ten Commandments*, 276.
78 Paul Tournier, *The Meaning of Persons* (New York: Harper & Row, 1957), 211f.
79 WA 30-1:244F [LSC:343].
80 Isaiah 54:5; 61:10; 62:5; Jeremiah 3:20; 22:32; 31:32; Hosea 2:7, 16; Mark 2:18-20 /Matthew 9:14f / Luke 5:33f; John 3:29; 2 Corinthians 11:2; Ephesians 5:25-32; Revelation 19:7ff; 21:2, 9; 22:17.
81 WA 30-1:245 [LSC:343].
82 WA 30-1:168 [LC:399].
83 WA 6:273 [LW 44:110].
84 Arlen Erdahl, Blue Earth, Minnesota.
85 WA 36:626 [LW 28:166].
86 WA 30-1:245 [LSC:343].
87 WA 30-1:171 [LC:401].
88 WA 30-1:174 [LC:404]; cf. WA 40-2:118-119 [LW 27:94]; WA 12:352 [LW 30:97].
89 WA 30-1:245f [LSC:343].
90 WA 30-1:85 [LW 51:161].
91 WA 30-1:180 [LC:408].
92 WA 30-1:247 [LSC:344].
93 Deuteronomy 4:24; 5:9; 6:15; Psalm 79:5; Ezekiel 39:25; Joel 2:18; Nahum 1:2; Zechariah 1:14.
94 WA 13:561 [LW 20:19].
95 WA 2:546 [LW 27:305].
96 WA 10-1-1:11 [LW 35:119].
97 WA 30-1:137-138 [LC:370].
98 WA 7:350 [LW 32:33].
99 Cf. William Barclay, *The Gospel of Matthew*, Vol. 2 (Philadelphia: Westminster Press, 1957), 24.
100 WA 49:598 [LW 51:341f].
101 WA 32:357 [LW 21:70].

[102] WA 10-1-1:11, 12 [LW 35:119, 120]; cf. WA 17-2:7 [HK 4.1:9].

[103] WA 33:37 [LW 23:28].

[104] WA 46:657-665 [LW 22:139-148].

[105] WA 40-1:209 [LW 26:117].

[106] WA 16:371-372, 373, 374 [LW 35:164, 165]; cf. WA 42:608 [LW 3:85]; WA 14:621-622 [LW 9:81]; etc.

[107] WA 18:81 [LW 40:98].

[108] WA 18:80 [LW 40:97]; cf. WA 50:331, 471 [LW 47:90, 110]; WA 2:580 [LW 27:355].

[109] Philip S. Watson, *Let God Be God!* (Philadelphia: Muhlenberg Press, 1947) 158.

[110] WA 39-1:455; cf. WA 14:632 [LW 9:94]; WA 43:213 [LW 4:149-160].

[111] WA 40-1:479-480, 673-674 [LW 26:308-309, 448]; To give us "a pattern . . ." WA 39-2:274; cf. WA 44:703 [LW 8:170]; WA 30-1:178 [LC:407]; WA 39-1:542; WA 26:204 [LW 40:277]; WA 18:693 [LW 33:150].

[112] WA 40-1:431, 523-525, 534-537 [LW 26:276, 340-341, 349-350]; cf. WA 40-2:352ff [LW 12:328ff, 374]; WA 2:498 [LW 27:232]; WA 39-1:356, 432, 474, 500, 510, 513.

[113] WA 40-1:368 [LW 26:232]; cf. WA 56:272 [LW 25:260]; LW 27:230ff; 32:23, 246; 38:158; etc.

[114] WA 40-1:537 [LW 26:350].

[115] WA 41:130 [LW 13:271].

[116] WA 23:622 [LW 20:297].

[117] WA 50:262 [LW 34:201].

[118] WA 10-1-1:715 [LW 52:277]; cf. WA 44:329 [LW 7:37]; WA 3:282 [LW 10:232].

[119] WA 32:353-354 [LW 21:66]; cf. [WA :4:391 [LW 11:532].

[120] WA 47:83 [LW 22:358].

[121] Jude 3.

[122] WA 40-1:128-129, 130 [LW 26:63, 64].

[123] See Kenneth Scott Latourette, *A History of Christianity* (New York: Harper & Brothers, 1953), 151ff.

[124] WA 10-2:389 [LW 43:24, 25].

[125] WA 40-1:343-344, 345 [LW 26:214].

[126] WA 10-1-1:216 [LW 52:67].

[127] WA 30-1:250 [LSC:345].

[128] WA 30-1:250 [LSC:345].

[129] WA 33:286, 388 [LW 23:181]; cf. WA 8:608 [LW 44:296f]; WA 40-1:130, 163-164 [LW 26:64, 88]; WA 8:111 [LW 32:235]; WA 39-1:91 [LW 34:160]; etc.

[130] WA 40-2:421, 422 [LW 12:376-377, 377f].

[131] Oscar A. Anderson, Augsburg University.

[132] WA 40-1:361-362 [LW 26:227-228]; cf. WA 41:231 [LW 13:344]; WA 5:68 [LW 14:342]; WA 33:611 [LW 23:377]; WA 19:486 [LW 36:338].

[133] WA 41:109 [LW 13:253]; cf. WA 46:669 [LW 22:153].

[134] WA 19:207 [LW 19:55]; cf. WA 20:26 [LW 15:22]; WA 32:515 [LW 21:260].

[135] *Journal*, 15 June 1741.

[136] WA 18:164 [LW 40:175]; cf. WA 51:127, 128-129, 133 [LW 51:374, 376, 379].

[137] WA 44:77 [LW 6:104].

[138] WA 33:127 [LW 23:84].

[139] WA 39-1:175 [LW 34:137] cf. WA 51:211, 212 [LW 13:160, 161].

[140] Cf. WA 40-1:418, 443, 447 [LW 26:267f, 284, 287]; WA 40-2:394f [LW 12:358]; WA 6:291 [LW 39:63]; WA 10-1-1:210 [LW 52:62]; WA 46:21 [LW 24:321]; WA TR 1:191 [LW 54:71].

[141] WA 43:28 [LW 3:214]; cf. WA 26:337 [LW 37:224]; WA 11:410f [LW 39:308].

[142] WA 33:127 [LW 23:84].

[143] WA 40-2:306 [LW 12:88].

[144] WA 40-1:447 [LW 26:287].

[145] WA 19:583-584 [LW 14:244-245]; cf. WA BR 2:431, 433 [LW 48:375, 379]; WA 42:566-567 [LW 3:24-25]; WA 40-2:48-49 [LW 27:38-39].

[146] WA 40-1:182, 212-213 [LW 26:99-100, 119].

[147] WA 18:652 [LW 33:88]; cf. WA 17-2:233 [HK 1.2:176].

[148] "Jesus is Lord" (Romans 10:9; 1 Corinthians 12:3); "Jesus is the Son of God" (1 John 4:15; 5:5); "Jesus is the Christ" (John 20:31; 1 John 5:10); Then they were baptized "in the name of Jesus Christ" (Acts 2:38).

[149] "With God, the Three in One" (from hymn, "The Church's One Foundation"); "great One in Three" (from hymn, "Come, Thou Almighty King"); "God in three persons, blessed Trinity" (from hymn, "Holy, Holy, Holy").

[150] Raymond Brown, *The Gospel According to John* (Garden City, Doubleday, 1970), 632.

[151] WA 40-1:98 [LW 26:42]; See John 4:34; 5:26ff; 6:37ff; 7:16, 28f; 8:26ff, 42; 10:18;, 32, 37f; 12:49; 15:15; cf. Matthew 10:40 / Luke 10:16; Mark 9:37 / Luke 9:48; Luke 4:18.

152 J. S. Whale, *Christian Doctrine* (Cambridge: Cambridge University Press, 1950,) 116.
153 WA 10-1-2:294 [HK 2.1:406f]; cf. WA 46:436.
154 Cf. WA 8:117-118 [LW 32:244].
155 Cf. WA 26:501ff [LW 37:361ff]; etc.
156 Leif Grane, *The Augsburg Confession: A Commentary* (Minneapolis: Augsburg Publishing House, 1987) 37.
157 Matthew 28:19; John 3:34; 14:15-16, 26; 15:26; Acts 7:55; 20:17ff; Romans 8:11; 14:17f; 15:15f, 30; 1 Corinthians 6:11; 2 Corinthians 13:14; Ephesians 2:18; 3:14ff; 5:18ff; 2 Thessalonians 2:13; Hebrews 9:14; 1 Peter 1:2; 4:14; 1 John 4:2; Jude 20-21.
158 Oscar Cullmann, *Die Christologie des Neuen Testaments* (Tubingen: J. C. B. Mohr, 1957), 300.
159 WA 40-2:458 [LW 12:403].
160 WA 40-1:75-76, 77 [LW 26:28].
161 Deuteronomy 6:4; Malachi 2:10, 15; cf. Deuteronomy 4:35, 39; 1 Kings 8:60; Isaiah 43:10; 44:8; 45:5-22; etc.
162 Romans 3:30; 1 Corinthians 8:4; Galatians 3:20; Ephesians 4:6; 1 Timothy 1:17; 2:5; James 2:19; Jude 1:25.
163 WA 33:81 [LW 23:55-56];cf. WA 42:295 [LW 2:48]; WA 40-1:80 [LW 26:30].
164 WA 30-1:190 [LC:419]
165 WA 46:554 [LW 22:21]; WA 42:15 [LW 1;18].
166 WA 42:15 [LW 1;18].
167 Hans Küng, *Credo* (New York: Doubleday, 1993) 152-153; *Christianity* (New York: Continuum, 1995) 95f.
168 *Credo*, 153
169 Ibid.,154.
170 WA 1:274 [LW 51:46].
171 WA 36:591-593 [LW 28:141]; cf. WA 11:457 [LW 27:171]
172 William Barclay, *The Letters to the Corinthians* (Philadelphia: Westminster Press, 1954), 169.
173 Cf. WA 43:391 [LW 4:355]; WA 43:561 [LW 5:192]; WA 44:605 [LW 8:36]; WA 40-2:205 [LW 12:13]; etc.
174 WA 32:414 [LW 21:140]; cf. WA 10-2:396[LW 43:30]; WA 42:96 [LW 1:128].
175 WA 43:564 [LW 5:197].
176 Leslie Weatherhead, *Why Do Men Suffer?* (Toronto: McClelland & Stewart, 1936), 39.
177 WA 30-1:247f [LSC:345]; cf. WA 30-1:183-184 [LC:412; WA 30-1:87, 94 [LW 51:163, 168].
178 See Herbert Girgensohn, *Teaching Luther's Catechism*, Volume I (Philadelphia: Muhlenberg Press, 1959), 134.
179 WA 44:647f [LW 8:94]; cf. WA 31-1:435-436 [LW 14:114]; WA 15:367f [LW45:326]
180 James Luther Mays, *The Lord Reigns* (Louisville: Westminster John Knox Press, 1994) 3-22.
181 H. G. Wells, *Mr. Britling Sees It Through* (New York: Macmillan, 1916) 406.
182 *Why Do Men Suffer?*, 229.
183 Proverbs 25:14; Proverbs 21:6; Job 21:34.
184 C. S. Lewis, *The Great Divorce,* (New York: Macmillan, 1946), 133f.
185 *Why Do Men Suffer?*, 90-91.
186 Ibid., 182.
187 Cf. Isaiah 63:9.
188 Paul Tournier, *The Strong and The Weak* (Philadelphia: Westminster, 1948/63), 186.
189 Adapted from a prayer by Sister Marilyn Kane, St. Luke's Catholic Church, St. Paul, Minnesota.
190 Francis A. Schaeffer, *Death in the City* (Chicago: Intervarsity Press, 1969), 100f.
191 Ibid., 101.
192 Ibid., 101.
193 WA 18:785 [LW 33:291]. WA 46:667ff [LW 22:150, 151, 152-153, 154].
194 WA 46:611 [LW 22:88]; cf. WA 45:616 [LW 24:170]; WA 312:146 [LW 16:206]; etc.
195 *A Commentary on the Holy Bible*, J. R. Dummelow, ed. (New York: Macmillan, 1908/52), xxx.
196 *Credo*, 18-19.
197 WA 42:3 [LW 1:3].
198 WA 42:17 [LW 1:22]; cf. WA 42:13, 17 [LW 1:16, 22]; WA 14:581 [LW 9:48].
199 WA 42:9 [LW 1:11]; cf. WA 3:407 [LW 10:347]; WA 13:574f [LW 20:32].
200 WA 42:13 [LW 1:16] cf. WA 13:547-548 [LW 20:4-5]; WA 18:497 [LW 14:163]; etc.
201 WA 43:222 [LW 4:120]; cf. WA 42:15 [LW 1:18]; WA 44:75 [LW 6:102].
202 WA 18:497 [LW 14:163].
203 Martin Buber, *Almanach des Schocken Verlags*, 5699 (Berlin, 1938), 20.

[204] Gerhard von Rad, *Old Testament Theology*, Vol. I (New York: Harper & Row, 1962), 146.

[205] Pages 91-93 are based on the following sources: William Barclay, *The Gospel of Matthew*, Vol. 1 (Philadelphia: Westminster Press, 1958), 1-8; Herman C. Weetjen, "The Genealogy as the Key to Matthew," *Journal of Biblical Literature*, No. 2, June, 1976, 95; D. W. Cleverley Ford, *An Expository Preacher's Notebook* (New York: Harper & Brothers, 1960), 25-29.

[206] WA 44:309, 310 [LW 7:10-11].

[207] WA 44:311 [LW 7:12].

[208] WA 44:312 [LW 7:14, 15] cf. WA 44:448 [LW 7:201].

[209] WA 10-1-1:77, 81 [LW 52:19, 22].

[210] WA 52:58 [HK 5:145].

[211] WA 52:46 [HK 5:117].

[212] WA 43:229 [LW 4:131]; cf. WA 42:356 [LW 2:134]; WA 43:371 [LW 4:326]; WA 45:640 [LW 24:198].

[213] WA 33:352 [LW 23:223].

[214] WA 40-2:508, 509 [LW 12:224, 225].

[215] *Christ the Center*, 115.

[216] *thauma*

[217] WA 30-1:249 [LSC:345].

[218] Cf. Luke 3:38; 2 Samuel 7:14/Psalms 2:7 & 89:26; Exodus 4:22/Jeremiah 31:7, 9/Hosea 11:1.

[219] Luke 3:38 (Adam), cf. Hebrews 2:14-18; Matthew 1:1 (David), cf. Luke 2:11, etc.; Matthew 1:1 (Abraham).

[220] Matthew 1:23; John 1:14; Colossians 1:19.

[221] WA 47:54 [LW 22:325]; cf. WA 40-2:256 [LW 12:51-52; WA 33:611 [LW 23:376-377].

[222] WA 45:549 [LW 24:97]; cf. WA 33:124-125 [LW 23:83]; WA 46:69-70 [LW 24:375-376].

[223] WA 5:68, 70 [LW 14:342, 343-344]; cf. WA 45:236-237 [LW 12:124]; Hans Küng, *Christianity*, 37.

[224] Otto Borchert, *Original Jesus* (London: Lutterworth, 1933) 74. Cf. Goethe's words in K. Lowith, *From Hegel to Nietzsche* (Constable, 1965) 15, "Who can demand that I love the cross if with that I am forced to share its burden?"

[225] Jürgen Moltmann, *The Crucified God* (New York: Harper & Row, 1974) 34

[226] Ibid., 37.

[227] WA 31-2:430 [LW 17:217].

[228] WA 45:236-237 [LW 12:124].

[229] Mark 10:45; Matthew 20:28; 1 Timothy 2:16; 1 Peter 1:18; Revelation 5:9.

[230] Hebrews 9:26; 10:12; 13:11-12; Ephesians 5:2.

[231] Matthew 1:21; Luke 19:10; John 12:47; 1 Corinthians 1:21; I Timothy 1:15; Titus 2:4; cf. Hebrews 2:15

[232] Galatians 3:1; 4:5; 5:1; cf. Roman 8:2

[233] Galatians 1:4; cf. Colossians 2:13-15

[234] Hebrews 2:14; 1 John 3:8.

[235] 2 Timothy 1:10; cf. Hebrews 2:15.

[236] Romans 5:10; Ephesians 2:16; Colossians 1:20; cf. 2 Corinthians 5:18

[237] Luke 9:22; 13:33; 24:7, 26; John 3:14; Hebrews 2:9, 14f.

[238] Roy Harrisville, *Fracture* (Grand Rapids: Wm. B. Eerdmans Publishing Co., 2006) 101.

[239] WA 40-1:569 [LW 26:373]; cf. WA 40-1:65, 297, 440, 441, 443, etc. [LW 26:21-22, 177, 281, 282, 284, etc.]; WA 8:21 [LW 13:21-22]; WA 31-1:418 [LW 13:377-378]; etc.

[240] Luke 23:34.

[241] Mark 15:34.

[242] Luke 23:46.

[243] John 19:30.

[244] Mark 10:45.

[245] Heinrich Bornkamm, *The Heart of the Reformation Faith* (New York: Harper & Row, 1965), 55.

[246] Isaiah 42:14.

[247] *The Crucified God*, 222.

[248] WA 5:50 [LW 14:316].

[249] *Why Do Men Suffer?*, 45 [30-53].

[250] Charles Dickens, *A Christmas Carol* (New York: Macmillan, 1950), 1.

[251] WA 32:436 [LW 21:165].

[252] WA 10-2:392 [LW 43:27]; cf. WA 32:436 [LW 21:165].

[253] WA 44:517 [LW 7:294].

[254] WA 10-2:392 [LW 43:27].

[255] WA 13:114 [LW 18:111-112].

[256] WA 45:522 [LW 24:67].

[257] WA 40-1:80 [LW 26:30]; cf. WA 40-1:77-78 [LW 26:28-29].

258 WA 28:429-430; cf. WA 36:483, 493, 557-558 [LW 28:60, 69, 116]; WA 33:104-105 [LW 23:70].

259 WA 36:605 [LW 28:150-151].

260 Exodus 13:21,22; 16:10; 19:9; 24:16; Leviticus 16:2; 1 Kings 8:11; etc.

261 Cf. WA 23:132, 142 [LW 37:64, 57].

262 WA 41:109 [LW 13:253].

263 Cf. WA DB 6:9 [LW 35:361]; cf. note 271.

264 Deuteronomy 11:11; 1 Kings 18:45; Psalms 68:8; 147:8; etc.

265 Genesis 1:8; 15:5; Psalm 19:1; etc.

266 Deuteronomy 10:14; 1 Kings 8:27; Nehemiah 9:6; Psalm 148:4; Ephesians 4:10; Hebrews 4:14; 2 Corinthians 12:2.

267 WA 23:135, 135-136 [LW 37:58, 59].

268 WA 16:371 [LW 35:164]; cf WA 54:237 [LW 41:301]; WA 18:389 [LW 46:69f]; etc.

269 WA 11:252 [LW 45:92]; cf. WA 19:629 [LW 46:99-100].

270 Omar Khayyam, *The Rubáiyát of Omar Khayyám*, First Edition, 1859, Quatrain 49 (New York: Random House, 1947), 34.

271 WA 3:17 [LW 10:14-15]; cf. WA 57-3:125 [LW 29:132]; WA 32:310 [LW 21:17];WA DB 6:9 [LW 35:361].

272 WA 30-1:249 [LSC:345].

273 See C. H. Dodd, *The Apostolic Preaching and It's Developments* (New York: Harper & Brothers, 1962).

274 Gerhard Forde, *Theology Is for Proclamation* (Minneapolis: Fortress Press, 1990), 85.

275 WA 10-1-1:9 [LW 35:117, 118]; cf. WA 56:168-169 [LW 25:148-149]; WA 12:259, 275 [LW 30:3, 19]

276 "Empowering *leaders*"—Genesis 41:38; Exodus 3:12; Numbers 27:18. "Energizing *the judges*"—Judges 3:10; 6:34; 11:29; etc. "Inspiring *the prophets*"—2 Chronicles 15:1-2; 24:20; Micah 3:8; etc. "Invigorating *skilled artists*"—Exodus 31:2-6. "Wholly enlivening"—1 Samuel 16:13.

277 Before the birth of Jesus—Luke 1:41, 67, 25-27. Empowering *John the Baptist*—Luke 1:15, 80. Wholly indwelling—Luke 3:22; 4:1, 8, 18. After the resurrection—Acts 2:4, 17.

278 WA 13:110 [LW 18:107]; cf. WA 42:423 [LW 2:228f]; WA 56:176 [LW 25:156].

279 WA 31-2:410 [LW 17:192].

280 WA 18:136 [LW 40:146]; cf. WA 42:184 [LW 1:248]; WA 26:506 [LW 37:366].

281 WA 45:472 [LW 24:13]; cf. WA 40-2:385-386 [LW 12:351-352]; WA 45:565-567 [LW 24:115-116].

282 WA 13:113 [LW 18:111].

283 WA 26:296-297 [LW 37:193]; cf. WA 23:182 [LW 37:88].

284 WA 18:136 [LW 40:213]; cf. WA 26:13, 14, 40, 41 [LW 28:230, 231, 268, 269]; WA 30-1:226 [LC:450].

285 WA 43:187 [LW 4:72]; cf. WA 31-2:118-119 [LW 16:168]; WA 45:616 [LW 24:170].

286 WA 10-2:393 [LW 43:28] cf. WA 30-1:91 [LW 51:166].

287 WA 7:69 [LW 31:371]; cf. WA 12:288 [LW 30:32f]; WA 32:422f [LW 21:149]; WA 40-2:37f [LW 27:30f].

288 WA 40-2:352, 353 [LW 12:328]; cf. WA 12:325-326 [LW 30:71]; WA 20:683 [LW 30:258].

289 WA 44:775 [LW 8:267]; cf. WA 31-2:434 [LW 17:224]; WA 20:622-624 [LW 30:229-230].

290 WA 2:535-536 [LW 27:289]; cf. WA 44:775 [LW 8:267]; WA 6:535 [LW 36:69].

291 Adolf Köberle, *The Quest for Holiness* (Minneapolis: Augsburg Publishing House, 1938), 151, 152. Cf. WA 14:63 [LW 30:190] WA 51:502 [LW 41:207].

292 WA 40-2:353 [LW 12:328-329]; cf. WA 45:615-616 [LW 24:169].

293 WA DB 7:13 [LW 35:371]; cf. WA 12:373f [LW 30:1189]; etc.

294 WA 8:123-124 [LW 32:253].

295 WA 40-1:368 [LW 26:232]; cf. WA 56:70, 269, 272 [LW 25:63, 258, 260]; LW 27:230ff; 32:23, 246; 38:158.

296 See Regin Prenter, *Spiritus Creator* (Philadelphia: Muhlenberg Press, 1953), 75.

297 WA 8:109, 111 [LW 32:232, 235].

298 WA 4:350 [LW 11:477]; cf. WA 4:313, 362, 364, 401 [LW 11:425, 494, 496, 541-542]; WA 56:441ff [LW 25:433ff].

299 WA 56:486 [LW 25:478]; cf. WA 56:239, 264 [LW 25:225, 251-252]; WA 2:536 [LW 27:289-290].

300 WA 3:47 [LW 10:53]; cf. WA 5:23 [LW 14:285].

301 *Spiritus Creator*, 97.

302 WA 56:264 [LW 25:251-252].

303 WA 7:337 [LW 32:24]; cf. WA 57:102.

304 Cf. WA 50:624-625 [LW 41:143ff]; WA 30-1:92 [LW 51:166-167].
305 WA 30-1:189 [LC:416, 416-417].
306 WA 50:625 [LW 41:144].
307 WA 10-2:393 [LW 43:28].
308 *The Interpreter's Dictionary of the Bible*, Vol. I (Nashville: Abingdon, 1962), 608.
309 WA DB 7:419, 420 [LW 35:410].
310 WA 50:628ff [LW 41:148ff]; cf. WA 6:301 [LW 39:75]; WA 42:624ff [LW 3:106ff[; WA 40-3:506f [LW13:90]; WA 31-1:232, 456 [LW 14:13, 135]; WA 11:408 [LW 39:305]; etc.
311 WA 50:629 [LW 41:150]; cf. WA 45:620-621 [LW 23:174-175; WA 8:491 [LW 36:145].
312 WA 6:560-561 [LW 36:107]; cf. WA 12:191 [LW 40:37]; WA 13:325 [LW 18:249].
313 WA 41:163, 165 [LW 13:301, 302].
314 WA 42:334 [LW 2:101]; cf. WA 31-2:145 [LW 16:205].
315 WA 42:423-424 [LW 2:229]; cf. WA 46:712-713 [LW 22:202-203].
316 Galatians 3:27-28; cf. Colossians 3:11; Romans 12:3-8; 1 Corinthians 4:6-7.
317 Romans 5:5; 8:9ff; 1 Corinthians 2:12-12; 6:19; 12:7/1 Peter 4:10; Romans 12:6-8; 1 Corinthians 7:7; 12:4-11; Hebrews 2:4.
318 1 Corinthians 12:4-11; 1 Peter 4:10-11; cf. Romans 12:4-8.
319 Ephesians 4:11-12; cf. 1 Corinthians 12:27-31.
320 WA BR 1:595 Luther refers here to 1 Peter 2:5, 9 and Revelation 1:4-5.
321 WA 6:566 [LW 36:116].
322 WA 12:317 [LW 30:63].
323 WA 10-3:309 [HK 2.2:376].
324 WA 8:486 [LW 36:138-139].
325 Paul Althaus, *The Theology of Martin Luther* (Philadelphia: Fortress Press, 1966), 314.
326 Mark 16:15; Luke 24:47; Acts 1:8; John 20:21.
327 WA 12:320, 319 [LW 30:65]; cf. WA 12:318-319 [LW 30:64-65]; WA 20:612 [LW 30:226].
328 WA 45:540 [LW 24:87-88].
329 James 5:16, 5:14; 2 Corinthians 1:11; Ephesians 6:18; 1Timothy 2:1-2.
330 WA 7:57 [LW 31:355].
331 WA 45:540 [LW 24:87]; cf. WA 32:488 [LW 21:228].
332 WA 45:540 [LW 24:87].
333 1 Thessalonians 5:21; Matthew 24:4; I John 4:1; Ephesians 5:10; 1 Corinthians 2:15, 13.
334 WA 6:410-413 [LW 44:133-136]; cf. WA 11:408-416 [LW 39:305-314]; WA 12:187ff [LW 40:31ff].
335 WA 6:412 [LW 44:135]; cf. WA 12:260, 271, LW 30:4, 15]; WA 14:32 [LW 30:168]; WA 20:736 [LW 30:291].
336 WA BR 2:522-523; cf. WA 46:21 [LW 24:321]; WA 42:515 [LW 2:353].
337 WA 17-2:7 [HK 4.1:9]; cf. WA 7:66 [LW 31:366]; WA 12:321 [LW 30:67]; WA 19:510 [LW 36:352].
338 WA 43:224 [LW 4:123].
339 WA 12:308 [LW 30:54]; cf. WA 1:530 [LW 31:86]; WA 8:252 [LW 39:23 5]; WA 12:185 [LW 40:28].
340 Ernst Käsemann, *Essays on New Testament Themes* (Philadelphia: Fortress Press, 1964/82), 63.
341 WA 12:319 [LW 30:65].
342 WA 12:179-190 [LW 40:21-34]; cf. WA 47:190 [LW 22:480].
343 WA 38:240 [LW 38:200]; cf. WA 41:187 [LW 13:317].
344 WA 8:495 [LW 36:149]; cf. WA 41:187, 207 [LW 13:317, 330-331].
345 WA 12:181 [LW 40:23]; cf. WA 47:190 [LW 22:480].
346 WA 12:179-190 [LW 40:21-34]; cf. WA 6:566 [LW 36:116].
347 WA 12:189-190 [LW 40:34-35]; cf. WA 11:451 [LW 36:298f]; WA 103:394f.
348 WA 12:190 [LW 40:35]. See pages 242-243. Luther's conviction that "to consecrate or to administer the sacred bread and wine . . . belongs to all." WA 12:182 [LW 40:24].
349 WA 6:566 [LW 36:116]; cf. WA 6:408 [LW 44:129].
350 WA 50:632f [LW 41:154].
351 WA 12:189 [LW 40:34]. WA 11:412 [LW 39:310]. WA 38:230 [LW 38:188].
352 WA 41:457.
353 WA 38:241 [LW 38:201].
354 WA 8:491 [LW 36:144-145]; cf. WA 42:334 [LW 2:101].
355 WA 12:308 [LW 30:54]; cf. WA 41:211 [LW 13:333].

356 WA 8:503 [LW 36:159]; cf. WA 32:535ff [LW 21:285ff]; WA 11:249 [LW 45:88]; WA 52:153 [HK 5:300f].

357 WA 6:408 [LW 44:129, 130]; cf. WA 60:240 [LW 13:195-196]; WA 23:663 [LW 20:346]; WA 40-1:544-545 [LW 26:356]; WA 12:130 [LW 28:43-44].

358 WA 11:413, 414 [LW 39:311, 312]; cf. WA 12:172, 189ff [LW 40:11, 34, 36ff]; WA 38:238 [LW 38:197]; WA BR 4:48ff.

359 WA 41:209 [LW 13:332]; cf. WA 12:177 [LW 45:177f].

360 WA 11:411 [LW 39:309]; cf. WA 49:590-591 [LW 51:335]; WA 47:191-192 [LW 22:482].

361 WA 15:721; LW 13:49, 331; 40:36, 37, 40; 36:304; 45:365; 51:335; WA BR 4:157-158.

362 WA 42:517 [LW 2:356-357]; cf. WA 40-1:577 [LW 26:379]; WA 33:567 [LW 23:352]; WA 42:639 [LW 3:128].

363 Marc Kolden, *The Christian's Calling in the World* (St. Paul: Centered Life, Luther Seminary, 2002), 12-13.

364 WA 8:606 [LW 44:298]; cf. WA 1:364 [LW 31:55-56]; WA 40-2:37f [LW 27:30]; WA 7:802 [LW 44:242].

365 WA 10-3:4 [LW 51:71]; cf. WA DB 6:9 [LW 35:361]; WA 47:114 [LW 22:393].

366 WA 30-1:207-208 [LC:433]; cf. WA 32:424 [LW 21:150,]; WA 30-1:105-106 [LW 51:178-179].

367 WA 30-1:105-106 [LW 51:178-179]; cf. WA 2:117ff [LW 42:65ff]; WA 44:490f [LW 7:258]; WA 32:481-482 [LW 21:220f].

368 Cf. *A Study of Hebrew Thought* (Tournai: Decslee, 1960).

369 WA 36:257 [LW 51:245]; cf. WA 36:266 [LW 51:252]; WA 46:760 [LW 22:248].

370 WA 36:662 [LW 28:190-191].

371 *Leadership Journal* (Winter, 1983): 35.

372 Luke 3:21; 5:16; 6:12; 9:18, 28-29; 10:21; 11:1-2; 22:17, 19, 41; 23:34, 46; 24:30; cf. 22:32.

373 Luke 11:1-4.

374 Luke 11:5-8.

375 Luke 11:11-13; 18:1-8;18:9-14.

376 Luke 6:28; 10:2; 20:45-47; 21:36; 22:40.

377 Luke 1:10, 13, 46-55, 67-79; 2:28-32, 37f.

378 Acts 1:14, 24; 2:42; 4:24ff; 10:1ff; etc.

379 WA 30-1:249 [LSC:346].

380 WA 45:68 [LW 24:241].

381 WA 46:85 [LW 24:393].

382 WA 45:540 [LW 24:88]; cf. WA 43:381 [LW 4:340]; WA 40-2:333 [LW 12:314f]; LW 21:235; 25:458.

383 WA 45:681 [LW 24:241]; WA 46:82f [LW 6:111]; WA 46:81 [LW 24:388f]; WA 30-1:95 [LW 51:169f].

384 Mark Twain, *Huckleberry Finn* (Berkeley: University of California Press, 1885/1985), 13.

385 WA 42:662 [LW 3:159].

386 Leslie Weatherhead, *Key Next Door* (New York: Abingdon Press, 1960) 107.

387 Leonard Griffith, *Barriers to Christian Belief* (New York, Harper & Row, 1962), 115.

388 George Buttrick, *Prayer* (Nashville: Abingdon-Cokesbury Press, 1942), 118.

389 WA 32:418 [LW 21:144]; WA 43:84 [LW 3:292] WA 19:560f [LW 14:217-218]; WA 51:606 [LW 43:230f].

390 New International Version (International Bible Society, 1978/83) 1036; J. B. Phillips, *Letters to Young Churches* (New York: Macmillan, 1948), 18.

391 Martin Buber, *Tales of the Hasidim: The Early Masters* (New York: Schoken, 1947/75), 215.

392 WA 51:623 [LW 43:240].

393 WA 53:442 [LW 47:167].

394 WA 38:364 [LW 43:200].

395 *Word and World,* Vol. 22, No. 1:90.

396 WA 6:20-22; cf. WA 46:83 [LW 24:390-391]; WA 2:126 [LW 42:75].

397 WA 30-1:193, 194 [LC:420, 421]; WA 42:500 [LW 2:333]; WA 43:84 [LW 3:291]; etc.

398 WA 30-1:195-196 [LC:423]; cf. WA 45:540f [LW 24:88]; WA 20:790f [LW 30:322f]; WA 38:360 [LW 43:194]; WA 18:317 [LW46:33]; WA 30-1:97 [LW 51:171].

399 WA 30-1:196 [LC:423]; cf. WA 32-2:237 [LW 16:320-321].

400 Hans Dieter Betz, *The Sermon on the Mount* (Minneapolis: Fortress Press, 1995), 388.

401 Isaiah 22:21; 63:16; 64:8; Jeremiah 3:4; cf. Jeremiah 3:19; Psalm 2:7; 68:5; 89:26; Malachi 1:6; cf. Tobit 13:4.

402 Cf. Jeremiah 10:10-12; 23:36; Psalm 18:46; 42:2; 84:2; Deuteronomy 5:26; Joshua 3:10; 1 Samuel 17:26; 2 Samuel 22:47; Daniel 6:20, 26; Hosea 1:10.

403 A modern version that regularly substitutes "Father-Mother" for the biblical term "Father" is *The New Testament and Psalms: An Inclusive Version*, (New York: Oxford University Press, 1994). For a critique of this version see "Probing an Inclusive Scripture" by Gail R. O'Day, *Christian Century*, July 3-10, 1996.

404 Helmut Thielicke, *Our Heavenly Father* (New York: Harper & Row, 1960), 9.

405 G. Dalman, *The Words of Jesus* (Edinburgh, 1903) 191f; Joachim Jeremias, *New Testament Theology* (New York: Charles Scribner's Sons, 1971) 61ff; Gunther Bornkann, *Jesus of Nazareth* (New York: Harper & Brothers, 1960) 128; etc.

406 *Our Heavenly Father,* 21-22 WA 32:420 [LW 21:146].

407 WA 30-1:[LSC:346]1 Kings 8:12, etc.

408 WA 32:420 [LW 21:146].

409 *A Brief Explanation of the Ten Commandments, the Creed and the Lord's Prayer* [1520] WA 7:220f [Works of Martin Luther (Philadelphia: A. J. Holman, 1915-32) Vol. 2:375].

410 "Atmosphere" (Psalm 68:8; 147:8; etc.); "celestial" (Genesis 22:17; 1 Kings 8:12; etc.); 'God of heaven' (Psalm 136:26; 1 Kings 8:23; etc.).

411 *Credo*, 162

412 James Limburg, *Psalms* (Louisville: Westminster John Knox, 2000), 260.

413 *Our Heavenly Father*, 48.

414 Ibid., 48.

415 WA 30-1:251 [LSC:346].

416 WA 30-1:251 [LSC:346].

417 WA 30-1:99 [LW 51:173]; cf. WA 18:528 [LW 14:203]; WA 6:217 [LW 44:39].

418 WA 2:87 [LW 42:27].

419 WA 2:92, 91-92 [LW 42:33].

420 WA 2:92 [LW 42:33].

421 *Word and World*, Vol. 22, 1 (St. Paul: Luther Seminary, Winter, 2002): 40-41.

422 WA 2:93 [LW 42:34, 35].

423 WA 13:641 [LW 20:111]; cf. WA 2:87 [LW 42:27-28]; WA 30-1:98f [LW 51:172-173].

424 The Sinai covenant is patterned along the lines of treaties such as the Hittite Suzerainty treaties of 3000 years ago. *Law and Covenant in Israel and the Ancient Middle East* (Pittsburgh: Presbyterian Board of Colportage, 1955). Cf. Delbert R. Hillers, *Covenant: The History of a Biblical Idea* (Baltimore: Johns Hopkins Press, 1969) 48ff.

425 Martin Buber, *Kingship of God* (New York: Harper & Row, 1967), 130.

426 Ibid., 130.

427 "Knowing the truth," John 8:32, 1 John 2:21, 2 John 1; "doing the truth," 1 John 1:6, cf. I John 3:18; "walking in the truth," 2 John 4, 3 John 3, 4.

428 WA 30-1:251-252 [LSC:346].

429 WA 30-1:200 [LC:427].

430 WA 18:694 [LW 33:153].

431 WA 2:95 [LW 42:37].

432 WA 2:96 [LW 42:38].

433 WA 2:98 [LW 42:41].

434 WA 30-1:251 [LSC:346].

435 WA 30-1:252 [LSC:347].

436 WA 30-1:252 [LSC:347].

437 Leslie Weatherhead, *The Will of God* (Nashville: Abingdon Press, 1944) 11ff.

438 *Why Do Men Suffer?*, 26.

439 Ibid., 42.

440 WA 32:29, 31 [LW 51:199, 200].

441 WA 2:99 [LW 42:42].

442 WA 7:337-338 [LW 32:24, 25] cf. WA 45:654 [LW 24:212]; WA 1:374 [LW 31:69]; etc.

443 WA 30-1:101-102 [LW 51:175].

444 The adjective is *epiousios*.

445 The phrase—*epi tav ousan*.

446 The word—*epiousa*.

447 The phrase—*epi ouai*.

448 The term—*epienai*.

449 Cf. W. F. Albright, & C. S. Mann, *Matthew* (Garden City: Doubleday & Co., 1971), 76.

450 WA 30-1:253 [LSC:347].

451 WA 30-1:253 [LSC:347].

452 WA 30-1:203-204 [LC:430].

453 WA 30-1:201 [LC:427-428]

454 WA 15:367-368 [LW 45:326].

455 WA 6:358 [LW 35:85]; cf. WA 47:19, 197 [LW 22:290, 489].

456 WA 30-1:253-254 [LSC:347].

457 Einar Billing, *Our Calling* (Rock Island: Augustana Press, 1955), 7.

458 WA DB 8:13 [LW 35:237];WA 46:684 [LW 22:170]; WA 47:19 [LW 22:290]; WA TR 1, 106 [LW 54:34].

459 WA 40-2:225 [LW 12:27].

460 WA TR 6, 6827; cf. WA 31 2:264 [LW 17:7].

461 WA 32:381 [LW 21:98]; WA 31-1:162 [LW 14:91]; WA 31-2:491 [LW 17:299]; WA 33:243 [LW 23:155].

462 *Let God Be God!*, 134.

463 WA 39-1:83 [LW 34:153].

464 WA 40-1:235 [LW 26:133]; cf. WA 2:494-495 [27:227].

465 WA 33:112 [LW 23:75].

466 WA 32:423, 424 [LW 21:149, 150]; cf. WA 31-2:22 [LW 16:31]; WA 10-3:251.

467 WA 32:424 [LW 21:151].

468 WA 32:425 [LW 21:152].

469 WA 26:202 [LW 40:274-275]; cf. WA 8:109 [LW 32:231-232].

470 Cf. Genesis 22:1; 1 Chronicles 29:17; 2 Chronicles 32:31; Judges 2:22, 3:1, 7:4; Psalms 7:6, 11:4-5; Proverb 17:3; Jeremiah 9:7, 17:10, 20:12; Zechariah 13:9; John 6:6; James 1:12.

471 The Greek noun in Matthew 6:13 and Luke 11:4, translated as "temptation" or "test" or "trial," is almost universally translated in Revelation 3:10 as "trial" or "ordeal."

472 WA 30-1:254 [LSC:347].

473 WA 30-1:254-255 [LSC:348].

474 The Didache, *The Library of Christian Classics*, Volume 1 (Philadelphia: Westminster, 1953), 174.

475 1 Chronicles 16:25-27; 29:11; Psalms 41:13, 73:18-19, 96:4-6, 145:11; Daniel 2:20; Jude 25; Revelation 4:11, 5:12-13, 7:12; cf. Ephesians 3:20-21.

476 WA 30-1:255 [LSC:348].

477 WA 2:126, 127 [LW 42:76, 77].

478 WA 23:244 [LW 37:126].

479 Ephesians 1:9; 3:3, 9; 5:32; Colossians 1:27; 1Timothy 3:16; Revelation 1:20; 17:7.

480 WA 2:509 [LW 27:249]; cf. WA 40-2:411 [LW 12:369f]; WA 6:373 [LW35:105]; WA 11:432 [LW 36:277]; etc.

481 WA 30-1:110 [LW 51:183].

482 WA 30-1:215 [LC:440]; cf. WA 19:390 [LW 19:192f].

483 WA 6:550 [LW 36:92].

484 WA 2:111 [LW 42:56].

485 WA 51:287 [LW 12:170].

486 WA 41:150 [LW 13:291].

487 WA 30-1:213 [LC:437]; cf. WA 42:667 [LW 3:166]; WA 43:32 [LW 3:220]; WA 26;156-157 [LW 40:242]; WA 6:530-531 [LW 36:62f]; WA TR 1, 306 [LW 54:113].

488 WA 38:240 [LW 38:199, 200]; cf. WA 47:211 [LW 22:505]; WA 52:169 [HK 5:308].

489 WA 42:667 [LW3:166]; cf. WA 43:32 [LW 3:220].

490 *Let God Be God!*, 161.

491 WA 42:294, 295 [LW 2:45, 46, 48]; cf. WA 42:184 [LW 1:248];WA 47:138f [LW 22:420]; WA 6:358f [LW 35:86].

492 *Infant Baptism in the First Four Centuries* (Philadelphia: Westminster, 1960), 24-40

493 Ibid, 32-36

494 . WA 1:113, 114 [LW 51:21,22]

495 1 Peter 3:18; 2 Corinthians 5:21; cf. Galatians 3:13; 1 Peter 2:24; see also WA 49:124 [LW 51:316]

496 WA 30-1:255 [LSC:348]; cf.WA 30-1:213 [LC:438]; WA 49:129-130 [LW 51:322-323] WA 38:239 [LW 38:198-199].

497 WA 30-1:112 [LW 51:185]

498 The Holy and Blessed Sacrament of Baptism, WA 2:727-737 [LW 35:29-43].

499 WA 2:727 [LW 35:29-30].

500 WA 6:531-543 [LW 36:64-81]; WA 30-1:220-222 [LC:444-446]; WA 13:432 [LW 19:121]; WA 56:57-58 [LW 25:50]; etc.

501 WA 2:732 [LW 35:35]

502 WA 2:727 [LW 35:29]; cf. WA 30-1:220 [LC:444f]; WA 2:742 [LW 35:50]; WA 6:531 [LW 36:64]

503 WA 6:534 [LW 36:68]

504 WA 30-1:256 [LSC:348]

505 WA 30-1:256f [LSC:349]

506 WA 30-1:257 [LSC:349]

507 Cf. WA 40-1:368 [LW 26:232]; etc.

508 WA 6:533 [LW 36:66]; cf. WA 12:282, 294, 296 [LW 30:27, 40, 41]

509 Cf. WA 18:139 [LW 40:149]

510 Cf. HK 2.1:188f; WA 2:727 [LW 35:29f].

511 *A New Catechism: Catholic Faith for Adults* (New York: Herder and Herder, 1967), 244.

512 WA 30-1:256 [LSC:348].

513 WA 30-1:256f [LSC:349].

514 WA 7:321 [LW 32:14]; cf. WA 2:733 [LW 35:38].
515 WA 6:527 [LW 36:59]; cf. WA 26:165 [40:253].
516 WA 6:533 [LW 36:67].
517 WA 2:732 [LW 35:36]; cf. WA 8:659 [LW 44:385].
518 WA 2:730 [LW 35:33].
519 WA 8:616 [LW 44:314].
520 WA 2:737 [LW 35:43]; cf. WA 311:250 [14:32]; WA 6:535 [LW 36:69].
521 WA 2:737 [LW 35:42].
522 WA 2:732 [LW 35:35].
523 WA 30-1:218 [LC:443].
524 WA 30-1:216 [LC:440]; cf. WA 7:322 [LW 32:16]; etc.
525 WA 30-1:216 [LC:441].
526 WA 30-1:222 [LC:446]; cf. WA 44:191 LW 6:258]; WA 32:424f [LW 21:151].
527 WA 6:536 [LW 36:70].
528 WA 2:733 [LW 35:37]; cf. WA 31:250 [LW 14:32]; WA 41:195 [LW 13:324]; WA 20:782 [LW 30:316].
529 WA 6:53 [LW 36:69]; cf. WA 20:782 [LW 30:316].
530 WA 26:162, 165 [LW 40:249, 252].
531 Again, we should not misunderstand the terms "the old me" and "the new self." See page 127.
532 WA 30-1:220, 221 [LC:445, 445-446]; cf. WA 44:191 [LW 6:258]; WA 33:531 [LW 23:330-331].
533 WA 30-1:221 [LC:446].
534 WA 6:528 [LW 36:59]; cf. WA 6:535 [LW 36:69].
535 WA 2:727 [LW 35:29]; cf. WA 10-3:49 [LW 51:92]; WA 31-2:697 [LW 15:234]; WA 33:452 [LW 23:284].
536 WA 30-1:221 [LC:445].
537 WA 2:732 [LW 35:36]; cf. WA 43:203 [LW 4:94-94]; WA 45:501, 661 [LW 24:44, 220]; WA 40:51 [LW 26:11].
538 WA 46:707 [LW 22:197]; cf. WA 45:690 [LW 24:250]; WA 14:63, 64 [LW 30:190]; WA 51:502 [LW 41:207].
539 WA 20:700 [LW 30:269]; cf. WA 11:251f [LW 45:91]; WA 32:425 [LW 21:152].
540 WA 26:155 [LW 40:241].
541 WA 30-1:217 [LC:442].
542 WA 30-1:216 [LC:441].

543 Alan Richardson, *An Introduction to the Theology of the New Testament* (New York: Harper & Brothers, 1958), 358.
544 Johs. Pedersen, *Israel: Its Life and Culture,* Volume II (Copenhagen: Branner Og Korch, 1926), 271.
545 *An Introduction to the Theology of the New Testament,* 359.
546 WA 42:621 [LW 3:102].
547 WA 42:622 [LW 3:104].
548 See pages 193-194.
549 See Herman Grossmann, *Ein Ja zur Kindertaufe* (Zurich: Kirchliche Zeitfragen Vol. 13, 1944) 14; cf. Jeremias, *Infant Baptism...,* 39-40, 48; Harald Sahlin, Omskarelsen I Kristus (Svensk Teologisk Kvartakskrift, 1947), 11ff.
550 WA TR 1, 365 [LW 54:55].
551 WA TR 1, 365 [LW 54:55].
552 *Infant Baptism,* 48-55; *An Introduction to the Theology of the New Testament,* 360-361; Oscar Cullmann, *Baptism in the New Testament* (London: SCM Press, 1950), 71-80; G Wohlenberg, *Das Evangelium des Markus* (T. Zahn, 1910), 272
553 The Greek word *koluo,* translated here as "prevent," is used in each of the biblical texts quoted here.
554 WA 26:158 [LW 40:245].
555 WA 26:168 [LW 40:256]; cf. WA 26:155 [LW 40:241]; WA TR 1:306 [LW 54:113].
556 WA 30-1:218 [LC:442].
557 WA 26:155 [LW 40:241].
558 Cf. WA 26:158 [LW 40:245].
559 WA 6:538 [LW 36:74]; cf. WA 44:719; [LW 8:192], WA 57-3:206 [LW 29:207]; WA 1:544, [LW 31:107]; etc.
560 WA 7:321 [LW 32:14]; cf. WA 57-3:169-170 [LW 29:172]; WA 7:387 [LW 32:54].
561 WA 7:321 [LW 32:15]; cf. WA 2:715 [LW 35:11]; WA 10-3:49 [LW 51:92].
562 WA 6:533-534 [LW 36:67]; cf. WA 10-2:324 [LW 43:53]; WA 30-1:109ff [LW 51:182ff].
563 WA 43:71 [LW 3:274]; cf. WA 7:321 [LW 32:15]; WA 38:231 [LW 38:189]; WA 10-3:142.
564 WA 43:71 [LW 3:274, 275]; cf. WA 30-3:165-166 [LW 38:87].
565 See Luke 11:52; Matthew 13:52; 16:19; 18:18; John 20:23.

566 The section on the Office of the Keys was added to the Small Catechism after Luther's death.
567 WA 30-2:505-506 [LW 40:375-376].
568 [LSC:349-351].
569 WA 26:507 [LW 37:368].
570 WA 19:520 [LW 36:359].
571 WA 10-3:61-62 [LW 51:98].
572 WA 6:546 [LW 36:86]; cf. WA 19:516 [LW 36:356].
573 WA 10-3:62 [LW 51:98-99].
574 WA 10-3:62 [LW 51:98-99]..
575 Florence L. Barclay, *The Following of The Star* (New York: G. P. Putnam's Sons, 1911), 343-344.
576 WA 30-1:260 [LSC:351].
577 Some less reliable manuscripts of 1 Corinthians 11:24 have inserted the word broken into Jesus' words, "This is my body which is for you." Luther writes, "This breaking must necessarily remain in the supper and in eating at the table and cannot mean anything else than that the body is distributed in the congregation, as one breaks bread and distributes it in the congregation." WA 18:199 [LW 40:209f].
578 WA 26:397-398 [LW 37:266-267].
579 The Blessed Sacrament of the Holy and True Body of Christ, WA 2:742-754 [LW 35:49-67].
580 WA 2:742, 743, 749 [LW 35:49, 50, 60].
581 WA 2:743 [LW 35:51].
582 WA 18:168 [LW 40:178].
583 WA 26:411 [LW 37:274-275].
584 WA 38:207 [LW 38:159].
585 WA 26:291-292 [LW 37:190].
586 WA 30-2:616 [LW 38:125].
587 WA 18:166-167 [LW 40:177].
588 WA 26:487 [LW 37:348].
589 Cf. LW 37:350, footnote 265; cf. WA 2:743 [LW 35:50f]; WA 26:493 [LW 37:356]; WA 11:437 [LW 36:282].
590 WA 7:324 [LW 32:16-17].
591 Hauspostille on Luke 22:7-20 [1534] *Luther's Sämtliche Schriften* (St. Louis, 1892) Vol. 13b:1844; [HK 5:454].
592 WA 26:394-395, 474 [LW 37:264-265, 332].
593 WA 30-1:260f [LSC:352].
594 WA 18:203-204 [LW 40:213-214].
595 WA 18:203-204 [LW 40:213-214].
596 WA 6:355, 360-361 [LW 35:82, 88-89].
597 WA 30-1:223 [LC:447].
598 WA 30-1:118 [LW 51:189]; cf. WA 26:506 [LW 37:367].
599 WA 30-1:226 [LC:450]; cf.. WA 1:595 [LW 31:193]; etc.
600 WA 6:363 [LW 35:91].
601 WA 11:432 [LW 36:277].
602 WA 11:432 [LW 36:277].
603 WA 47:219 [LW 22:516]; cf. WA 6:373 [LW 35:105]; WA 30-3:350 [LW 34:81]; WA 30-1:118 [LW 51:189].
604 WA 38:253 [LW 38:212].
605 WA 6:373 [LW 35:105].
606 WA 6:373-374 [LW 35:106].
607 WA 6:520 [LW 36:47].
608 WA 6:359 [LW 35:86].
609 Cf. WA 6:359 [LW 35:86].
610 Cf. P. Pfatteicher & C. Messerli, *Manual on the Liturgy: Lutheran Book of Worship* (Minneapolis: Augsburg, 1979), 17, 19.
611 WA 30-1:224-225, 227 [LC:449, 451].
612 WA 30-2:614 [LW 38:122].
613 WA 19:78 [LW 53:68].
614 WA 26:110 [LW 28:369].
615 WA 38:231 [LW 38:189].
616 WA 36:237 [LW 51:232].
617 WA 23:662 [LW 20:345].
618 WA 8:515 [LW 36:173].
619 WA 19:505 [LW 36:349].
620 WA 33:326 [LW 23:207]; cf. WA 33:326 [LW 36:183]; WA 12:180f. [LW 40:22]; WA 18:197 [LW 40:208]; etc.
621 WA 2:112 [LW 42:57].
622 WA TR 1, 234 [LW 54:90].
623 WA 11:433 [LW 36:277].
624 WA 12:35 [LW 53:11]; cf. WA 2:608 [LW 27:396]; WA 26:110 [LW 28:369]; WA 42:184 [LW 1:247f].
625 WA 19:505 [LW 36:349].
626 WA 38:199 [LW 38:151].
627 WA 1:604 [LW 31:210].
628 WA 6:232 [LW 44:57].
629 WA 30-3:350 [LW 34:82].
630 WA 40-2:259 [LW 12:54].
631 WA 26:217 [LW 40:293].

[632] WA 6:502 [LW 36:19]; cf. WA 26:498 [LW 37:360]; WA 33:65 [LW 23:46].
[633] WA 23:145 [LW 37:65]; cf. WA 30-3:125 [LW 38:27].
[634] WA 26:298, 300 [LW 37:195, 196].
[635] WA 30-1:261 LSC:352].
[636] WA 30-1:226f, 229, 230 [LC:450f, 453].
[637] WA 26:216 [LW 40-1:292].
[638] WA 7:386 [LW 32:54].
[639] WA 2:14 [LW 31:271].
[640] WA 30-1:222 [LC:447]; cf. WA 19:501 [LW 36:347]; WA 18:123 [LW 40:141]; WA 30-1:117 [LW 51:189]; etc.
[641] WA 26:220 [LW 40:296].
[642] WA 26:216 [LW 40:292].
[643] WA 19:521 [LW 36:359].
[644] WA 30-1:233 [LC:456-457].
[645] WA 30-1:222 [LC:447].
[646] Cf. WA 19:521 [LW 36:359].
[647] WA 7:317 [LW 32:12-13]; cf. WA 173:170 [LW 29:172]; WA1:544 [LW 31:106f]; WA 6:531-532 [LW 36:64-65].
[648] Anthony Wilhelm, *Christ Among Us* (New York: Paulist Press, 1975) 244.
[649] WA 33:190 [LW 23:123]; cf. WA 42:294 [LW 2:47]; WA 47:210, 210ff [LW 22:504, 505-509].
[650] WA 19:486 [LW 36:338]; cf. WA 26:312-313 [LW 37:202-203].
[651] WA 23:157 [LW 37:72].
[652] James Killgallon & Gerard Weber, *Life in Christ* (Chicago: Foundation for Adult Catechetical Teaching Aids, 1958), 143.
[653] WA 8:493 [LW 36:146-147].
[654] Van Doornik, Jelsma, & Van de Lisdonk, *A Handbook of the Catholic Faith* (Garden City: Image Books, 1956), 308.
[655] WA 6:365, 368 [LW 35:94, 98]; cf. WA 30-3:356 [LW 34:85]; WA 8:511ff [LW 36:168ff]; WA 12:211 [LW 53:26].
[656] *Christ Among Us*: 244, 348ff; *A Handbook of the Catholic Faith*: 311; *Life in Christ*: 183
[657] V. Staley, *Catholic Religion* (Harrisburg, Pennsylvania: Morehouse, 1983), 16, 26, 210; Anthony Hanson, *Beyond Anglicanism* (London: Darton, Longman, & Todd, 1965), 227; Urban T. Holmes, III, *What is Anglicanism?* (Wilton, Connecticut: Morehouse-Barlow, 1982), 54-55.
[658] *Evangelical Lutheran Worship* (Minneapolis: Augsburg Fortress, 2006), 111, 109.
[659] WA 30-1:223 [LC:448]; cf. WA 42:170 [LW 1:228].
[660] WA 38:240 [LW 38:199].
[661] WA 26:213 [LW 40:289].
[662] WA 30-2:614 [LW 38:122].
[663] WA 12:182 [LW 40:24].
[664] WA 12:182 [LW 40:24].
[665] *The Lord's Supper* (SCM Press, 1967) 103.
[666] Ibid, 104.
[667] WA 6:408 [LW 44:129]; cf. WA 7:58 [LW 31:356]; WA 31-1:211 [LW 13:65]; WA 50:632f [LW 41:154].
[668] WA 31-1:211 [LW 13:65].
[669] *Catholic Religion*, 210.
[670] *Ministry and Ordination*, Anglican-Roman Catholic International Commission (Canterbury, 1973) 9.
[671] Cf. WA 12:169-195 [LW 40:7-44]; WA 38:228ff [LW 38:185ff]; WA 6:406ff [LW 44:127ff]; etc.
[672] Heinrich Bornkamm, *Luther in Mid-Career, 1521-1530* (Philadelphia: Fortress Press, 1983),129.
[673] WA 6:512 [LW 36:36].
[674] Cf. *Manual on the Liturgy*, 226ff.
[675] WA 6:516 [LW 36:41].
[676] *Manual on the Liturgy*, 232.
[677] WA 30-2:614 [LW 38:122-123].
[678] WA 23:270 [LW 37:142].
[679] *Manual on the Liturgy*, 242.
[680] WA 6:367, 373, 374 [LW 35:97, 105, 106]; cf. WA 6:522-523 [LW 36:50].
[681] WA 12:171 [LW 40:9].
[682] WA 11:433 [LW 36:278].
[683] WA 7:320 [LW 32:15].
[684] WA 30-1:224-225 [LC:449].
[685] WA 30-1:227 [LC:451].
[686] WA 30-2:601 [LW 38:104].

WORKS OF MARTIN LUTHER CITED

WA	LW	
1:111-115	51:17-23	Sermon: Psalm 19:1 [21 Dec 1516]
1:273-277	51:44-49	Sermon: John 11:1-45 [19 Mar 1518]
1:353-374	31:55-56	Heidelberg Disputation [1518]
1:525-628	31:83-252	Explanations of the Ninety-five Theses [1518]
2:6-26	31:259-292	Proceedings at Augsburg [1518]
2:80-130	42:19-81	An Exposition . . . Lord's Prayer . . . Laymen [1519]
2:452-618	27:153-410	Lectures on Galatians 1-6 [1519]
2:727-737	35:29-43	The Holy and Blessed Sacrament of Baptism [1519]
2:742-758	35:49-73	The Blessed Sacrament . . . Body of Christ [1519]
3:15-31	10:11-34	Lecture on Psalm 1 [1513]
3:37-64	10:42-75	Lecture on Psalm 4 [1513]
4:305-393	11:414-534	Lecture on Psalm 119 [1515]
5:47-74	14:313-349	Commentary on Psalm 2 [1518]
5:125-199		A Study of Psalm 5 [1519]
6:20-22		A Good Interpretation . . . Our Father [1519]
6:36-60	45:273-308	Trade and Usury [1524]
6:202-276	44:21-114	Treatise on Good Works [1520]
6:353-378	35:79-111	A Treatise on the New Testament . . . [1520]
6:404-469	44:123-217	To the Christian Nobility . . . German Nation [1520]
6:497-573	36:11-126	The Babylonian Captivity of the Church [1520]
7:49-73	31:333-377	The Freedom of a Christian [1520]
7:194-229	WML 2:354ff	Brief Explanation: 10 C., Creed, and L. Prayer [1520]
7:308-456	32:7-99	Defense and Explanation of All the Articles [1521]
7:795-802	44:235-242	Sermon: Instruction of Consciences [1521]
8:43-128	32:137-269	Against Latomus [1521]
8:482-563	36:133-230	The Misuse of the Mass [1521]
8:573-669	44:251-400	The Judgment of . . . Luther on Monastic Vows [1521]
8:676-687	45:57-74	A Sincere Admonition. . . to All Christians. . . . [1522]
10-1-1:8-18	35:117-124	A Brief Instruction . . . Look for in the Gospels [1521]
10-1-1:58-95	52:7-31	Kirchenpostille: Christmas Eve, Luke 2:1-14 [1521]
10-1-1:180-247	52:41-88	Kirchenpostille: Christmas Day, John 1:1-14 [1521]
10-1-1:555-728	52:159-286	Kirchenpostille: Epiphany, Matthew 2:1-12 [1522]
10-1-2:293-306	HK 2.1:405-454	Gospel: Trinity Sunday: John 3:1-15
10-2:11-41	36:237-267	Receiving Both Kinds in the Sacrament [1522]
10-2:375-406	43:11-45	Personal Prayer Book [1522]

10-3:1-13	51:70-75	Sermon: Invocavit Sunday [9 Mar 1522]
10-3:13-20	51:75-78	Sermon: Invocavit Monday [10 Mar 1522]
10-3:58-64	51:97-100	Sermon: Remin. Sunday [16 Mar 1522]
10-3:304-312	HK 2.2:370-389	Gospel: 12th Sunday after Trinity: Mark 7:31ff
11:245-280	45:81-129	Temporal Authority . . . [1523]
11:408-416	39:305–314	That a Christian Assembly. . . Right to Judge [1523]
11:431-456	36:275-305	The Adoration of the Sacrament [1523]
12:35-37	53:11-14	Concerning Order of Public Worship [1523]
12:169-195	40:7-44	Concerning the Ministry [1523]
12:232-244	45:141-158	An Exhortation to Knights [1523]
12:259-399	30:3-145	Sermons on 1 Peter [1522]
13:88-122	18:79-123	Lecture on Joel, Chapter 2 [1524]
13:547-664	20:3-152	Lectures on Zechariah (Latin) [1526]
14:15-74	30:151-199	Sermons on II Peter [1523]
14:545-744	9:11-311	Lectures on Deuteronomy [1523/25]
15:360-378	45:317-337	Exposition of Psalm 127 . . . Riga [1524]
15:716-721		Sermon: 21st Sunday after Trinity: John 4:47f
16:363-393	35:161-174	How Christians Should Regard Moses [1525]
17-2:5-15	HK 4.1:7-19	Epistle: 1st Sunday After Epiphany: Rom. 12:1-6
18:62-125	40:79-143	Against the Heavenly Prophets - I [1525]
18:134-214	40:144-223	Against the Heavenly Prophets - II [1525]
18:492-498	14:155-163	Commentary on Psalm 38 [1525]
18:600-787	33:15-295	The Bondage of the Will [1525]
19:72-113	53:61-90	The German Mass [1526]
19:185-251	19:3-104	Lectures on Jonah [1526]
19:482-523	36:335-361	The Sacrament of the Body and Blood. . . . [1526]
19:582-594	14:243-256	Commentary on Psalm 94 [1526]
20:7-203	15:3-187	Notes on Ecclesiastes [1526]
20:599-801	30:221-327	Lectures on I John [1527]
23:64-283	37:13-159	. . . "This Is My Body". . . . [1527]
23:485-664	20:155-347	Lectures on Zechariah (German) [1527]
26:4-120	28:217-384	Lectures on I Timothy [1527-28]
26:144-174	40:229-262	Concerning Rebaptism [1528]
26:195-240	40:269-329	Instructions . . . Visitors of Parish Pastors. . . . [1528]
26:261-509	37:161-372	Confession Concerning Christ's Supper [1528]
28:425-439		Sermon on John 20:1ff [12 June 1529]
30-1:57-121	51:137-193	Ten Sermons on the Catechism [1528]
30-1:125-238		The Large Catechism [1529]
30-1:243-264		The Small Catechism [1529]
30-2:465-507	40:325-377	The Keys [1530]
30-2:595-626	38:97-137	Admonition Concerning the Sacrament. . . . [1530]
30-3:331-388	34:67-104	Commentary on the Alleged Imperial Edict [1531]
31-1:189-218	13:41-72	Commentary on Psalm 82 [1530]
31-2:261-585	17:3-416	Lectures on Isaiah, 40-66 [1528-30]
32:28-39	51:197-208	Sermon on Cross / Suffering [16 Apr 1530]
32:299-544	21:3-294	Sermons: Sermon on The Mount [1531]
33:3-675	23:3-422	Sermons on John 6-8 [1530-1532]
36:237-254	51:241-243	Sermon 1 Thessalonians 4:13-14 [22 Aug 1532]
36:482-696	28:59-213	Commentary: 1 Corinthians 15 [1534]
38:195-256	38:147-214	The Private Mass . . . Consecration of Priests [1533]

38:358-375	43:193-211	A Simple Way to Pray [1535]
39-1:2-126	34:151-196	Disputation Concerning Justification [1536]
39-1:175-180	34:137-144	Disputation Concerning Man [1536]
39-1:418-485		2nd Antinomian Disputation [12 Jan 1538]
39-2:187-203	34:303-321	Licentiate Exam: H. Schmedenstedt [1542]
39-2:257-283		Dr. Disputation: T. Fabricius and S. Lituanus [1544]
40-1:52-688	26:3-461	Lectures on Galatians 1-4 [1535]
40-2:1-184	27:3-149	Lectures on Galatians 5-6 [1535]
40-2:193-312	12:3-93	Commentary on Psalm 2 [1532]
40-2:315-470	12:303-410	Commentary on Psalm 51 [1532]
40-2:472-610	12:147-300	Commentary on Psalm 45 [1532]
41:79-239	13:227-348	Commentary on Psalm 110 [1535]
41:454-459		Sermon: Wed. St. Luke's Day [1535]
42:3-263	1:3-359	Lectures on Genesis 1-5 [1535/36]
42:263-549	2:3-399	Lectures on Genesis 6-14 [1536/37]
42:550-673	3:3-175	Lectures on Genesis 15-17 [1538/39]
43:1-137	3:176-314	Lectures on Genesis 18-20 [1538ff]
43:137-430	4:3-409	Lectures on Genesis 21-25 [1539]
43:431-695	5:3-386	Lectures on Genesis 26-30 [1541/42]
44:1-304	6:3-407	Lectures on Genesis 31-37 [1542/44]
44:304-581	7:3-377	Lectures on Genesis 38-44 [1544]
44:581-825	8:3-333	Lectures on Genesis 45-50 [1545]
45:204-250	12:97-136	Commentary on Psalm 8 [1537]
45:465-733	24:5-298	Sermons on John 14-15 [1537]
46:538-789	22:3-274	Sermons on John 1-2 [1538]
47:1-231	22:274-530	Sermons on John 3-4 [1539]
47:757-772	51:291-299	Sermon on Soberness and Moderation [1539]
49:124-135	51:315-329	Sermon on Matthew 3:13-17 [2 Apr 1540]
49:58-615	51:333-354	Sermon: Dedication - Castle Church, Torgau [1544]
50:262-283	34:201-229	The Three Symbols... of the Christian Faith [1538]
50:312-337	47:65-98	Against the Sabbatarians [1538]
50:509-653	41:9-178	On the Councils and the Church [1539]
51:267-295	12:147-179	Commentary on Psalm 23 [1532]
51:585-625	43:219-241	Appeal: Prayer Against the Turks [1541]
52:41-49	HK:5:109-120	Hauspostille: 27 Dec 1534, Luke 2:15-20
52:58-64	HK:5144-152	Hauspostille: 25 Dec 1534, Luke 2:10-12
53:417-552	47:137-306	On the Jews and Their Lies [1543]
56:1-528	25:3-524	Lectures on Romans [1515-16]
57-3:98-238	29:109-241	Lectures on Hebrews [1517-18]
Br 1:594-595		Letter: George Spalatin (18 Dec 1519)
Br 2:522-523		Letter... Altenburg (8 May 1522)
DB 6:2-11	35:357-362	Preface to the New Testament [1546]
DB 7:3-27	35:365-380	Preface to the Epistle to the Romans [1546]
DB 7:407-421	35:399-411	Preface to the Revelation of St. John [1546]
DB 8:11-31	35:235-251	Prefaces to the Old Testament [1545]
TR 1 234	54:90	Authority of the Minister Resides in the Office [1533]
TR 1 365	54:55-58	"The Word of God and the Sacraments" [1532]
TR 6 6827		"The Forgiveness of Sins"

ACKNOWLEDGMENTS

The material in this book was gathered over the years that I worked and studied with confirmation age students—one of the favorite parts of my ministry. Recently, as I looked over photos of these confirmation classes, many memories came to mind! Here are three memories from three different congregations:

> I asked a class of students, "What is God's Word?" And a youngster named Colleen responded, "God's Word is what God says." Someone might say, "Well, of course!" But Colleen's answer struck me then and strikes me now as profound in its simplicity.
>
> Bernt was one of the most intelligent fellows I ever had in class. The thing is, Bernt seldom came to class prepared. But once his classmates began to discuss the day's topic, he quickly caught on and made a solid contribution to the class. I remember saying on one occasion, "Bernt, if you would bother to prepare, you would be a world beater." Actually he was already. He listened and joined in as his classmates taught him. Today, he is an ardent Christian.
>
> Amy and Emily, two sharp young people, loved to try to get me off topic by asking tough questions or making audacious comments. The result was invariably a stimulating session—the kind I have always enjoyed.

I could relate many more recollections from the nearly 700 catechism students I worked with over the years. Their lives, questions, and contributions have strongly influenced the material cited here.

Special thanks to my good friend Jim Limburg for writing the foreword for this book. And special thanks as well to Karen Walhof for her encouragement, her suggestions, and the time, energy, and skill she has invested in editing and publishing this book.

www.ingramcontent.com/pod-product-compliance
Lightning Source LLC
Chambersburg PA
CBHW062033120526
44592CB00036B/1902